THE GOOD
ALTERNATIVE TRAVEL GUIDE

THE GOOD
ALTERNATIVE TRAVEL GUIDE

Exciting Holidays for Responsible Travellers

Second Edition

Mark Mann
with Zainem Ibrahim

for

TourismConcern

Earthscan Publications Ltd
London • Sterling, VA

Second edition first published in the UK and USA in 2002
by Earthscan Publications Ltd

Copyright © Tourism Concern and Mark Mann, 2002

First edition (*The Community Tourism Guide*) 2000

A catalogue record for this book is available from the British Library

ISBN: 1 85383 837 3

Typesetting by PCS Mapping & DTP, Newcastle upon Tyne
Printed and bound by Creative Print and Design Wales, Ebbw Vale
Cover design by Susanne Harris
Cover photos: Christopher Gow/Symbiosis Expedition Planning, Guy Marks/Tribes
  Travel, Paul Miles, Lisa Young

Tourism Concern
Stapleton House, 277–281 Holloway Road
London N7 8HN, UK
Tel: +44 (0)20 7753 3330
Fax: +44 (0)20 7753 3331
Email: info@tourismconcern.org.uk
Web: **www.tourismconcern.org.uk**

For a full list of publications please contact:

Earthscan Publications Ltd
120 Pentonville Road
London N1 9JN, UK
Tel: +44 (0)20 7278 0433
Fax: +44 (0)20 7278 1142
Email: earthinfo@earthscan.co.uk
Web: **www.earthscan.co.uk**

22883 Quicksilver Drive, Sterling, VA 20166–2012, USA

Earthscan is an editorially independent subsidiary of Kogan Page Ltd and publishes in
association with WWF-UK and the International Institute for Environment and
Development

This book is printed on elemental-chlorine free paper

'The quest of the responsible traveller should be to learn, to be understanding, to share, to contribute – rather than to act as a consumer who seeks maximum gratification at minimum expense.'

Rolf Wesche/Andy Drumm, from *Defending our Rainforest*

'The fact that indigenous people want to insert themselves in the market does not mean that they disappear as peoples.'

T Tapuy, coordinator of RICANCIE, Ecuador

'When we speak of ecotourism, we speak of us – our people, our lives and the way we do things. This is what ecotourism means to us.'

Edgar Boyan, Lokono community member, Guyana

'When you enter our lands, you become part of us. The land, the creatures, the forest, you and I become one.'

Stanley Sam, Ahousaht elder, Canada

'The raw material of the tourist industry is the flesh and blood of people and their cultures.'

Cecil Rajendra, human rights activist, Malaysia

CONTENTS

FOREWORD:
TOURISM CONCERN – PUTTING
PEOPLE IN THE PICTURE

So you're planning your next holiday. It's been a fraught and busy year; you've thought it over and decided that even though the money's tight, you deserve to spoil yourself a bit. Yes, this is the year you're actually going to do that long-postponed big adventure – no holds barred.

In this delicious frame of mind, the last thing in the world any of us wants is to have our dream planning interrupted by some squeaky, small voice of conscience whispering: What about the environment? What about human rights? What about the poverty? Don't you care that *you* might be making things worse by going *there*?

In truth, you probably do care. But, you rationalize, there's nothing you personally can do about any of that stuff, and staying away won't stop anyone else from going, so you might as well go anyway. That's where Tourism Concern can make the difference. For more than a decade it has pursued two big aims: firstly, to get the tourism industry to recognize that it is creating serious problems and should be doing something about them; and secondly, to tap into tourism's huge potential in order to spread its benefits far more even-handedly.

Tourism Concern was founded in 1989 on a simple premise: our holiday destination is always somebody else's home, and the people who live there are not merely part of the scenic backdrop to our fabulous holiday experience. They matter.

It's a very basic notion. And if you turn it around, it makes instant sense. How many of us have caught ourselves cursing inconsiderate tourists congregating in coachloads in a narrow high street? Or lengthening the lunchtime queues at busy bank counters or ticket offices? Or booking out the one hotel you always stay in on the bank holiday weekend? Or marching up and down your local beauty spot until the path is as busy as a motorway and twice as ugly?

Local people matter. Yet the failure to recognize it has sparked local protests and campaigns the world over against tourism development. So Tourism Concern has been trying, since its inception, to fill in the seductive but empty images of paradise in the travel brochures by putting people back in the picture. We do this through a mixture of research, education, lobbying, campaigning, tackling the industry head-on, and getting together with like-minded people. And our work is producing results. The industry and even governments are starting to take the problems of tourism much more seriously.

Some of the ideas we've pioneered – such as fair trade and educational videos for holiday-makers – have been taken up by bits of the industry. We are no longer a lone voice. Voluntary Service Overseas (VSO) and Action for Southern Africa (ACTSA) have both run campaigns to highlight how little of the money we spend on our holidays benefits the local people whose areas we visit. The first of our two aims, then, is showing signs of being realized – today there is much broader recognition of tourism's tendency to create problems. We have even started to tackle the tricky bit: finding solutions.

TOURISM CONCERN'S ORIGINS

Tourism Concern started life in 1988 as an informal network run from my home in Gateshead. In the 1980s, I'd become involved with European groups supporting a new network, the Ecumenical Coalition on Third World Tourism (ECTWT), then based in Bangkok. They all wanted tourism to lead to 'just, participatory and sustainable development' and were challenging the international tourism industry to change its ways.

In 1988 the time seemed right to create a British group to support and publicise what the ECTWT was doing. We began contacting people in Britain who might want to join in a fresh critique of the tourism industry, and Tourism Concern was officially launched as a membership organization in September 1989.

The fledgling organization instantly ran into an image problem. This was 1989, and the green movement was riding the crest of a wave of public popularity. It was hard to convince people that this wasn't yet another campaign hitching a ride on the environmental bandwagon. Actually, we would have had an easier time if we *had* limited ourselves to campaigning for rare animals and plants threatened by tourism's heavy footprint.

Yet we have always been clear that our definition of environment is much broader than that: it includes people, their environments, economies, cultures, societies and their basic rights. In any case, experience has shown that environmental solutions rarely work unless the people who actually live in that particular environment are consulted and involved.

In little over ten years, Tourism Concern has grown from a small group of individuals into a national membership organization. Members include concerned holiday-makers, teachers and students, academics, journalists, people from the tourism industry and development workers – and, of course, people who live and work in holiday destinations. We hold an annual conference, have a quarterly magazine, and run debates and seminars. We have produced affordable videos and education materials for teachers and students to help them understand the issues in tourism. We have an extensive website and a vast library of books, papers, magazines and other documents.

The voluntary coordinator who started out running the show from her home has given way to a full-time director and specialist staff, generously housed by the Business School of the University of North London.

PART OF A GLOBAL NETWORK

Tourism Concern is a small voice. But it is not alone. When it was set up, groups across the world were already challenging the conventional view of tourism as a 'passport to development'. Individual groups have come and gone, but the global network remains a reality and a source of real strength.

People from all over the world find their way to our office, to share their experiences and to ask for our advice and support. On occasion, we've been lucky enough to play a hand in the birth of local campaigns. The Indian state of Goa was one such case. Tourism Concern was set up just when it was receiving its first charter flights from Europe, bringing unprecedented numbers of package tourists. Local Goan groups were already sounding alarm bells about what uncontrolled package tourism might mean. They asked us to raise the issue with tour operators and tourists in Britain.

We have since developed strong links with Goan organizations and have relayed their worries and views to the UK tourist industry and public. While we can't claim total success, we have generated publicity and awareness in Britain, which has added weight to local efforts to challenge damaging development.

NOT AN ANTI-TOURISM CAMPAIGN

Although we are often called up by journalists when they want an 'anti-tourism' quote, Tourism Concern is not against tourism. Most of our members became involved precisely because they love travelling, so it would be hypocritical of us to tell others not to travel. In any case, we realize that people will still go on holiday, whatever Tourism Concern says.

What we *are* about is developing a fairer, more responsible and sustainable tourism industry – one that benefits local people just as much as ourselves and doesn't degrade environments – and we seek to work *with* the tourism industry rather than against it. We don't believe that considering the welfare of local people has to mean a 'worse' holiday. Indeed, the central message of this book is that, in the right circumstances, tourism *can* support local people, cultures, environments and economies, while still being exciting and enjoyable for us.

MOVING FORWARD

Campaigning for change in the tourism industry

Drawing on information from our global partners about the damage that badly-developed tourism causes, we lobby the tourism industry, the British government and international tourism organizations for ethical and fairly-traded tourism. Our public campaigns range the world and have included highlighting the displacement of people from their homes in East Africa for tourism and conservation, and support for Aung San Suu Kyi's call for tourists and tour operators to boycott Burma until democracy is restored. Our latest campaign highlights the often-appalling working conditions of trekking porters in countries such as Nepal and Peru.

Making holiday-makers more aware

We also seek to make holiday-makers more aware of their impact on the places they visit. We do this in various ways including having a strong presence at exhibitions, creating a lively video for independent travellers, developing codes of behaviour for travellers, publishing a quarterly magazine and producing stimulating educational materials for schools and universities.

Exploring fair trade in tourism

Increasingly, however, our work is focusing on the concept of fair trade. As with fairly-traded coffee or tea, we want to encourage more equitable business partnerships that benefit tourists, tour operators and hosts alike. But tourism is a more complex and varied business than coffee or tea. So, with organizations and companies from both Europe and the developing world, we are exploring how fair trade might work in the mainstream tourism industry. We hope that, one day, you will be able to walk into a travel agent and buy a well packaged, thoroughly enjoyable, certified 'Fair Trade holiday'.

Patricia Barnett
Director
Tourism Concern

Alison Stancliffe
Founder and original coordinator
Tourism Concern

Tourism Concern is a small but dynamic membership organization. If we are to make the tourism industry fairer and more sustainable, we need your support to help fund our work and to strengthen our voice. You can find information about joining Tourism Concern on our website.

Tourism Concern
Stapleton House
277–281 Holloway Road,
London N7 8HN
☎ +44 (0)20 7753 3330
🖷 +44 (0)20 7753 3331
✉ info@tourismconcern.org.uk
🖥 **www.tourismconcern.org.uk**

PREFACE TO
THE SECOND EDITION

Most community tourism projects are small ventures with limited finances and, often, limited business experience. Inevitably, some fail. So, for this new edition of the guide, we've added new projects and removed ones that no longer exist. Where necessary, we've updated contact details for existing projects.

Since the first edition came out two years ago, there has been growing interest in community tourism, and the idea that it can be a tool for conservation and development while offering travellers more rewarding encounters with local people than conventional tourism. More projects have sprung up, more conservation and development organizations are supporting community tourism ventures and more tour operators have begun to market community tours and guesthouses.

A recent MORI poll for the Association of British Travel Agents (ABTA) found that 85 per cent of UK holiday-makers thought it important not to damage the environment, 71 per cent thought tourism should benefit local people and 64 per cent said they would pay between £10 and £25 more for their holiday if it benefited local people, charity or the environment. A separate survey (Tearfund: *Tourism: An Ethical Issue*, 2000) found that half of UK holiday-makers would pay an average of 5 per cent more for their holiday if it meant fairer wages for local people or protecting the environment.

These findings hint at a potentially greater demand for fairer and more sustainable tourism. The thing that will make the tourism industry sit up and take notice, however, is not surveys but 'bums on seats' – hard evidence that responsible tourism really can sell. This guide offers you a chance to provide that evidence – and to discover a great new way of travelling into the bargain.

INTRODUCTION: STRANGE
BIRDSONG IN THE JUNGLE

This guide contains two of the best holidays I've ever been on. The first was in the Australian Outback, about 300 kilometres from Uluru (or Ayer's Rock, as it used to be called). If nowhere has a middle, this was it, with no major town for thousands of kilometres in any direction. The vast night skies were filled with shooting stars and the desert was alive with plants and animals, drawing on the unseen water reserves buried beneath the flaming red earth. Secret waterholes made perfect swimming pools to cool off in during the heat of the day.

The second was in the middle of the Ecuadorean Amazon, deep inside the world's greatest rainforest. There was certainly no shortage of water here. On one occasion we even found ourselves up to our necks in soupy brown flood-water, as we tracked a herd of wild boar through the forest. At night, we spread our sleeping mats on an open wooden platform and drifted into sleep to the sounds of crickets and frogs and strange birdsong.

Two dramatic, and dramatically different, settings. What links them is that both holidays were run by the local aboriginal/indigenous communities: people who still live in remarkable natural places and who still feel and understand the rhythms of nature. Through them, I learned to see places I would other-wise have regarded as wildernesses as *homes*. Places where people have lived for thousands of years.

WHAT TYPE OF HOLIDAYS WILL YOU FIND
IN THIS BOOK?

- Tours that have local grassroots involvement and benefits.
- Holidays with a high level of interaction with local people and cultures.
- All budget and comfort levels, from roughing it to luxury.
- Many 'green' tours featuring wildlife, wilderness regions, etc.
- Small-group travel, not mass package tours.
- Tours you can book before leaving home and tours you can arrange locally.
- Tours lasting from half a day to three weeks.
- Village stays with indigenous and rural communities in the developing world.
- Community-run campsites, lodges, hotels, museums, cultural centres, etc.

I also realized that a 'responsible' or 'ethical' holiday didn't have to be boring. Instead, these community-run tours were a great way to get closer to the people and cultures I was visiting. A chance to step off the tired tourist treadmill for a few days. And they showed me that a 'tour' didn't have to mean being stuck with 30 other tourists, herded in and out of places I didn't really want to see anyway. Instead, I found myself with a few like-minded visitors, with time to relax, to appreciate our surroundings and to get to know our hosts.

Since then, I've discovered that these two holidays are part of a new but growing movement: a movement that lacks a clear name but which is most commonly described as 'community tourism'. These holidays permit us to visit wonderful places in ways that benefit the people who live there and help preserve the natural beauty that attracted us in the first place. They get beyond the bland facade of mainstream tourism and offer us a real insight into local life. They show us living cultures instead of the fake, out-of-context 'cultural shows' served up with dinner in tourist hotels. And they take us to some of the most beautiful places on the planet.

WHAT ARE COMMUNITY-BASED HOLIDAYS?

Gone are the days when a 'politically correct' holiday meant listening to a lecture on tractor production statistics in a Cuban workers' cooperative. Tour operators (and local communities themselves) have realized that people don't go on holiday to listen to lectures about poverty. Instead, the trips in this guide offer you a chance to *do* something positive while still having a rewarding, enjoyable, fun... holiday.

In fact, our directory contains an incredibly diverse range of holidays in over 40 countries, linked by a common thread of local involvement and benefit. Most are small-group tours or small, locally run lodgings. They allow you to get to know local people in a way that package tourism and big hotels don't. Many trips take you to beautiful wilderness areas. There are drumming holidays in Senegal, language schools in Central America and Kenya, treks in Nepal, horse riding in Arizona, sea-kayaking or snorkelling in the South Pacific, and much more. And, as it happens, our directory *does* contain holidays in Cuba, but ones that focus on the island's fabulous musical wealth and vibrant culture.

Nor does community tourism have to mean sleeping in mud huts and not washing for a week. There are tours and lodgings here to suit all comfort levels and budgets, from backpacker trips for £5 a day to £200-a-day luxury safari lodges.

Finally, the guide includes holidays you can book before you leave home and tours that you can easily arrange locally. For each entry in our directory, we provide details of how to book or get more information.

HOW THIS BOOK IS ORGANIZED

Section One of this book introduces the issues and principles of community tourism. It also includes a chapter, 'Being there', that describes visits to a few community tourism projects. Section Two is a directory of community-based holidays. This is divided into tour agencies in the UK and other Western countries ('Outbound operators') and tours, guesthouses and lodges in individual destination countries ('Local tours by country'). A 'Holiday-finder index' is included to help you match holidays to your own interests. Section Three contains a directory of responsible tourism organizations and resources and some guidelines for responsible tourism, in case you would like to know more about the issues raised in this book.

INDEPENDENT TRAVEL OR PACKAGE TOUR?

As well as complete holidays, the Holiday Directory features local tours and guesthouses that you can visit while travelling independently. Each directory entry includes contact details, and most are easy to arrange locally. Even if you generally prefer to travel independently, a few days spent in a community on one of these community-based projects can add an extra dimension to your holiday – and bring more benefit to local people.

SPONSORS

The following tour operators 'put their money where their mouth is' to help finance this new edition of the Guide: **Dragoman, Muir's Tours, Rainbow Tours, Specialist Trekking** and **Sunvil Discovery**. Without their generous support, this new edition would not have happened.

ACKNOWLEDGEMENTS

Many people helped to make this book a reality. We'd like to thank Patricia Barnett, Director of Tourism Concern, for supporting this project, and Christine Franklin, Barbara Gehrels, Stuart Hume, Michael Lomotey, Lara Marsh and Sue Wheat, for making Tourism Concern an enjoyable place to work.

Kirstie Jones, Diana Bewley and Martine Grove helped check and research tours. Many other people provided information on individual countries and regions, either for the first or second editions or both. They include: Judy Bennett (Kuna tourism in Panama), Roger Diski and Liz Dodd (southern Africa), Judith de Witt (Madagascar), Deborah McLaren (US), David Lovatt Smith (Kenya), Jenny Lunnon (Dominican Republic and Haiti), Rolf Wesche and Andy Drumm (Ecuador), Ron Mader (Mexico), Chris McIntyre (Namibia), Paul Miles (Solomon Islands), Dominic Hamilton (Venezuela), Trish Nicholson (Australia and New Zealand), Ricardo Oliveira (Brazil), Peter Eltringham (Belize), Jean McNeil (Costa Rica) and Martin Mowforth (Central America). Jane Taylor helped solve a minor editorial crisis.

Thanks to the following for permission to reproduce the articles in 'Being there': Andrew Eames, Jan Fairley, Mike Gerrard, Chris McIntyre, Paul Morrison, Mike Peterson/Dorobo Safaris, Belinda Rhodes, Lisa Sykes, *The Times*, *The Sunday Times*, *Independent on Sunday*, *Wanderlust*, *Traveller*, *Evening Standard*.

We are also grateful to Christopher Gow/Symbiosis Expedition Planning, Guy Marks/Tribes Travel, Paul Miles and Lisa Young for permission to use their photographs.

Mark Mann and Zainem Ibrahim

DISCLAIMER

These tours have been researched through a mixture of personal visits, email, the internet and Tourism Concern's many contacts among travellers, journalists, academics and travel-industry professionals. We've tried to check that the tours we include genuinely benefit local communities, but it would be virtually impossible to inspect every tour ourselves. Even if we did have the time and resources to visit all of these projects, deciding exactly what is beneficial to local people can still be complex and contentious. We cannot *guarantee* that we've got it right in every case.

Tourism Concern neither endorses nor condemns tourism *per se*. If tourists are going to visit the developing world or indigenous territories, we believe that community-based tourism is a better alternative to mainstream tourism. But there are real dangers in this form of tourism, as in any other: if tours are not carefully planned in consultation with local people, then people and cultures can become just another marketing commodity, helping tourism to invade remote corners of the globe. And even the most worthwhile projects bring changes and have costs – even if it's only the pollution created by a long-haul flight to get there in the first place.

For these reasons, **inclusion in this guide does not constitute an official Tourism Concern 'seal of approval'**. (This disclaimer applies to both editorial listings and advertisers.) As an independent organization, Tourism Concern does not represent any interest within the tourism industry and does not officially endorse *any* tour operators. No tour operator may claim to be supported, endorsed or recommended by Tourism Concern. Finally, all prices are for guidance only and no responsibility or liability is accepted by Tourism Concern as a result of reliance on information in this guide.

SECTION ONE

COMMUNITY TOURISM – THE ISSUES AND PRINCIPLES

TOURISM AND THE DEVELOPING WORLD

THE GLOBAL ECONOMY

One day soon, somewhere deep in a rainforest in South America or Borneo or Central Africa, a few nervous men and women will step into a muddy clearing in the jungle. Cautiously, they will accept the steel machetes or cooking pots being held out by a government-sponsored anthropologist, before hurrying back into the safety of the forest.

The encounter will not be marked by any great fanfare. It will probably not make the news. Yet it will be a significant landmark in human history. The last 'uncontacted' tribe on earth will have been caught in our global web and an era of exploration, invasion and global integration that began when Columbus first set eyes on the Americas will be over. For the first time, the entire human race will be connected in one all-embracing cultural and trading network.

As this era of human history comes to a close we are left with a dominant social and economic system that ignores human and environmental costs. A system that destroys communal life because of its demand for a mobile labour force. That creates mental illnesses and stress by sucking people into huge, anonymous cities. That discourages people from growing their own food because doing so doesn't involve selling anything (and therefore doesn't show up as profit in economic statistics). A system that puts a greater value on a pile of dead wood than on a living forest.

Beginning with the triangular colonial trade in slaves and sugar, a Western-dominated global economy has imposed itself on the world. This is the so-called 'free market': imposed by deceit and force, from the brutality of the conquistadors and the gunboat diplomacy of the British Empire to CIA-backed coups and the financial bullying of the International Monetary Fund.

The engine that drives this system is trade. Almost all human societies have engaged in some form of trade, but the global economy is unique in its scope and the way it aggressively destroys local self-sufficiency and replaces it with global trade relationships that defy common sense. These are trade relationships in which an apple transported halfway around the world via a massive infrastructure of expensive planes, airports, trucks and roads can still cost less than the same apple grown a few miles from your home.

Until the last few decades, many rural and indigenous communities in the developing world remained on the periphery of this global economy, living largely self-sufficiently. But now, because of massive improvements in modern communications, even the most remote tribe is being forced into the global marketplace. Many once-isolated communities face the end of self-sufficiency. Many of these communities now have no choice but to become involved in trade. But the terms of this trade are heavily weighed in favour of the West, which controls the capital that oils the system. Almost all of the world's major banks and stock markets are found in the West (or Japan), as are most of the shareholders of the increasingly dominant transnational corporations.

This global economy shapes – distorts – all exchange between the 'developed' and the developing world. It explains why it is *us* visiting *them*. Why *we* have the money and the consumer choice and *they* don't.

Tourism is a form of trade. It is a part of the global economy and thus bound to reproduce the inequalities and distortions of the larger system. This book aims to highlight a more positive type of holiday – one that brings benefits to local communities. However, as long as tourism takes place within this unreformed, Western-dominated global economy, even the best community tourism projects will never be perfect.

ESCAPING ESCAPISM

'Escape to the sun.' 'Leave your worries behind.' 'Get away from it all.' The marketing clichés of the tourist brochures sell us holiday fantasies cut off from real life: a parallel universe where everything bad is magically suspended for two weeks. But, for the people we visit, tourism can be anything but an escape. We can walk away from the problems that tourism creates, but they can't. It may be our holiday, but it's their home.

We need to forget tourism's escapist fantasy and accept that our holidays take place in the real world – and have a real effect on real people.

Letting go of this fantasy can also be an opportunity – not only to help the people we visit, but for ourselves as well. Community tourism can still be an escape; the holidays in this book can take you to truly beautiful places, and about as far from the daily grind of offices and traffic jams as it's possible to get. And many of these trips feature nothing more demanding than lying on a tropical beach or taking photographs of wild animals. But going on holiday, with our eyes open, to the *real* world also helps us to make friends across cultural divides; to engage more fully with the places we visit; to understand the lives of the people we visit. In short, to explore this endlessly complex and fascinating world in which we find ourselves. Escaping from 'escapism' allows us to move beyond the superficial fantasies of the tourism industry towards richer – and ultimately more rewarding – holidays.

THE WORLD'S BIGGEST INDUSTRY

Tourism is, or will soon be, the world's biggest industry. It is estimated to provide something like one in every ten jobs on the planet. It accounts for 7.9 per cent of worldwide export earnings, more than any other industry.[1] If tourism were a country, it would have the second largest economy in the world after the US. Behind the escapist fantasies, tourism is big business.

It's a complex industry too: a hydra-headed monster that embraces the large and the small, from huge corporations such as British Airways to family-run guesthouses or women braiding tourists' hair on a beach. Tourism can mean anything from rambling in Snowdonia to family trips to Disneyland, sun'n'booze packages to Spain or Greece, middle-class villas in Tuscany, all-inclusive Caribbean resorts, skiing in the Alps, wildlife safaris in Africa, or jungle tours in the Amazon.

Although Tourism Concern as an organization also examines tourism issues in Europe and Britain, this particular book is mainly about tourism to the developing world,[2] which accounts for almost a third of global tourism. A third of the world's biggest industry is still big business and still very complex. A rainforest tour in Borneo, for instance, raises different issues to an all-inclusive resort in Barbados.

According to the British Tourism Authority, 1998 was the first year in which British tourists took more holidays abroad (29 million) than in the UK (27 million).[3] In 1971, by comparison, only 8 million Britons went abroad and 34 million took holidays in Britain.

A recent phenomenon: a brief history of tourism

There have always been explorers, adventurers and traders, but modern tourism (from a British perspective, at least) might be said to have begun with the 'Grand Tour' of Europe in the 18th century, when it became fashionable for young British aristocrats to spend a year or so taking in the monuments, art and salons of continental Europe.

For the working classes it was the industrial revolution of the 19th century, with railways and paid holidays for factory workers, that provided their first chance to travel, although right up until the 1950s a holiday for most working class people generally meant a 'day out' in the country or at the seaside.

In 1841, Thomas Cook, the 'father of package tourism', organized his first train excursions in the Midlands, taking tee-totallers to meetings of the Temperance Society. In the 1850s, he branched out into rail trips to the continent. For most people, however, holidays still meant the British seaside or countryside. It wasn't until the advent of cheap air travel in the 1960s that the age of mass international tourism really began, with the first modern holidays in the sun to Mediterranean destinations such as Majorca or the Costa Brava in Spain. In the 1960s, too, small numbers of hippies and adventurous travellers set off with their backpacks to explore more exotic destinations such as Indonesia, Nepal and India, where you could live for next to nothing and find inexhaustible supplies of cheap dope. The 'Hippie Trail' was perhaps the first example of modern tourism in the developing world. While the number of Western travellers was small, they often had a disproportionate impact on local economies and cultures because of their high visibility and (relative to local people) high spending power.

Where hippies and backpackers blazed a trail, mainstream holiday development soon followed. The island of Ko Samui in Thailand, for instance, went from being an 'undiscovered' hippie hangout in about 1980 to a package tour destination with an airstrip and modern hotels by the end of that decade. The same thing has happened in Hawaii, Ibiza, Goa, Bali, Mexico's Yucatán peninsula, Fiji, the Sinai, Kenya and elsewhere. Today, it is happening in Kerala in southern India, in Zanzibar and in many other places.

Two developments – apart from the general post-war increase in disposable income and leisure time in the West – have fuelled this growth. One was the falling cost of air travel and the introduction of a generation of faster, wide-bodied planes in the 1970s. These permitted the extension of cheap charter flights and package holidays beyond the Mediterranean to such developing world destinations as Mexico, the Caribbean or The Gambia.

The second was that the tourism industry began to get involved in independent travel. Agencies such as Trailfinders and STA began selling cheap, convenient round-the-world air tickets that took much of the risk and uncertainty out of independent travel. Guidebooks such as the Lonely Planet series

INTERNATIONAL TOURIST ARRIVALS: 1950 TO PRESENT

WORLD TOURIST ARRIVALS (MILLIONS)

	1950	1960	1970	1980	1990	2000
	25.3	69.3	159.7	284.8	425	699

TOURIST ARRIVALS IN DEVELOPING COUNTRIES (MILLIONS)

	1950	1960	1970	1980	1990	2000
	–	–	–	50.3	–	191.9

Source: WTO[4]

allowed visitors to get by in almost any country, with little or no knowledge of the local language or culture.

Tourism to the developing world has grown so rapidly over the last three decades that it's easy to forget many older people in these new tourist destinations grew up without ever seeing a white person. Many are still struggling to understand this strange intrusion into their lives.

And the future? The World Tourism Organization (WTO) predicts that international tourist numbers will rise to 1.5 billion by 2020 – more than double their present level.

Who travels?

International travel remains the preserve of a few. The World Tourism Organization estimated that, in 1996, only 3.5 per cent of the world's population travelled abroad. Approximately 80 per cent of these international travellers came from just 20 countries – 17 European nations plus the US, Canada and Japan.[5]

Domestic tourism *is* growing rapidly in some developing nations – especially in larger countries with substantial middle classes such as India, China, Mexico and Brazil and emerging economies such as Korea, Thailand and Malaysia.[6]

But in smaller or poorer developing nations that lack a sizeable middle class, most tourism development and planning targets high-spending Western tourists rather than locals. Luxury hotels, all-inclusive resorts, golf courses, airports, safari parks and theme parks all cater predominantly for the demands of rich Westerners.

TOP TOURISM MARKETS, 2000		
	TOURIST SPENDING (US$ BILLION)	% OF GLOBAL TOURISM SPENDING
United States	65	13.7
Germany	47.6	10.0
United Kingdom	36.6	7.7
Japan	31.5	6.6
France	17.2	3.6
Italy	15.5	3.2
Canada	12.4	2.6
Netherlands	11.8	2.5
Combined share of tourism spending		**49.9**
Source: WTO		

Who works in tourism?

Jobs in tourism are typically badly paid and insecure, with notoriously poor conditions – both in the developing world and in rich countries such as the UK. Because tourists need attention around the clock, tourism often requires long and antisocial working hours. Of course, there's the benefit of free travel for some, but most tourism workers don't even get to travel: they work in hotels, bars, restaurants, amusement parks, car-hire offices and the like. Many jobs in tourism are seasonal, with many workers only employed during a high season that lasts just a few months.

In the developing world, local people may be employed for a year or two in the construction of a new resort, but only a few of them will be kept on once the resort actually opens – and then mainly in low-skilled, low-status roles such as porters, maids, kitchen staff, waiters and cleaners. Most management jobs are filled by Westerners or other outsiders. People need training to manage a hotel or resort, and it's usually cheaper for the resort company to bring in someone who is already trained.

As in other industries, women working in tourism earn less than men and are heavily concentrated in part-time, low-skilled jobs. They are less likely to be promoted or trained for management roles.

Who profits?

Next time you go on holiday, ask yourself who owns the hotel or airline, or the tour agency who booked your holiday, or who supplied the drink with your dinner. Who is making money from your holiday? In fact, much of what we spend on holiday – even in the developing world – ends up back in Western countries. This is known as leakage. On holiday, most of us stay in hotels owned by a Western company. We drink imported spirits, beers and soft drinks. We eat food imported to cater for Western tastes. If we are staying in an 'all-inclusive' resort we may not leave the hotel complex during our entire stay. If we do, it may be on a half-day sightseeing trip in an imported, hotel-owned coach.

Leakage means that our holidays often generate more money for Western companies than for people in the countries we visit. Even the World Bank (a generally conservative observer) estimates that an average of 55 pence out of every £1 we spend on holidays in developing countries returns to the West.[7] Much of the rest goes to businessmen drawn from national elites. Only a few pence 'trickles down' to the ordinary people who live in the rural and seaside villages in which you are actually staying.

Power and ownership in tourism is increasingly concentrated in the hands of a small number of transnational corporations. Out of 35 million overseas holidays taken by British holiday-makers in 1999, more than half – 19 million – were package tours.[8] Four companies (Thomas Cook, Airtours, First Choice

THE 'BIG FOUR' IN THE UK TRAVEL INDUSTRY

	THOMSON	AIRTOURS	FIRST CHOICE	THOMAS COOK
High street *travel agents*	Thomson Preferred Agents, Lunn Poly, Budget Travel, Pegasus, Sibbald, Travel House	Going Places, Go Direct, Travelworld, Flightdeck, Holidayline, LateEscapes	Travel Choice, Hays Travel, Bakers Dolphin, Holiday Express	Thomas Cook, ARTAC, Worldchoice
Tour operators	Thomson Holidays, Austravel, Crystal, Headwater, Jetsave, Magic Travel, Portland, Simply Travel, Skytours, Spanish Harbour, Tropical Places, etc	Airtours Holidays, Aspro, Tradewinds, Bridge, Panorama, Cresta, Eurosites, Jetset Europe, Leger Holidays, Manos, etc	First Choice Holidays, 2wenties, Eclipse, Falcon, JWT, Flexiski, Hayes & Jarvis, Sovereign, Suncars, Unijet, Travelbound, etc	Thomas Cook Holidays, Club 18–30, JMC Holidays, Time Off, Neilson, Style Holidays, Skiers World, etc
Cruise lines	Thomson Cruises	Airtours Sun Cruises (+ partnership with Carnival Cruises)	First Choice Cruises (+ alliance with Royal Caribbean)	
Airlines	Britannia Airways	Airtours International	Air 2000	JMC Airlines

Sources: www.travelmole.com; Tourism Concern

and Thomson) sold roughly three-quarters of these trips. The table below shows the main subsidiaries owned by these four companies. In November 1999, the European Commission prohibited Airtours' proposed takeover of First Choice, on the grounds that it would have left the remaining 'big three' in a position of 'collective dominance' of the UK travel industry. However, in 2000, Thomson was bought by the German giant, Preussag, while Thomas Cook was taken over by another German operator, C&N – making Preussag and C&N the two largest tourism businesses in Europe.

If you go into a Lunn Poly shop, book a holiday with Austravel and fly to Australia with Britannia Airways, in reality you would be dealing exclusively with Thomson – or, rather, with Preussag. This phenomenon, where one company is involved at every step of your holiday, is known as 'vertical integration'. And it's a similar pattern worldwide, with a dozen or so transnational corporations controlling a large share of the global tourist market.

GLOBAL AIRLINE ALLIANCES

ONE WORLD	SKY TEAM	QUALIFLYERS	STAR
British Airways,	Delta, Air France,	SwissAir, Air Europe,	Lufthansa, SAS, United,
Aer Lingus, Quantas,	Aeromexico, Korean Air	Turkish, CrossAir, Sabena,	Thai, Air Canada, Varig,
American, Cathay Pacific,		TAP, AOM	Singapore, Air New Zealand,
FinnAir, Iberia, Lan Chile			All Nippon Airways, Ansett,
			Austrian, British Midland,
			Lauda

Source: Travel Mole, 2001

Within the airline business, too, a recent spate of mergers and 'alliances' (in which airlines agree to integrate flight networks, share planes on certain routes and so on) has left four giant partnerships controlling much of the world's air travel.

* * *

International tourism, then, is an industry dominated by a few large corporations, almost all based in the West. This industry caters for a market of tourists largely drawn from 20 Western countries. In other words tourism – and especially international travel – is predominantly a Western pastime.

NEGATIVE IMPACTS OF TOURISM

Tourism can promote respect for different cultures and encourage us to care about what happens to people in faraway countries. It can create jobs and put money into local economies. It can help rural and indigenous communities preserve their culture. These potential benefits are explored in the next chapter.

Too often, however, tourism to the developing world only adds to the difficulties facing local people. Here are some of the ways that tourism can affect local people.

Displacement

Images of local and indigenous people – especially 'exotically' dressed tribal people – are commonly used in tourist marketing to sell destinations. Pick up a brochure for holidays in Kenya and the chances are that it will contain a picture of a few Maasai tribesmen in 'traditional dress', probably jumping up and down. Yet Maasai communities in Kenya have been evicted from their land to make way for the country's famous national parks, such as Amboseli. Most environmentalists now agree that their presence wasn't harming the wildlife. The Maasai themselves feel they were forced to move because they were 'in the way' of tourist development that benefited the Kenyan government and businessmen in Nairobi.

The Maasai are not unique. All over the world, poor rural communities standing in the way of profitable tourist development have been thrown off their land. In Tanah Lot in Bali, farmers claim that the government forced them to hand over their farms for a golf course and hotel by shutting off irrigation to their fields. In Goa, developers of the 5-star Taj hotel complex persuaded the government to serve compulsory purchase orders on people in 17 villages, all of whom had previously refused to sell their land.

On the other hand, in the Peruvian Amazon, communities of Yagua Indians have been coerced by tour operators to move in the opposite direction, closer to tourist lodges, so that tourists could photograph them more conveniently. Removed from their traditional hunting land, the Yagua have become dependent upon tourism.

In Malaysia, shop owners on the coastal road near the jetty at Kuah were forced to move because the Tourist Development Committee considered them an eyesore. A tourist shop and restaurant were built in their place.

In Burma, thousands of people were forcibly relocated by the governing State Law and Order Restoration Council (or SLORC: now renamed the State Peace and Development Council or SPDC) to clear the way for tourist development in Pagan, whose monumental collection of temples is one of the country's big tourist draws.

Individually, these may not sound spectacular. A few insignificant villagers moved on here or forcibly bought out there. That's just the point: that poor local people are regarded as insignificant when they stand in the way of tourist developments that will generate money for governments and business interests. And these are not isolated examples: there are thousands of similar stories.

Cultural degradation

Tourism may encourage begging and 'hustling', or transform traditions of hospitality into commercial transactions, lacking the kindness and generosity they once contained. Locals may aspire to Western lifestyles and adopt the materialistic values of their Western visitors. Tourism may reduce cultural traditions to meaningless tourist attractions. Sacred dances become after-dinner shows in luxury hotels. Such shows might, in theory, keep cultural traditions alive, but they are all too often stripped of meaning and significance to become parodies of the real thing.

Tourism can encourage prostitution, as it has in Thailand. In a study of 100 schoolchildren in Kalutara, Sri Lanka, 86 children had their first sexual experience aged 12 or 13 – the majority with a foreign tourist. In Thailand, impoverished families, often from the northern hill tribes, sell their daughters into prostitution, largely to cater for the sex-tourism industry.

Distorting local economies and social structures

Tourism may lead to dependence on income from tourists. A farmer may neglect his crops because he can earn more money by guiding tourists. However, unlike farming or hunting, tourism does not in itself produce food to feed people or materials to clothe and house people. Tourism is a service industry that depends upon fashions and trends in distant countries. Local people in the developing world have no control over the global tourist market. Fashions change. A kidnapping in another part of their country may frighten tourists away. What does the farmer do then, if he hasn't prepared his land – or if he sold his land to invest in his new tourist business?

Tourism can also undermine established social structures. If a young boy can earn more guiding backpackers to cheap hotels than his teacher earns from teaching, will his teacher still command respect? Similarly, a young tourist guide may find himself the richest person in his village simply by mastering a smattering of English and taking a few tourists for a walk. He can distribute money or gifts and hand out jobs as porters and cooks, for instance. Will he – and the rest of his village – still defer to the traditional chief or elders, who may have little economic power in this new world? These traditional community authorities may be bypassed by the hustle of free-market tourism.

Environmental degradation

Air travel is extremely polluting. It's also growing rapidly and scientists predict that, by 2015, half the annual destruction of the ozone layer could be caused

'The impacts of global warming have been and will continue to be worst felt in poor, developing regions, through increased incidents of drought, flooding and freak weather. Any short-term 'development' of these countries through tourism must be set against the catastrophic effect already seen and still anticipated from global warming. There is no such thing, in real terms, as ecotourism. If we travel, we should do so in the knowledge that our tourism brings with it environmental damage.'

Source: Joanna Griffiths, environment editor, *Guardian Unlimited* (www.guardian.co.uk)

by air travel. A return flight from London to New York produces more carbon dioxide per passenger than the average British motorist does in an entire year and fuel emissions high in the upper atmosphere have a far greater effect on the ozone layer than emissions at sea level.

To be truly 'green', then, we ought to take our holidays as close to home as possible, with the minimum amount of travel.

Travellers worried about their environmental impact can donate to either **Future Forests** or the **Carbon Storage Trust**.[9] You pay a voluntary levy, based on the length of your flight, and these organizations will plant trees and take other measures to absorb the carbon dioxide your journey produces. (The theory is that planes emit carbon dioxide, while trees absorb it. However, not all scientists agree that this will work in practice – see www.chooseclimate.org.)

At a localized level, the best defence of many wilderness regions has been their inaccessibility: a new road or airstrip to service a remote 'eco-lodge' may threaten this. New infrastructure such as roads or airstrips may also open up wilderness to more destructive activities such as settlement, farming or logging.

CONTRIBUTION OF AIR TRAVEL TO GLOBAL WARMING, IN 'SUSTAINABLE EMISSION YEARS'

London to Sydney	2.58 years
New York to Kathmandu	1.84 years
London to Lima	1.52 years
London to New Delhi	1.13 years
London to Madrid	0.25 years

Note: A sustainable emission year is the total fossil-fuel a person can use in a year without contributing to global warming, if everyone on the planet used fuel equally. Anything over 1 is thus unsustainable. Figures assume a return economy 747 flight at 80 per cent capacity.

Source: Dr Ben Matthews (www.chooseclimate.org)

Hotels often pump untreated sewage into rivers and oceans. In the Sinai, hotels dump rubbish in the desert, out of sight of the tourists. Trekkers and trekking companies discard their litter as they go – as has happened at Everest Base Camp or along the Inca Trail in Peru. Coral is damaged by clumsy snorkellers or by tourist boats dropping their anchors. Deforestation and soil erosion occurs in Nepal as already scarce trees are cut down so that trekkers can have hot showers. It is estimated that the average trekking group uses as much firewood in two weeks as a local family uses in six months.

Throughout the 1990s, an average of 350 new golf courses were built worldwide every year, many in holiday destinations such as Thailand or Goa. It's estimated that golf courses in such countries need around 1500 kilogrammes of chemical fertilizers, pesticides and herbicides each year. Building golf courses usually means clearing away well-adapted native species and replanting imported grasses, which often have no defence against local diseases and therefore require extra pesticides. The health of local people can be affected by drinking water or eating fish from rivers contaminated by toxic run-off from golf courses.

Diversion of scarce resources upon which local people depend

The development of hotels, or other tourist facilities such as golf courses, may divert scarce resources away from local people. For example, a single golf course in Thailand can use as much water as 60,000 rural villagers. Hotels and golf courses may draw so much water from the local water table that it is severely depleted. Village wells run dry and villagers – usually women – have to walk for hours to fetch water for their own use. (As with many of these negative tourism impacts, the extra burden tends to fall disproportionately on women.)

All-inclusives – hotels which contain all the facilities that tourists needs within their grounds – not only exclude most local people from a share of the profits, but also deny them access to land and beaches from which they may once have swum or fished themselves, or where their children used to play.

Disease

With remote tribal groups, visitors risk introducing diseases to which the tribe has no immunity. In extreme cases, tribal people have died from contact with Western tourists.

* * *

If you'd like to know more about these issues, see Tourism Concern's website at www.tourismconcern.org.uk

ACCEPTING THE TRUE COST OF OUR HOLIDAYS

We tell opinion polls that we want better social services, then vote for tax cuts. We say we want organic food, then buy the cheaper stuff on the next shelf. And we talk about more socially responsible, environmentally friendly holidays... then book the cheapest package tour we can find.

It's hard to resist a bargain. But cheap holidays, like cheap food and lower taxes, mean that corners have to be cut. Hotels are built without proper sewage treatment plants. Rubbish is dumped in fragile areas, rather than carried out. Staff are underpaid and laid off out of season.

Tour operators argue that they have no choice. They say holiday prices have been driven down by less scrupulous competitors. If they invest properly in being 'green' and in making sure they don't disadvantage local people, then they will have to charge more for their holidays. But (the tour operators argue) consumers are only interested in the bottom line. If a company raises prices to pay its workers a better wage, then customers will simply switch to another operator who *has* cut corners to keep prices down.

Many people in the tourism industry privately acknowledge that cut-price tourism is unsustainable. It degrades each destination before moving on in search of the next 'unspoilt' paradise. And tourism is growing rapidly. If it causes problems now, what will it be like in 50 years' time, with four or five times the present number of tourists?

Is it possible to imagine a type of tourism that leaves a place just as beautiful as it finds it? Where tourists can keep on coming, year after year, without degrading the local environment and undermining local cultural values? A tourist industry that is non-destructive and sustainable?

Tour operators say it's up to us to prove that we are really willing to pay more for sustainable holidays. Only then will the mainstream tourism industry begin to take notice and put more emphasis on behaving responsibly. The holidays in this directory are small in scale and may not, in themselves, have much impact on global tourism statistics and problems. But they may be a way in which you can demonstrate that there is a demand for more responsible, less damaging, holidays.

NOTES

1 World Tourism Organization (WTO) figures. The WTO estimates that tourism is the main source of foreign currency in 38 per cent of countries in the world and one of the top five export categories in 83 per cent of countries.
2 See the Glossary at the end of this book.
3 A holiday, in this case, meaning a stay of over four nights. However, if one includes all trips of at least one night, Britons take about three times as many domestic as

international holidays – 75.3 million in 1999 compared to 36.6 million foreign trips. (Note: there is some variation between figures for UK outbound tourism produced by different organizations.)

4   The WTO statistics count 'arrivals' rather than the number of people who travel, so one person making two overseas trips in a year counts as two arrivals. Thus, although there were 698 million international arrivals in 2000, the number of people travelling internationally would have been considerably less. WTO figures are for all international journeys, including business travel, but exclude domestic tourism (holidays taken in one's own country). No accurate statistics exist measuring domestic tourism, but it has been estimated to be something like three to five times greater than international tourism.

5   Most of these travellers were heading for other Western countries. The most popular overseas destination countries for British tourists are, in descending order: Spain, France, the US, Greece, Portugal, Italy, Ireland and Cyprus (Office of National Statistics, 2001).

6   In 1994, for instance, India, South Africa and Brazil received 1.88 million, 3.66 million and 1.7 million international visitors respectively, but the number of domestic 'tourist nights' in these countries was estimated at 135 million, 12 million and 96 million respectively (WTO).

7   Studies for individual countries have put the figure for leakage at 40 per cent in India, 60 per cent in Thailand, 70 per cent for Kenya and up to 80 per cent in the Caribbean.

8   *Travel Trends* 1999, Crown Copyright 2000.

9   See Resources directory.

COMMUNITY TOURISM: AN ALTERNATIVE

COMMUNITY TOURISM DEFINED

The idea of community tourism is simple: you can help local people and still have a good holiday, simply by going on tours that involve local communities. In other words, it is mutually beneficial trade. In practice, however, there is no one single model for community-based tourism and the projects in our directory are owned and managed in a variety of ways. Rather than lay down a rigid set of rules for community tourism, this chapter discusses the general principles that lie behind such holidays.

Who and where?

This guide is mainly about tourism to the developing world. Of course, the principles of community tourism (local benefit, consultation, sustainability) apply everywhere, but the impact of tourism – for good or bad – is arguably greater in the developing world, where many countries are coming to depend upon tourism as one of their main foreign currency earners. In any case, it's much harder to talk about 'communities' in Western countries, with their mobile and largely urban populations.

Most of the tours and projects we list are rural. Although many people in the developing world now live in cities, the idea of community is hard to apply in an urban context. Few tourists want to spend their holiday in developing world cities anyway, so urban tours are pretty thin on the ground.

While also including non-tribal tours, this book places a special emphasis on tribal people. This is not because tribal people are any more special than non-tribal people. However, as tribal people are more likely than non-tribal people to live communally (that is, after all, what 'tribal' means[1]), it's not surprising that they feature strongly in a book about communally organized tourism. They are also, on the whole, more vulnerable to the impacts of tourism. Tourism sees tribal culture as a selling point. Tourists seek out tribal people whether or not tribal people want to to be visited – for example, on 'hill-tribe treks' in northern Thailand. Tribal communities often find it hard to cope with the volume of tourists trying to visit them. Tribal peoples are also more likely to live in 'ecotourism' destinations such as rainforests or deserts: 'ecotours' often enter tribal land without permission. And because tribal communities often live very differently from Westerners, tourists are more likely to disrupt local life or give offence than in more acculturated communities. Tourism Concern recommends that you only visit tribal territory on tours that are run by – or have been authorized by – the communities themselves. We include tribally and indigenously run tours even in Western countries such as the US (see box below).

FIRST NATIONS

First Nations is a collective term for Native Americans in the US and Canada, Australian Aboriginals and New Zealand Maoris. Why are they included in a directory of developing world tourism? Because, in many ways, they have more in common with indigenous people elsewhere than with the European societies who have colonized their lands. They often suffer developing world levels of poverty – one recent study reported that Australian Aboriginals had the worst health statistics of any ethnic group on earth. Like other indigenous people, many First Nations still live in 'wilderness' areas; still live in tribal communities; still preserve close ties with the land. They also face similar obstacles when starting businesses: lack of education and business experience, discrimination by governments and white society. And tourists want to visit them for the same reasons that we want to visit indigenous people elsewhere: to experience non-Western attitudes, customs, spirituality, etc.

What is a community?

In this book, a 'community' means a mutually supportive, geographically specific, social unit such as a village or tribe where people identify themselves as community members and where there is usually some form of communal decision-making. The breakdown of such traditional, locally based communities in the West and the urban developing world – largely due to the global economy's demand for a mobile labour force – is one of the reasons why this book is mainly about the rural developing world, where most people still spend most of their lives in one village or tribe.

What is a community-based tour?

The obvious definition would be: 'tours owned and run entirely by local communities'. At present, however, this is too limiting: some of the most successful projects involve non-community partners such as non-governmental organizations (NGOs) or commercial tour operators. Others may be set up by individual community members: sometimes this works well and sometimes it creates divisions within the community. For these reasons, we've adopted a broad definition of what counts as community-based to include anything that involves genuine community participation and benefits. (I'll discuss what these benefits might be later in this chapter.)

PRACTICALITIES

What sort of holiday can you expect?

Community tours tend to be small-group trips run by small specialist operators. You won't find mass package tours where you travel in large groups and stay in identikit hotels. These are holidays for people who want to get away from the crowd, not be part of it. Many of these tours are nature based. Others emphasize local life and culture. Many combine both. They allow you to experience different lifestyles and to meet local people in a relaxed, unhurried atmosphere. And they are extremely varied. There are beaches in Brazil, wildlife in Kenya, drumming in Senegal, dancing in Cuba, Spanish lessons in Guatemala, trekking in Nepal, sea-kayaking in Samoa, horseriding in Arizona, yak-trekking in Mongolia, and much more. The 'Holiday-finder index' in Section Two of this guide will help you find a holiday to suit your interests.

Mud hut or luxury lodge?

The directory includes a wide range of comfort levels. Some of the safari lodges in Africa, for instance, are about as upmarket and luxurious as it gets. Other trips involve sleeping in mud huts or under the stars. Some communities have comfortable guesthouses; in others you do as the locals do – even if that means heading off into the bushes when you need the toilet. Prices vary accordingly. Individual directory entries indicate the level of comfort, price and facilities you can expect.

Efficiency

Some trips will run smoothly. Others can be less reliable. Many travellers find that a degree of unpredictability is 'all part of the fun', but you may disagree if you're on a tight schedule. Usually, the more you pay, the more efficiency and punctuality you can expect. You can reasonably assume that a tour which has a UK agent, fax, email and website is more likely to run punctually than a tour that you reach by throwing a stone across a river to attract attention. But many people want to visit remote rural and indigenous communities precisely to get away from things like efficiency and punctuality. You can't have it both ways. So take a moment to decide what sort of holiday you really want.

BETTER HOLIDAYS FOR YOU

Let's be clear. The holidays in our directory are definitely that. Holidays! Of course, if all you want is sex, sun and booze without too many annoying foreign people, then maybe Club 18-30 or Ibiza would be better choices. But if you've read this far, you probably see a holiday as an opportunity to discover new places and explore different cultures. If so, community tourism offers some special rewards.

Cultural contact

Meeting people from different cultures can be one of the pleasures of travel. Community-based tours provide more opportunities than mainstream tours to get closer to local culture and to spend time with local people in a relaxed, unhurried atmosphere. You will have more time to develop friendships and see what life is really like for your hosts. These tours are a way to get beyond the artificial 'cultural shows' that you find in tourist hotels, or the typical 20-minute coach tour stop in a local village to buy handicrafts. And you can expect a warmer welcome because local people know that they are benefiting from your visit. Even backpackers will find that a few days on a locally booked community tour can provide an extra degree of insight into local life and culture, often for little more than it costs to travel independently.

Exciting destinations

Our directory lists hundreds of tours in over 40 countries. Many take you to beautiful natural places: rainforests, deserts, tropical beaches and coral reefs, towering mountain ranges and African plains. You can visit remote tribal communities in the Amazon rainforest or experience everyday life in rural Asian villages. You can see mighty ruins of ancient civilizations and some of the most amazing wildlife on earth.

Local knowledge

You'll have the privilege of seeing these places in the company of the people who know them best – the people who live there. For instance, tours run by indigenous communities often make a feature of their traditional knowledge of local wildlife or medicinal plant uses: knowledge built up over thousands of years of living in that particular environment.

Helping the people you visit

There is satisfaction in contributing to the efforts of local people to build a better life for themselves: a feeling of solidarity and shared ideals. It may be intangible but, as many 'community tourists' have discovered, it could be the thing that makes your trip truly memorable.

An 'indigenous message' for us

The tours in this book illustrate that (apart from Antarctica) there are few truly uninhabited regions of the planet. Most of what we think of as wilderness – rainforests and deserts and so on – has been home to people for thousands of years. These areas are, in fact, managed environments. In many cases, the indigenous people who live in these places have simply managed their environments better than we in the West, using them productively yet preserving their natural beauty and richness. If we in the West are to relearn a less destructive way of life, then we must learn from their example. Community tours to indigenous communities can be a source of inspiration. They can show Western visitors that a 'sustainable lifestyle' and 'living with nature' are practical realities, not just utopian concepts.

An attitude to travel

This book is more than just a list of tours. It is also about an attitude to travel. Even if you prefer to travel independently, the principle of community tourism can point you towards richer and more rewarding holidays. The idea is mutual benefit – better holidays for you and better holidays for local people. By contributing more, you get more yourself.

HOW COMMUNITY TOURISM DEVELOPS: UNPLANNED AND PLANNED

Community tourism tends to develop in one of two ways, each of which raises slightly different issues.

Unplanned

In the first, unplanned, scenario, an area is 'discovered', first by adventurous backpackers and then by commercial operators who notice the emerging market. At first, local communities may be bemused by this invasion, reacting to tourism rather than planning and controlling it. They offer accommodation because tourists and tour operators ask them for this facility and because of traditional rules of hospitality: as a result, a variety of informal arrangements spring up between tourists, operators and local people. As local people start to understand what tourists want (and how much they really pay), they begin to seek more control of tourism in their territory. In this scenario, community tourism develops as a response to tourism. Often communities will develop partnerships with those operators who make the effort to consult them properly.

We might also call this scenario 'demand-led', because local tourism is driven by consumer demand. Community tourism projects that develop in this way have few marketing problems, since backpackers are turning up anyway. But a local pattern of exploitative, disruptive tourism may already be established and hard to change.

Planned

The alternative, planned, scenario typically involves an NGO (or the community itself, or occasionally a commercial operator) who identifies tourism as a potentially sustainable source of income for a community that is engaged in a more environmentally harmful activity (for instance, overfarming poor soil, logging, etc). The NGO/operator/community tries to develop a community-based tourism project before the backpackers and commercial operators move in.

These projects aim to preempt the harmful impact of unplanned tourism. But because both local community and NGOs may lack experience in tourism, they can struggle to deliver an attractive product to the tourist. Prices are often set wishfully high. Inexperienced guides don't understand what tourists want. Things don't run on time.

We might also call this scenario 'supply led'. The supply (the tour) is there before the demand (the tourists), hence the second problem for these projects – attracting tourists. Planned/supply-led projects often aim to bypass the low-paying backpacker market in favour of a more upmarket clientele, who will bring more money with less disruption. Reaching this market requires high initial investment in installing upmarket accommodation and infrastructure, plus glossy advertising and marketing deals with upmarket travel agents. All this is expensive and may lie outside the experience of the NGO.

TEN PRINCIPLES FOR COMMUNITY TOURISM

1 Community tourism should involve local people. That means they should participate in decision-making and ownership, not just be paid a fee.
2 The local community should receive a fair share of the profits from any tourism venture.
3 Tour operators should try to work with communities rather than individuals. Working with individuals can create divisions within a community. Where communities have representative organizations these should be consulted and their decisions respected.
4 Tourism should be environmentally sustainable. Local people must benefit and be consulted if conservation projects are to work. Tourism should not put extra pressure on scarce resources.
5 Tourism should support traditional cultures by showing respect for indigenous knowledge. Tourism can encourage people to value their own cultural heritage.
6 Operators should work with local people to minimize the harmful impacts of tourism.
7 Where appropriate, tour operators should keep groups small to minimize their cultural and environmental impact.
8 Tour operators or guides should brief tourists on what to expect and on appropriate behaviour before they arrive in a community. That should include how to dress, taking photos, respecting privacy.
9 Local people should be allowed to participate in tourism with dignity and self-respect. They should not be coerced into performing inappropriate ceremonies for tourists, etc.
10 People have the right to say no to tourism. Communities who reject tourism should be left alone.

BETTER HOLIDAYS FOR LOCAL PEOPLE

While community tourism has much to offer tourists, the uniting principle is the idea of local benefit. Here are some ways in which these holidays can help local people.

More of your money stays in the local economy

This is the most obvious benefit. It may mean that your guide or porter is paid more. It may mean that you (or your tour operator) pay a fee into a community fund. It may mean local people own the tour company. It may mean that tourists provide a market for other small local businesses, such as carvings, clothes, crafts, jewellery, snacks or restaurants. Such businesses may also open up new employment opportunities – especially for women, since working part-time from home or within their village often fits well with childcare and other responsibilities. Thus, community-based tourism can give women more economic and social independence.

Even so, the chances are that local people will see only a fraction of the money you spend on your holiday. They do not get any of your airfare, which is most people's single largest holiday expense (but see **North-South Travel** in the chapter on UK/General Tour Operators). If you book with a UK-based agency, much of the cost of your trip inevitably goes on marketing, administration and UK office staff. Yet even a few extra pounds paid locally could be the difference between poverty and security to someone in rural Peru or Zimbabwe.

Not harming the environment: beyond ecotourism

When used by tour operators to sell their tours, ecotourism can be a vague concept. It can simply mean looking at trees or animals. In practice, most so-called ecotours do little to protect the environment – and little or nothing to improve the well-being of local people.

In fact, such nature tours ('ecotourism-lite', as they've been dubbed) tend to simply ignore local people. Look at the brochures of many ecotour companies – or even trips run by some non-profit environmental organizations – and you'll notice a strange absence of people. Instead, ecotourism operators sell images of exotic animals and empty landscapes, or present indigenous people as if they were another exotic species of wildlife to be pointed at and photographed. Notions of sustainability and responsible tourism are understood in terms of preserving the environment or wildlife, rather than in terms of helping local people.

In reality, the two go together. Few 'wildernesses' are really as devoid of people as the brochures suggest and if ecotourism ignores the human presence it is of little use as a conservation tool. Such tourism simply puts extra pressure on fragile areas, using up scarce resources and leaving more rubbish. Community-based ecotourism, on the other hand, allows local people to benefit from conservation and can be a valuable conservation tool. Here's why.

A sustainable economic alternative for local people
In parts of Africa, local people have killed elephants for their ivory, or rhino for their horns, because they have no other income. In the Amazon or Borneo, local communities have logged (or sold logging rights) or signed deals allowing oil companies to drill for oil on their land. In Brazil, communities clear land to farm by burning forest. These people understood the harm they were doing...

COMMUNITY TOURISM OR ECOTOURISM?

The US-based Ecotourism Society defines ecotourism as: 'responsible travel to natural areas that conserves the environment and improves the well-being of local people'. Many of the tours in this directory fit this definition. But community tourism is a distinct (if overlapping) concept: it means 'tourism that involves and benefits local communities'. Community tourism doesn't have to be nature-based. Communities may offer cultural tours or simply run local guesthouses. In general, community tourism puts the emphasis on people, while arguing that it is only by putting people at the centre of the picture that true conservation solutions will be found.

but everyone has to eat. Community-based tourism may offer local people a more environmentally sustainable alternative.

Indigenous land rights can protect 'wilderness'

Many indigenous communities, in particular, still live in areas rich in plant species and wildlife. These wilderness regions are now threatened by a host of 'development' pressures, from oil companies, loggers, miners and ranchers to tourism or governments desperate for hard currency to fund debt repayments to Western banks. Indigenous people have a claim to ownership of their traditional lands, based upon the simple fact that they have lived there for centuries. These indigenous land rights (if accepted by governments, who usually dispute them) can block harmful development. Without the presence and resistance of indigenous people in the Ecuadorean Amazon, much more of that country's rainforest would have been destroyed.

But most indigenous communities are no longer able to live self-sufficiently. If conservationists want them to say 'no' to harmful development, they must offer them an alternative means of feeding their families. Tourism may be that alternative. In many places, tourism is a central pillar of emerging alliances between local communities and conservation organizations.

Supporting tribal / communal structures

Tourism can easily disrupt complex communal relationships, especially in tribal and indigenous cultures. While change may be inevitable, tour operators should work within existing social structures to allow communities to change on their own terms. And operators have a responsibility to ensure that any tourists they bring into communities also understand and respect these social structures.

This demands a long-term commitment from tour operators. Internal community relations may be hard for outsiders to grasp, and decision-making may be slow and complex. Many indigenous people are being forced to adapt quickly to new situations and concepts (such as a money-based economy), while the very future of their culture may depend upon the choices they make. In these circumstances, people should not be rushed into quick decisions. Traditional decision-making within indigenous cultures is often a slow process: people may have to walk for hours or even days to attend a meeting and debates may be loosely structured and last for days, involving many meetings and rituals (to consult ancestors and guiding spirits, for instance).

Community consultation can therefore be frustrating, expensive and time consuming for a tour operator. It may result in a less profitable tour. A tour operator may be impatient to get things moving and be tempted to work with a few cooperative individuals – even if they do not represent the whole community. It is a test of a tour operator's commitment to community tourism that it takes consultation seriously.

The reason that most of the communities in this guidebook have turned to tourism is that they realize they have to adapt. Across the globe, development means traditional self-sufficiency is rarely possible. Even many remote tribal communities must now become involved in the market economy.[2] Without a source of local income, community members will have to move to cities to look for work, joining the ever-increasing army of underemployed squatters in the makeshift shanty towns that surround most developing world capitals. If too many people leave, the community will disintegrate. Its former members will be cut off from their roots, culture and support networks. This has already happened in much of Europe and North America, and it may be one reason why depression, stress and mental illnesses are on the increase in the West despite our material prosperity. Community tourism may help keep communities together.

Allowing local people to participate in tourism with dignity and pride

This means not being pressured into performing inappropriate rituals for tourists. It means being able to put local viewpoints to tourists. It ensures that local people are not seen as tourist exhibits or photo opportunities. It means children seeing their parents involved in decision-making and working as teachers and guides rather than as porters or beggars. Self-respect, although intangible, can make a real difference to the quality of people's lives.

Many indigenous communities have been subjected to years of propaganda from governments, educators and missionaries, telling them that their traditional culture (animism, hunting, etc) is primitive, inferior and even evil. Meeting tourists who are interested in, and respectful of, their culture can be a surprise to many indigenous people. It can encourage them to reevaluate their

---

COMMUNITY OR LOCAL?

A key principle of community tourism is *buy* local: eat locally-grown food in locally-owned restaurants, stay in locally-run guesthouses, buy locally-made souvenirs, use local guides, and so on. In principle, the more locally you spend, the more good it is likely to do. Yet, as any independent traveller will realize, there are many thousands of family-run guesthouses and restaurants around the world that are not listed in this book. Many are excellent, but the benefits of such private enterprises are not *always* shared evenly and this can create local inequalities and tensions. We believe communally-owned tourism, where benefits are shared equitably and everyone in the community has a stake in the venture, is an even better alternative.

---

own attitude towards their traditions. The 1997 ToDo! Awards report for the Shawenequanape Kipichewin – an Anishinabe camp and cultural centre in Canada – notes that: 'Thanks to the visitors' high regard for traditional First Nations culture, young Anishinabe have become conscious of their own values, which is the greatest achievement of the project.'

Defending community land rights

There are countless cases of people being forced off their land so that governments, rich businesspeople and Western corporations can move in and exploit its natural and mineral wealth. Sometimes people are forced out to make way for tourism itself, as we saw in the previous chapter.

Publicizing a community's presence
Community tourism can assert a community's land rights simply by making its presence more widely known. Tourists who have visited a community are more likely to take a continued interest in what happens to its people, and advertising a community's presence in tour brochures makes it harder for governments to pretend a community does not exist.

Giving communities an economic value
Governments look at wild areas and, instead of seeing natural beauty and richness, they see economic vacuums. Even when people are living sustainably in these areas, governments see no money changing hands, no profit, no export earnings. A tourism project at least registers on the economic statistics. It attracts tourists, who bring in foreign exchange and go on to visit other parts of the country. For the same reason, governments are also more likely to tolerate indigenous culture if it attracts tourists.

DIFFICULTIES AND DANGERS

A job in tourism may sound glamorous – a chance to travel. But for people in poor developing world communities, it's not like that. For a start, tourism to them doesn't mean the chance to travel. Many of these communities see tourism not as a glamorous adventure, but as the least harmful option open to them. Even the best community-tourism project will cause some disruption and bring change. But we have to ask: 'would the alternative have been better'?

Practical difficulties

Rural and indigenous communities face practical problems in running their own tourism projects. To overcome these, they often work with a commercial tour operator or an NGO. These are some of the practical problems.
- They lack capital: to invest in infrastructure, advertising, training, etc. Therefore their 'product' may not match that of commercial rivals. Their guesthouse may not be as comfortable, their boats not as fast.
- They may not be used to Western business practices: the need to keep accounts, to reinvest profits, to advertise, to work to precise timetables.
- They may not understand tourists: after all, what is the point of tourism? Why do we want to visit their village? What do we want to do, now that we're here? Many local people may not realize that our societies are very different from theirs, and are amazed that we are willing to pay to watch them catch a fish or carry out some other everyday task.
- They lack access to tourist markets: based in remote parts of the developing world, how do these communities reach tourists in Europe or North America? (This book is intended to help them do just that.)

Potential dangers

All change is unpredictable. There are many pitfalls for communities who get into tourism. Even a successful project can create new problems. Tourism inevitably involves exposure to Western people and Western ideals and this will inevitably change traditional and indigenous cultures. Even development agencies may impose Western values – insisting, perhaps, that women participate in activities from which they were traditionally excluded. Should we force cultures to change practices we dislike?

Even as well-intentioned tourists, we may still bring our Western values and hang-ups: the value we place on money and material gain; our cynicism; our secular scepticism; our belief in individual freedom over communal obligations; our liberal attitudes towards sex and drugs, and so on. And tourists,

DEGREES OF COMMUNITY PARTICIPATION

Responsible tours

These are tours run by commercial tour operators who behave responsibly towards local communities. A share of the profits may be given to local community projects. Local people are trained as guides and properly paid. While better than most commercial trips, they are still controlled by outsiders. Responsible tours are often ecotours, with more emphasis on wildlife and nature than on culture.

Partnership tours

Here, tours run in partnership between the local community and an 'external partner' – maybe a responsible commercial operator or an NGO. This covers a variety of arrangements in which the local community has some say in – but not total control over – planning and managing tours. The external partner cushions the impact of tourism on the community and provides business or marketing skills that the community lacks. But, like responsible tours, they depend on the good faith of the external partner. These tours are likely to offer tourists more cultural insight than normal holidays.

Community tours

These are tours set up, owned and run entirely by the local community. This is the 'purest' type of community tourism, but not all communities are able to run their own tours. They may have problems with marketing or understanding what Western tourists want. Even a sudden influx of cash can create problems in a community unused to the cash-economy. Some community-owned ventures employ an outside manager to overcome these problems.

with their gadgets and self-confidence, can be unwitting propagandists for a Western lifestyle. People who can afford exotic foreign holidays are, in a way, the 'successes' of Western society. The people we visit don't see the 'failures' – the alcoholics, the addicts, the homeless, the people in prisons and psychiatric institutions.

Tourism can also remove self-sufficiency. People may neglect other tasks, such as tending the fields or going to school, to focus their energy on their successful tourism scheme. But tourism depends on Western consumer trends. If tourists stop coming – maybe because of a changing exchange rate or a terrorist threat – the community may have nothing to fall back on.

There is also the danger that tourism will turn once practical cultures into fossilized tourist attractions. Rituals and survival skills may lose their meaning if they become simply tourist shows. When ritual becomes divorced from functionality, a practical way of life is on the way to becoming a dead 'museum culture'.

Lastly, tourism can destabilize a community. It may give individuals an influence that clashes with traditional structures. It may create jealousies and resentment. After all, money can be destabilizing even for us – and we're used to dealing with it.

Is it genuine... and who decides?

Does a new village school or health centre make up for the loss of traditional knowledge of culture? What if increased income leads to more materialistic, less communal values? Weighing up the benefits and costs of a community tourism project is a subjective and contentious business.

Who makes these decisions? Ideally, it should be the community itself. But communities are often internally divided. In such circumstances, *what* we hear about a project may depend on *who* we talk to. In many cases, our information comes from commercial tour operators who work with local communities. While most of these operators are undoubtedly sincere, a few may be using the pretence of community involvement to sell purely commercial tours. In Kenya and South Africa, white ranch-owners have converted their farms into game reserves which they claim to be 'community projects' simply because they employ local people. Some of these reserves may genuinely involve the local community and bring real benefits to local people, but others are simply perpetuating the old colonial order of a white land-owning elite and low-paid black workers.

How do we decide what is genuine and what is a sham? All we can do is gather as much information as possible about each project, from as many people as possible, and make a judgement. The line between genuine community tourism and tokenism can be a fine one, and we may have made mistakes in compiling our directory. That is one reason why we don't officially 'recommend' any tours. We welcome your comments, good or bad, on any tour we list.

* * *

Community tourism won't save the world. But it might help some local communities improve the quality of their lives. It might help protect fragile natural regions until we develop a saner approach to the environment. And it might help to demonstrate a consumer demand for fairer, more sustainable holidays – a demand that could eventually change the mainstream tourism industry too.

NOTES

1   See the glossary at the end of this book.
2   In the few cases where tribal communities are still able to live self-sufficiently, they usually show little interest in tourism and we recommend that you don't visit them.

BEING THERE

So much for Theory. But what are community-based holidays like in practice? These articles might give you a better idea of what it's like to be a tourist on a community-based tour. All of these trips are featured in the Holiday Directory.

ECUADOR: AT HOME IN THE AMAZON

This article of mine appeared in *The Times* in March 1997. It describes a visit to a **Siecoya** community on the Aguarico River in the Ecuadorian Amazon. This exact tour no longer runs, but the same community still take visitors. (See **Pirana Tours**, Ecuador.)

What is Ramiro thinking about, I wonder, as we crash clumsily along the rainforest path behind him. For us, our walk reveals a thousand new sensations: giant tree trunks, insects camouflaged as leaves, the sounds of birds and frogs and crickets, splashes of colour among endless shades of green – scarlet flowers, strange yellow fruits, white fungus on rotting logs, electric blue butterflies.

But Ramiro has walked this way a thousand times before. This is where he grew up. So maybe he is thinking about his wife and three young children. Or of rebuilding his house, which burned down last week while he was out hunting. Or is he thinking of the oil company Occidental, who want to build an oil well where we now stand? Ramiro says he will die fighting rather than let the oil workers move in.

Ramiro, a stocky 28-year-old dressed in T-shirt and football shorts, is a Siecoya Indian. This beautiful stretch of primary rainforest along the Aguarico ('rich water') river in the Oriente, Ecuador's part of the Amazon, is Siecoya land. The Siecoya have fished, hunted and farmed here for centuries. Today, like the neighbouring Cofan and Siona, the once-feared Huaorani and the Achuar, they number less than 1000. (Two other indigenous groups, the Shuar and Quichua, are slightly more numerous.)

Ramiro still hunts and fishes, but nowadays he is also a tourist guide. He has little choice. Since the 1970s, oil companies, loggers and settlers have seized huge tracts of forest. The hunting is poorer and the Siecoya's freedom to move through the forest is gone. Increasingly, they have to find alternatives. Most, such as working for the oil companies or logging, involve destroying the forest. Only tourism seems to offer a sustainable future.

Although Ecuador has many jungle tours, few involve or benefit the indigenous Indians, the rightful owners of the forest. It's our loss, too, since the Indians – who know the rainforest better than anyone – have much to teach us. But this trip is different. It is run by the Siecoya themselves.

The itinerary is much the same as for other 'jungle tours'. We see macaws and toucans and monkeys swinging through the canopy. We travel in dugout canoes at night to spot caimans. We fish for piranha. We learn about the different ecosystems in the forest (of which 'jungle' is only one – the dense growth along riverbanks or in clearings left by fallen trees). It is not so much the details as the overall feel that is different. The feeling of being not in a wilderness, but guests in someone's home, with children and pets running around your feet, women cooking, neighbours visiting.

We learn how the Siecoya use the forest. For instance, they have controlled their own population with a plant that is a contraceptive in small doses and makes women sterile in larger amounts. They can stitch wounds with a particular type of ant. Holding it so that it pinches the wound shut, they break off the body, leaving the head and pinchers fixed in place.

But this is no fantasy trip to a make-believe paradise. We also learn about the politics of the forest and the pressures on the Siecoya to abandon their traditional life. In fact, the ultimate aim of these tours is to help the Siecoya maintain their way of life and remain in the forest – not only by generating income, but also by encouraging the children to value their culture, by seeing outsiders eager to learn about it too. Alongside the economic pressures, for example, well-funded missionary groups such as the Summer Institute of Linguistics have undermined respect for traditional ways by teaching that shamanism and hunting are primitive and evil.

It's not just the Siecoya's future at stake. It's vital for the forest itself that it continues to be inhabited by people who value it and know how to manage it sustainably. The Indians' presence is a major factor keeping the oilmen out of Ecuador's remaining primary forest. But the situation is precarious. Occidental recently persuaded the Siecoya's president to sign a contract to build their oil well, with a road connecting it to the town of Coca, in return for five outboard motors and a well. Luckily, he was able to retract his signature in front of lawyers, but no one thinks Occidental will give up. Yet Ecuador's oil reserves will barely see out the century.

It was time for us to go. Ramiro and his wife Betty waved to us from the little beach in front of their home. As we set off in the motorized canoe, they were soon swallowed up by the endless wall of living green forest, mirrored in the brown waters of the Aguarico.

Despite their problems, I left with a sense of hope. I'd learned that the Amazon is neither uninhabited nor a wilderness. People have lived here for millennia (evidence of settlement dates back to at least 5000BC) and humans are as much part of the rainforest as are birds and insects. The forest has its dangers, of course, but the 'savage jungle' of Western imagination is

more a reflection of our own mistrust of nature – an attitude that has led us into environmental crisis. Seeing the forest as the Siecoya do, as a home, a provider of food, shelter, materials and medicines, reminds us that there is another way. Man can live harmoniously with nature, without having to destroy it. And that, ultimately, is worth more than any holiday photos or exotic souvenirs.

(Sadly, the community leaders *did* subsequently sign an agreement – in controversial circumstances – with the oil company allowing exploratory oil drilling on their land, which they are now trying to retract.)

FIJI: FIJI GIRL SMART IN SEX

This is another article of mine, which was published in *The Times* in December 1996. It describes a trip to **Navala** village in the hills of Vitu Levu, where the village takes in visitors for overnight stays.

There are three Fijis. The palm-fringed tourist beaches are one. Navala, where I was headed, belongs to the second: a traditional Fijian village tucked away in the hills of Viti Levu, Fiji's main island.

To reach Navala, you must go through a third Fiji – bustling coastal towns full of the Indian migrants who now comprise half the population. The town where I changed buses, Ba, could be in India, with the scent of aromatic spices drifting from the shops, Indian sweet stalls beside the road, women in sarees, curry houses and signs in Hindi and Urdu.

Leaving Ba, the old British Leyland bus roared off in a cloud of dust and exhaust fumes. It struggled up steep inclines, tilting at alarming angles. The sugar plantations of the hot coastal plains gave way to rugged hills, with cliffs of black volcanic rock jutting out of dry yellow grass. And then, in a valley over a last hill, was Navala.

The village, on a grassy sloping riverbank, is one of the few in Fiji still built entirely of *bures* (pronounced boo-rays). About 60 of these thatched huts stood in neat rows, surrounded by flowers, coconut palms and vegetable patches. Children ran between them. Some youths played touch rugby. Men carrying machetes returned from the sugar fields, and fires burned in the surrounding hills – part of a wild boar hunt. It looked beautiful, a self-contained world.

Guests traditionally stay with the chief. I was shown inside his *bure*: one room, the floor covered in palm mats, empty except for a bed and a wardrobe. On the wall were family photographs and pictures of the Fijian prime minister and the Pope.

The chief was rotund and greying, in jeans and sweatshirt. He invited me to drink some 'grog'. Grog, or *yaquana* – made from the ground root of the kava plant (*Piper Methysticum*) – is the traditional Fijian brew, drunk mainly by men. It is slightly narcotic and numbing. I'd heard that too much causes one to lose all muscular control, so I was disappointed to find we were still coordinated when diner arrived – a tasty stew of wild pig, fresh from the hunt. I slept on a mattress on the floor, as did the chief's son, John, his wife and their child. I guess I wasn't important enough for the bed, which remained empty.

Next morning, everyone went to church "cos we catholics, see' (most Fijians are protestant). Having heard that visitors are often asked to deliver a sermon, I explored the village instead, accompanied by the inevitable entourage of skipping and giggling children. A woman invited me into a *bure* full of about 20 girls – 'the village netball team'. They were large girls – they could have been the wrestling team – with equally big laughs. They all had wild, electric-shock, Don King hairstyles, as if they'd been plugged into the village generator. The conversation soon reached a familiar stage.

'You married?'

'No.'

'Oh.' A pause. 'Single?'

'I have a girlfriend.'

In developing world villages, people go by the principle that any single Western gentleman, presumably in possession of a good fortune, must be in want of a wife. For solo travellers, a girlfriend or boyfriend is a necessary fiction. Mine wasn't working.

'Your girlfriend in Fiji?'

'No, she's in England.'

'You take girlfriend in Fiji?'

'But I'm only here for one night.'

'You take Fiji girlfriend for one night. You take (pointing to a quiet girl in the corner) Alessi.'

I must have appeared hesitant, for she persisted.

'Fiji girls smart in sex, you know.'

I think she was joking. (Fiji is not, I should point out, a sex-tourism destination.) Still, I wasn't entirely sure, so I declined politely and escaped to the river to teach the children to skim stones.

For once, Fiji is a place where the colonial legacy seems positive. Christianity ended years of rampant cannibalism. The British never invaded but were asked to take over the islands in the mid 19th century by the fearsome Chief Cakabu (said to have personally killed and eaten 80 men) to stop bloody intertribal warfare. They initially turned down the offer.

The first governor, Sir Arthur Gordon, decreed that no land could be sold to a non-Fijian and no native labour could be used on the new sugar plantations. He also left the traditional village chief system in place. As a result, Fijian culture is the best preserved in the South Pacific.

The other side of Britain's laudable decision not to exploit native labour was the importation of Indian workers. Someone had to keep the sugar mills supplied and Sir Arthur wasn't about to do the job himself. Denied access to land, the Indians in Fiji developed an industrious business ethic and now run the economy.

Two more contrasting cultures are hard to imagine. The Indians are hard-working, eager to make money and keen for progress. The Fijians are relaxed and conservative. The Indians can only rent land from Fijians, which they resent: they complain that they work hard while the Fijians do nothing but drink grog and live off the profits.

The British also installed an abiding affection for two of their favourite upper-class institutions, the royal family and rugby, both almost obsessions in Fiji. The most common questions I was asked (after 'Where you from?' and 'You married?') were: 'You play rugby?' and 'How is Princess Di?'

In the morning I left. I caught a bus down the pot-holed road to the Indian supermarkets and saree shops of Ba, and then back to my tourist paradise. In two days I'd learned just a little about Fiji, but it was more than I would have in a month on the beach.

AUSTRALIA: SYDNEY'S FORGOTTEN ABORIGINAL HERITAGE

This unpublished article of mine describes a day trip in Sydney with an Aboriginal guide, Rodney Mason, who operates **Dharawal Tour**.

'My ancestors', says Rodney Mason, 'were standing right here watching old Captain Cook when he arrived. They were here to meet that old bugger Captain Phillip too, when he landed – shook 'im by the leg, an' all. The "first contact" – that was us, mate. And we're still here today.'

We are standing on the shore of Botany Bay, now a suburb of southern Sydney, looking across to the flagpole on the far shore that marks the spot where Cook made that historic landing. The houses behind us, says Rodney, are the homes of his people, the Dharawal. The same Dharawal who watched Captain Cook sail his strange ship into this very bay, over two centuries ago.

'This was all Dharawal country', Rodney continues, 'from Sydney Harbour right down the south coast. Now most of us live here. Too bloody expensive up near the city. People think you only find Aboriginal people out in the desert, painted in ochre or whatever. But you don't have to go to no bloody desert to find Aboriginals. We're right here in Sydney, mate.'

Rodney is a tall, tough-looking, tattooed Aboriginal man, with a beard last seen on tour with ZZ Top and oil on his jeans from fixing his van.

'Getting a flash new one next month', he tells me, 'Did my heavy vehicle licence the other day.'

Rodney runs Dharawal Aboriginal Tours. His aim is to introduce tourists to Sydney's forgotten Aboriginal history. When the first Europeans arrived there were people living in every part of Australia, not just in the remote deserts. However, persecution that at times amounted to ethnic cleansing, European diseases and the sheer volume of white immigrants quickly overwhelmed the Aboriginals in places such as Sydney. Today it is easy to overlook their presence. To do so would be like visiting London and ignoring everything that happened before Queen Victoria.

In fact, Sydney was home to a number of Aboriginal tribes, divided into three language groups – the Ku-ring-gai on the northern shores, the Dharug on the western plains towards the Blue Mountains and the Dharawal on the southern coast. Each of these subdivided into smaller clans, bound together by a complex system of relationships and obligations.

Today, most Aboriginals in Sydney do not belong to any of these groups. They migrated into the city from other parts of Australia, having been driven off their traditional lands by settlers or forcibly separated from their families. For years in the middle part of this century, government policy was to remove Aboriginal children from their parents and place them with white foster parents. The Dharawal of Botany Bay, on the other hand, have probably been here for thousands of years and, even as the suburban sprawl of southern Sydney enveloped them, they have managed to keep alive their connection with their traditional land.

Rodney runs trips from Bondi Beach, deep in the heart of tourist Sydney, to Botany Bay and into the Royal National Park, an area of bushland immediately south of Sydney. It's a unique opportunity to learn about Aboriginal culture, on the doorstep of the nation's biggest city.

We start off by looking at some Aboriginal rock art on the cliffs overlooking Bondi Beach. (There is Aboriginal rock art to be found throughout Sydney.) Whales and fish are etched into the rock on the cliffs. These figures represent both signposts – 'supermarket signs' as Rodney calls them – indicating the types of fish or animals to be hunted in the area, and also include totem animals. Each Aboriginal clan would have had a totemic animal, connected to an ancestoral creation story. (A clan had certain responsibilities for protecting its totem animal, ensuring that they were not overhunted.) The Dharawal, according to Rodney, are 'whale people', because whales migrating along the coast would have their babies in the waters just off Bondi, within their territory.

Next stop is Botany Bay to see where Cook and Phillip landed, as well as a French expedition which spent six weeks camped in the Bay. Rodney says that many Dharawal families still have artefacts that were given to their ancestors by the original settlers – watches, spoons, plates, jewellery, coins or swords. Ironically, perhaps (since the settlers no doubt thought they were giving away worthless trinkets), these have now become valuable antiques, and Rodney says he sold a couple of old muskets to buy his van. They have been handed down through the years and kept in mint condition, and there are plans to establish a Dharawal museum at Botany Bay to display them and to tell the history of the community. Rodney relates some of these stories, handed down through the generations, of settlers and sailors from the first fleet who jumped ship and married into the Aboriginal community.

Then we drive down towards the Royal National Park. The road south follows the ridge of a hill. The route, Rodney says, is an older Aboriginal track. This would have once been a well-worn path through the bush, used by people moving up and down the coast. Such tracks are known as 'dreaming tracks' or 'songlines' and are part of a vast network of tracks that criss-cross the whole of Australia. Dreamtime stories describe the landmarks along these paths, acting as oral guidebooks that allow a traveller to find his or her way around the country. Rodney claims his great-grandfather walked to Sydney from Arnhemland (which is like walking from London to Cairo) to marry into the Dharawal clan.

Our final destination, the Royal National Park, is the second oldest national park in the world and protects an area of rivers, waterfalls, coastal cliffs and red-gum bushland. This coastal woodland is a reminder of the landscape of Sydney as it was before the arrival of Europeans. Here, away from the skyscrapers and traffic, we can see the natural environment in which traditional Aboriginal culture developed. It's very beautiful, with cool swimming holes and waterfalls hidden in the forest.

Rodney shows us 'bush tucker'. In fact, the word indicates more than just food. 'Aboriginals divide plants into four classes', he explains. 'You've got food, fibre, medicine and weapon plants. In the old days, your survival depended upon that knowledge.' Next, he takes us to a high outcrop of flat rocks. This, Rodney says, was a sacred site.

'People get the wrong ideas about sacred sites, see. Really, they're just places were Aboriginals can come and perform their ceremonies. Look at this place: you can see for miles all around. Once you understand the land, it's obvious why someone would pick it.' He was right. It was exactly the sort of spot that called out to you to have a rest and take in the view.

Sitting here, I can imagine how Dharawal life must once have been: living off the land and hunting, gathering, fishing. Retelling mythical stories around the campfire – stories that contained vital information about where to find food and shelter. Walking along 'dreaming' trails that led to water holes and rivers, pathways worn through the dense bush by thousands of years of repeated use. A life deeply tuned into nature and the land.

But it's time to head back to Bondi and off into the urban jungle. And I find myself thinking that, while Sydney is undoubtedly a beautiful city, the land on which it stands must have been much more beautiful when it was still all Dharawal territory.

NAMIBIA: FRUIT FROM THE DESERT

This is an article by Chris McIntyre, from the February/March 1998 issue of *Wanderlust*, about **Damaraland Camp** in Namibia. (Damaraland is marketed in the UK by **Sunvil**. For information about *Wanderlust*, call 01753-620 426 or visit www.wanderlust.co.uk.)

'I applied for a job as a guide, but I was good at entertaining guests – and so trained for the bar. But I still want to be a guide, so I've built a small water bowl near my tent. I watch the birds, and learn to identify them from a book.'

Franz Coetzee's bird-bowl seemed a long way from the Savoy, where a waiter filled our glasses as we listened for the British Guild of Travel Writer's Silver Otter award to be announced. I wondered if all this pomp would make any difference to Damaraland Camp, or Franz's rural community there that ekes out its living on the fringes of the Namib desert.

The trip to London had certainly affected Franz, who had seldom stopped smiling. Until now, his longest journey had been as a child, when his parent's community had been displaced from South Africa and trekked into Namibia. They settled in the arid, semi-desert region of Damaraland. 'It was good that we came to Damaraland', he said. Despite entering an area already occupied with Damara people, 'We mixed with those people, and we accepted each other,' he assured me. Franz and his family stayed on, when most returned to South Africa, two years ago. 'We won our land back, but my parents wanted to stay in Namibia. I don't know anything more. So I stayed also.' After finishing school, he searched for a job. 'I went to town, with no luck. To Walvis Bay, as my sister was there. There is a really big problem with unemployment. I decided to go back to Damaraland to concentrate on farming.'

Like most of his community, Franz lived by tending cattle, sheep and goats. Damaraland may be spectacularly beautiful, but its land is poor for farming. Rocky hills and minimal rainfall mean a difficult life. There is game around, and sometimes he would hunt springbok, or even zebra, kudu or oryx. Occasionally he would glimpse the area's desert-adapted black rhinos – but elephants were a different story. 'They visited the water points during the night and our vegetable gardens on the farm. I remember once, a month before the harvest, a lot of elephants came, damaging the farm. The dogs barked, and we became nervous. We just stood. You can do nothing to an elephant. You can't even chase him away. You just clap your hands, but stay out of the way.' Though rare, these desert elephants meant nothing to Franz when compared to his vegetables.

Then things started to change. A government survey visited farms, explaining how they could benefit directly from the wildlife and tourism. Eventually the 70 households in Franz's community established themselves as custodians of the land, forming the Ward 11 Residents Association – with its own constitution and membership. They then sought investors, and after two years of tortuous negotiations, involving the whole community, they settled on an agreement with Wilderness Safaris – one of Southern Africa's best safari operators. Wilderness would build Damaraland Camp, and train local people as staff to run it. The community gets the jobs, and 10 per cent of the profits. After ten years, ownership of the camp will revert to the community.

Franz is enthusiastic about the benefits, and to date the community has N$57,000 in the bank.

'We will try to renovate our local clinic, and have donated N$2,000 to the school for a photocopier. At first it was just a loan, but later we said, "Just donate it." It's for our children.' But he recognizes that the next challenge is to decide how to use the increasing revenues. 'Farms which have had windmills damaged (by elephants seeking water) will be the first to get help. And there are other problems – predators like jackal catch goats and sheep.'

Gradually, attitudes towards wildlife have changed. Now Franz tells stories about elephants over breakfast, before guests go out on safari. The community knows how to deal with them, and nobody kills wild animals to eat – they're worth more alive as attractions for visitors.

Almost two years since it started, Damaraland Camp is now one of the most popular camps in Namibia. Except for two managers from Wilderness, all the staff are from the community – and next year will start training to replace the existing managers. Franz explained that his work of 'entertaining guests' meant 'telling them about yourself – visitors usually want to know about our traditions.' With a ready smile and a disarming line in chat, it's clear why he was perfect for this.

Later that evening, the winner was announced: the city of Dubrovnik, for its restoration work. Damaraland Camp was highly commended, followed by Madikwe Game Reserve, in South Africa, which has a similar approach to conservation. Franz's smile never wavered – clearly the award would make no difference to that. But why was this project so special? Surely all camps should be run like this?!

PHILIPPINES: KINGS OF THE SWINGERS

This article by Belinda Rhodes, about an indigenous **Aeta** community's own 'jungle survival tour' appeared in *Traveller* magazine in 1997. (*Traveller* is a magazine for members of Wexas Travel Club, 020-7581 4130, www.travelleronline.com.)

As we glide over Subic Bay towards its languid little airport, a vast, tropical forest slides into view, its foliage creeping snug to the edge of a placid turquoise sea. From above, I can only guess at what the forest holds, but its apparent impenetrability hints at wild animals and vicious reptiles.

Just a few hours later I am strolling towards an opening in the dense forest wall. 'Do you have bug juice?' asks Pepito Tabradillo, my jungle guide. I envision blood-thirsty mosquitoes lurking behind every gentle palm frond and every innocent leaf, and obediently smear myself with repellent. When I offer some to the diminutive Pepito he simply chuckles, 'Oh, they've bitten us too much already!'

Entering the deep, dark underworld of the rainforest unarmed and without a map is clearly not going to be the leap into the unknown for Pepito and his partner Gary Duero that it is for me. Their scanty preparations consist of putting a handful of rice into the leg-pockets of their camouflage trousers and sliding sharp hunting knives under their belts.

Tribesmen of the Philippines' Aeta cultural minority, Pepito and Gary walk nonchalantly in the direction of the jungle, weaving rope from stringy tree bark as they go. To them, this rich forest on the west coast of the island of Luzon represents a bountiful wellspring of food, water, shelter and equipment. It contains every item they could possibly need, and they are about to share these secrets with me.

Subic Forest, 10,000 hectares of lush, lofty jungle, lies inside the old perimeter fence of the former US naval base at Subic Bay, 160 kilometres north-west of the Philippines capital Manila. Because the land was off-limits to Filipino hunters and loggers for the five decades the Americans held the base, the forest has remained virtually untouched. Meanwhile, roughly three-quarters of the rainforest, which used to cover the rest of the Philippines, has been lost to the ravages of the tropical hardwood industry. There is virtually no virgin forest left in the country and environmental groups are struggling to preserve what little remains.

One reason the US navy kept Subic Forest intact was in order to use it for jungle survival training. Infantry preparing to serve in the Vietnam War came here to learn potentially lifesaving lessons from the Aeta tribesmen. They could have had no better teachers: the Aeta have lived in the region's forests for centuries and consider it their ancestral domain. Many a pilot returned to Subic from the Vietnam War to thank the Aetas for teaching him how to find fresh water, catch birds, treat snakebites and recognize the 'compass tree' whose leaves always show which way is south.

But now that the former naval base has been turned over to the Philippines for civilian use, the fun-loving Aetas show tourists the ropes – including the type that Tarzan swung from. Jungle tours, which can be custom designed to be as easy or difficult as visitors require, are proving immensely popular amongst a local population previously unaccustomed to taking an interest in their natural environment.

'Subic Forest provides people from urban areas their first chance to see a real rainforest,' says attorney Mary Mai Flor, legal officer at the Subic Bay Ecology Centre. 'Nowhere else in the Manila area is there anything like this. When visitors go inside, they're pretty impressed. Not many Filipinos knew that the Aetas trained the marines, so now tourists are flocking to see those demonstrations,' she adds.

Swinging their hunting knives about their heads, Gary and Pepito beat a path through thick vegetation, constantly glancing back to check that I am following. When they see me stooping and wriggling through the small tunnel they have cut between the lianas and spiky shrubs, they let out hoots of laughter. 'The trail is only Aeta-size!'

Small, athletic and as fleet-of-foot as Zola Budd, these spirited people find constant amusement in the fact that their Caucasian visitors are twice their size and certainly more than twice as clumsy. 'White men walk like buffalo, breaking everything and scaring the animals!' they laugh. They scamper lightly through the forest on bare feet, now and then shinning up a tree trunk to survey the forest canopy.

Pepito gives the first lesson in jungle lore: how to make an 'emergency hat'. He skilfully folds two large bangaba leaves, pins them with a twig and puts the creation over my head. 'Princess hat!' he chuckles, watching everything but my chin disappear. It will protect me from insects and camouflage my white skin which might otherwise alarm the wildlife. Next we must find fresh water inside the hollow chambers of a bamboo trunk. By carefully slicing just beneath one of the solid bands around the trunk, and a few inches above, he carves out a cylindrical cup full of clean, cool water.

Lessons follow in how to make traps for different kinds of animals – a sprung noose for a feral chicken, a pit trap for a boar – and tips on how to detect where the animals live. 'Even if you know how to make a trap, you'll have no food if you don't know the tactics of the animals,' says Pepito.

As we walk, the Aeta teach me to identify trees, vines and ferns – some for fun and some for their nutritional or medicinal value, from soup and edible berries to poultices and headache cures. The bark of one of the tall elegant dipterocarps which dominate the forest can be scraped off to make what Gary calls an 'Aeta band-aid'. Held over a wound for half an hour, it will stop the bleeding. The trunk of the *Ficus nota*, locally known as the tibig tree, holds gallons of fresh water. The bark of a tough shrub can be used to make improvised shoes.

The value of this forest, one of the few remaining large stands of triple-canopy rainforest in the Philippines, was acknowledged long before the Americans handed it over in 1992. Filipino botanists and zoologists could hardly wait to delve into its leafy depths and see whether it still held natural secrets long since destroyed in other parts of the Philippines.

The Subic Ecology Centre is now working on an inventory of the flora and fauna in the forest. Preliminary results have revealed 292 plant species, some of which are endangered and some of which are only found in one or two other places in the country. It is thought there are some species in the forest which have never before been identified in the Philippines. 'This highlights the importance and urgency of preserving the forest,' says attorney Flor.

Amongst the birds, mammals and reptiles often seen in Subic's jungle are wild pigs, civet cats, parrots, owls, eagles, vipers and pythons. The Aeta have reported seeing a red-and-black striped snake, whose identity has not yet been established. Monkeys (Philippine macaques), which used to loiter at the roadside ready to ambush American picnickers, have been encouraged to return to their natural lifestyle and now forage and breed in the dense forest canopy.

The wildlife did, however, suffer badly during the massive eruption of Mount Pinatubo in 1991. Ashfall from the volcano, 30 kilometres north-east of Subic, was dumped on the forest destroying the canopy and making the ground soil sandy and dry. Although rainforest vegetation is fast growing, it will take some time for the forest to make a full recovery.

Just after noon Pepito and Gary lead me to a clearing by a waterfall where we stop for lunch. While huge ochre-coloured butterflies bat around our heads, I am treated to a masterful demonstration of the versatility of bamboo and the dexterity of the Aeta with hunting knives. In what seems like seconds they carve cooking pots, plates, knives and forks from bamboo trunks, make a water carrier and a shelter from bamboo poles and create fire with bamboo tinder.

Gary comes leaping up from the river bank with pieces of greenery and a handful of what look like small brown stones, and a few minutes later we are served fern and snail soup in bamboo cups. Over lunch Pepito recalls his terrors during the eruption of Mount Pinatubo. The volcano is the Aetas' god and the resting place of their ancestors' spirits, so the tribespeople were deeply shocked when it apparently turned its wrath on them. Pepito was at work on the naval base when the sky went black and the earth began to tremble with the earthquakes which accompanied the eruption. He walked 20 kilometres through the ashy darkness to be with his family during the catastrophe.

When the dust settled, the Aeta found that some of their number had been lost in the explosion. Because there was no mention in the Aetas' oral history of Pinatubo being a volcano, thousands of them were living on its upper slopes where they practised slash-and-burn farming. Many hundreds were forced to flee to evacuation camps in the lowlands and have not yet been able to return. It is feared that these Aeta will eventually forget their traditions, tribal rituals and knowledge of the rainforest.

This makes it all the more vital to practise and preserve the ways of the forest, say Gary and Pepito. Although even they watch the odd TV show, drink the occasional Coca-Cola and don't actually live in the forest most of the time, they are proud in the knowledge that they have the survival techniques born in the jungle. 'Believe it or not, my family once stayed in there for three whole years. The American marines used to get mad in the jungle sometimes; they wanted to go downtown. But this is our home, and we want to take care of it.'

MOROCCO: WINDS OF CHANGE

The following is an extract from an article by Paul Morrison in the August/September 1999 issue of *Wanderlust* magazine. It describes a trip to the **Rif Mountains** of Morocco. This project is marketed in the UK by Tribes Travel. (For information about *Wanderlust*, call 01753-620 426 or visit www.wanderlust.co.uk.)

Abdu's brother and his wife had been unlucky in a way that was hard to imagine. 'Their first five children died,' he told me with a shrug. 'They just got sick.'

Their latest baby had made it, so far at least, though problems in labour had meant his four brothers had had to carry his sister-in-law on a blanket for three hours to reach the road that led into town for medical help. I had started by asking Abdu why he had left his village in the northern Rif Mountains, and ended by wondering why anyone would stay. But he was the only one in his village to go to school, and it was this education that was his passport to life in the city and a job in tourism.

'I am intelligent!' he declared with a grin, and he was. He was also smart enough to know how lucky he was. Here in the High Atlas Mountains, to the south of his new home in Marrakesh he could appreciate what a difference a lucky break can make.

I was travelling in a party of three, along with Abdu, as guide and interpreter, and Rhazi, the visionary director of a unique Moroccan tour company – Tizi-Randonnées. What makes Tizi-Randonnées so different is its concern to regenerate remote communities such as the one where Abdu grew up. They still offer their clients the kind of outdoor and cultural experiences that Morocco has in abundance, but behind the scenes the philosophy is refreshingly different.

'I wanted to ensure that the funds that visitors spent went to the local community,' Rhazi explained as we stood on the roof terrace of the guesthouse overlooking the village of Aroumd. The clouds had parted to reveal the mountains, dusted in snow, towering over a fertile valley where women stood in the river beating colourful clothes against the dark volcanic boulders. And at first glance this apparently timeless scene could be another rural community caught in the past. It's the satellite dishes that give it away.

Aroumd was like many remote villages in the Atlas. Trekkers sometimes pass through on their circuits, or parties of seasoned skiers visit as they head to the slopes of Toubkal further up the valley. But this was not enough to keep the youngsters from leaving for the city – like Abdu. What turned it around in Aroumd was a project initiated by Tizi, but with local people in control, that sought to breathe life back into the village. With a promise of materials secured from a development association in Rabat, it was up to the villagers to raise the balance of funds. All 200 households gave what they could. In 1997 electricity was brought to every home, and seven freshwater fountains were installed, fed by a small reservoir above the village.

'Before we had big problems for water,' Mohammed explained. 'When it snowed we would heat snow, but when there was no snow the women would go with a donkey to collect water from the river down in the valley, or from a spring much higher up the hillside.'

Mohammed was born in the village, where he lives with his wife and five children, and makes a living as a guide. A true Atlas man, he speaks only Berber, a tongue of which Arabic Moroccans like Abdu have little knowledge. Rhazi (who spoke French, but no English) bridged the gap, and between the four of us we were able to have a slow but revealing conversation.

'People are now very happy and feel healthier as the water is purified – we already have fewer problems of sickness for children.' I thought of Abdu's brother's family and looked again at Mohammed, who grinned at us from beneath his black woollen hat with Chicago emblazoned on the front. This symbol of the outside world somehow complemented his brown striped *djellaba* (the traditional robe) and, like the satellite dishes on the mud-walled homes, hinted at the changes in the village.

'My wife likes action films,' declared Mohammed.

But TV was not killing the art of conversation in Aroumd for the simple reason that there were no programmes in Berber, so no one could understand what was being said. Instead, it offered a glimpse, however unreal, of an outside world. 'I recently spoke with an 80-year-old man in the village,' said Rhazi, 'who had never been beyond the mountains. "Before I was blind, but now I've seen things!" he told me.' Mohammed told us he believed his children would now stay in the village, whereas in the next valley most of the village teenagers leave for the city.

Tourism, even on a small scale, is playing a part in keeping Aroumd alive. They have rebuilt the school, reworked irrigation channels, and even bought their own bull (the previous two, being shared with other villages, died from overwork). And a similar project is underway in the north, in Abdu's village.

But Rhazi realizes that he couldn't sell tours to foreign visitors just on the strength of the projects. People come to Morocco for a good time, and in the High Atlas this means walking through magnificent scenery. So after lunch we took off along a pilgrims' trail to a holy shrine in the mountains. The path twisted upwards towards the distant peak of Toubkal, and the sun burned our faces through the cloud cover. On the way we passed straggles of bizarrely clad skiers picking their way between the rocks with their poles as they returned from the high-country lodge. In their bright skiwear and clompy boots they looked like spacemen who'd missed their landing site. Their sport is not the only hazard in the mountains – in the summer of 1995 a flash flood swept hundreds to their deaths in this valley, but the atmosphere was peaceful on that warm March afternoon. The scenery was stark and magnificent, with a feel of the Himalayan foothills. As we strolled back into the village at the end of the day it was hard to comprehend how close we were to Europe.

Facilities for travellers are still fairly simple, and not for someone who insists on a hot shower in an ensuite bathroom. But the scenery and insight to local life more than compensated. Our *gîte* was comfortable enough, and the local food was excellent. Lunch and dinner centred upon the *tagine* – a stew of vegetables, herbs, spices and meat cooked in the traditional clay vessel of the same name. And despite warnings in the guidebooks to the contrary, my vegetarian equivalent was easily obtained and equally delicious. All meals were followed by 'Moroccan whiskey' – a teeth-tormenting sweet tea made from a stew of Chinese tea leaves and fresh mint, supplemented by a fistful of sugar. It's a taste I found myself getting to like after a few days, though noticing the brown stains on the teeth of many Moroccans, I was pleased that the habit was short lived.

Like all the mountain settlements I saw, Aroumd was made from the earth and stone around it, giving the impression of having been hewn out of the rock. From the air these settlements must be virtually invisible, blending into the landscape in perfect camouflage. Where the rock was red with iron, so were the houses, but Aroumd was made of a dull grey-brown volcanic stone, which would have made the village seem sombre were it not for its spectacular setting. One morning I woke early and walked along its narrow paths across to the eastern side, where the morning sun was driving the chill from the air and wafts of rising smoke caught the dawn light. Here I witnessed the decoration of the village in a flash of colours guaranteed to wake up the senses.

Although most villagers in the High Atlas are devout Muslims, theirs is not a faith that requires dressing down and covering up. Berber culture predates the Arab invasion 13 centuries ago and is strongest in the mountains of Morocco. Here, the women wear bright dresses and scarves, with their faces usually uncovered, revealing a rosy flush to the cheeks that seems to typify mountain people the world over. This sense of colour clearly extends to the home – as I walked out that morning onto the sunkissed side of the village I was greeted by the scene of women spreading out rugs and bedcovers on their rooftops and hanging them from windows. The patchworks of reds and greens and pinks and blues gave the village a festive air. A flock of red-beaked choughs was performing aerial displays above the rooftops, the birds cawing to each other as they circled upwards on the morning thermals.

On our final evening in Aroumd, Abdu announced that we would have visitors after dinner. The tables were dragged to the walls and the chairs rearranged in the centre. Moments later, figures appeared in the doorway and soon the small room was alive with chatter as half a dozen local men assembled around the fire to warm the skins of their tambourine-shaped drums and argue about nothing in particular. The atmosphere of the room was transformed into a lively bar, but there was no alcohol fuelling the spirits, just sweet tea. Mohammed served the guests, as four young girls filed in and took their seats against the wall. The teenagers sported brightly coloured cardigans and chattered away quietly, turning to smile at us at intervals with their eyes down. The guys puffed their chests out and assembled on the other side of the room.

One fellow, Barim, was the joker in the pack, sending his companions into convulsions of laughter with a single phrase; yet as it turned out he was also the nearest the musical group had to a leader. Holding his drum in front of his mouth, he started to sing an improvised rant that led to a chanting refrain by the men, followed by a response from the girls – a sort of vocal tennis match, as each side threw choruses back and forth. The girls' high voices and harmonies made them sound almost oriental. The men played their drums in a variety of rhythms with their fingers and palms. Mohammed sat behind and joined in by banging a saucepan with a pair of spoons.

The sound soon attracted more faces at the doorway and Barim decided that it was time to take to the floor. He enticed a reluctant girl to join him, and before I had a chance to resist I was there as well, partnered by young Mina from the house next door, who was trying to contain her laughter as she tutored me in the steps. It looked easy, just a shuffle back and forth, but then she shook her shoulders in a manner and speed that I could only comically imitate. At ten o'clock the music ended, the girls disappeared without a word, and the room returned to normality.

As we drove out of the mountains the next morning I reflected on life in Aroumd and was satisfied that our incursion into this remote community had brought benefits that travel does not always bestow. It wasn't just the project that was making a difference, but also the policy of Rhazi's company, which meant, for instance, that everyone involved gets a fair wage. Tourism can be a fiercely competitive game and it is often those on the ground who feel the squeeze. But Tizi pays everyone, from porters to guides, at the top end of the local going rate for the job.

TANZANIA: DOROBO SAFARIS

Dorobo Safaris is a safari company in Tanzania that works closely with local communities. Although not describing an actual tour, this extract from one of their newsletters, written by David Peterson (a Dorobo director), captures the way that interaction with local people can add an extra dimension to our experience of a place.

One day near the beginning we were hunkered around one of those everlasting acacia fires in the crisp dawn of South Maasailand. The 'old man', pushing 80 and with eyesight shuttered by cataracts, turned to Thad and Daudi and said, 'We're low on water, you guys better go down and fetch some from that pool in the riverbed.' That sounds pretty straightforward but you've got to imagine the racket that was emanating from that pool. For the last several hours, camp music had been lions' throaty growls punctuated by buffalo bellows and the volume was high.

'But there's lions down there,' we said.

'So what, we need water, just walk down there assertively and fetch some.'

So we did walk down there assertively until at 30 metres we were faced by eight very feisty, vocal and aggressive lions, whose tails were ramrod stiff and thrashing the bushes, a clear prelude to a charge. 'When the tail stops, the charge starts.' At that point our assertive walk while still facing the lions somehow changed direction and we ended up back in camp.

Without water!

'Where's the water?'

'Those lions are right next to the water, are very aggressive and won't give way.'

'No excuse. You guys backing off like that are teaching those lions bad manners. You can't let them get away with it. Now you walk in there assertively and get that water!'

Three times we walked assertively and three times we found ourselves back in camp with no water. The old man was totally disgusted and disappointed. Now, it's true we needed water. We didn't even have enough for a second round of morning *chai*. And we did trust and respect the old man and felt pretty badly about letting him down. But facing that moving wall of growling lion just felt too much like forever foregoing another cup of tea anywhere.

The decision to move camp and look for alternative water was painful but at this point obligatory. As we were packing up, we saw another Dorobo man approaching camp, still out of the old man's vision. We quickly went out to meet him to get a second unbiased opinion. 'What do you do if lion are very aggressive and keep you from getting water?' we asked. Without hesitation the Dorobo answered. 'You walk in there assertively until they back off.' 'Show us,' we said, and he replied, 'Let's go.'

Despite the second corroborating opinion, our assertive walk was accompanied by some inner trepidation. We walked right into the waterhole without raising a single growl. We kept walking to where the lions had been thrashing with their tails. No lions. They had just left, which explained why the growling stopped just after we left camp. There in the middle of a patch of trampled grass and broken bush lay the horns, skull and vertebrae of an old buffalo bill. He had been a worthy adversary for several hours of bellowing resistance until he continued his journey through the food chain.

Although we will always wonder what would have happened if the lions had not finished feeding and left before we finally walked in there, the old man taught us a lot and we have on several subsequent occasions walked assertively in our encounter with lions. Mike and Daudi on two separate Mzombe River walks ran into what was almost certainly the same very tenacious lioness who had cubs. While her cubs and cohorts slipped away, she faced our large group of clients and porters with continuous growling and repeated half-way charges. Every slow hominid step backwards only brought her several quick steps forward. Five minutes of this scenario brings one close to adrenaline depletion and in the end it was the old man's assertive walk which, at closer than 20 metres, finally led her to slink off with a throaty backward glare to join her cubs and companions.

This story is a roundabout way of introducing the 'old man' who played a primary role in the naming and defining of Dorobo. The old man's name was Mzee Mori. An Iraqw tribesman by birth, he was a Dorobo by inclination and lifestyle. By the time we met him in the mid 1970s, he was kind of 'king of the Dorobo' within a large area of south Maasailand in that he'd taught most of the younger Dorobo the art of gathering wild honey and was respected by being tithed a portion of honey each season. He died in 1984, well into his 80s, in his sleep and most likely after partaking of a healthy gourd of well-brewed honey beer.

The old man left us with an intimate relationship to a particular piece of God's real estate. He showed us all the elephant highways, the important larger waterholes, the springs and river courses, baobabs that held water cisterns, baobabs that consistently attracted wild bees to their natural cavities, hollowed baobabs and rock overhangs one could escape to for shelter. Based on Aldo Leopold's definition that 'the best ownership of land is knowledge of land', we 'owned' some 20,000 square kilometres of South Maasailand. When we imagine heaven for the old man, baobabs, waterholes and elephant are very prominent.

Just as importantly, or more so, the old man with his unique perspective of looking and feeling left us with a spiritual, aesthetic and playful relationship with country and its critters. Whenever we'd come to a waterhole, the old man would scoop up a handful of water, look, taste and smell the water and give his assessment. 'This water's too dirty for elephant; it's only fit for buffalo.' Then we'd proceed to circuit the waterhole and analyse track and spoor, which invariably confirmed his earlier assessment.

One time, we filled a jerry can with water from a particular raunchy seepage and brought it back to camp where the old man was tending the fire. We brewed tea and laced the cups with more than normal amounts of milk and sugar to mask the water flavour. The old man took a sip and broke out with a huge grin. 'Buffalo piss, much better tasting and much healthier than cow piss.'

There were 500 to 800 elephants drinking at one of the big waterholes and the bush and woodland all around were totally thrashed. As we approached the waterhole we saw lovely unscathed *Acacia tortilis* trees ringing the edge. 'Don't tell me elephant don't have a sense of aesthetics. Look how they've left those acacia untouched.'

One night sleeping around the fire, we woke to a persistent birdcall. We asked why that bird was calling in the middle of the night. 'God put that bird there to fill the heads of people alone in the bush so they wouldn't go crazy with their own thoughts.'

Dorobo is a collective name for hunter-gatherer peoples found in remnant groups scattered throughout both Kenya and Tanzania Maasailand. It is likely that before the advent of Bantu and Cushitic agriculturists and Nilo-Hamitic pastoralists, the land was sparsely peopled by hunter-gatherers. These early folk were either assimilated by or pushed out by agriculturists but were able to coexist as hunter-gatherers within the production mode of extensive pastoralism as practised by the Maasai.

All Dorobo, regardless of ethnic background, have been culturally influenced in varying degrees by the stronger, dominant Maasai culture. So, for example, the Dorobo the old man hung out with have lost all vestiges of their own language and speak only Maa. They live as poor Maasai within Maasai kraals except when they are off on their honey gathering forays. Most have no wives as poor Maasai men marry available Dorobo women. The future of these Dorobo as a group is pretty clear. Further south, where Maasai expansion occurred later, there are groups of Akie Dorobo who still speak their own language, but only in private amongst themselves; otherwise they speak Maa. These Dorobo live in their own kraals and practice a mix of hunting and gathering, livestock and agricultural economic options.

Although Dorobo are within the greater Maasai cultural and economic sphere, they and their lifestyles are openly and disparagingly considered inferior by Maasai. Yet the Maasai depend upon Dorobo to perform cultural rites of circumcision, for provision of honey to brew beer for ceremonial occasions and as a fallback in times of drought, disease and famine. Many Maasai survived the great rinderpest cattle plague in the early 1890s by running to, and living with and as, Dorobo hunter-gatherers.

Our relationship with the old man and his Dorobo associates was an important reason why we chose the name Dorobo for our safari business. The fact that Dorobo is not one ethnic group but rather many unified by a common lifestyle – a lifestyle characterized by fitting in with and working as part of natural systems – was also a compelling reason. Lastly, we hope in some small way that our name and philosophy of doing business has or will help some Dorobo folk to stand with dignity as Dorobo.

EGYPT: WIND, SAND & STARS

This article by Mike Gerrard appeared in *The Independent on Sunday* in June 1997. It describes a tour to the Sinai desert in Egypt with UK operator **Wind, Sand & Stars**.

'You mean we're not staying in a five-star hotel?' Louise asked. Louise, aged 66, had never slept in the open before and wasn't expecting to do so on the first night of our trip to the Sinai desert. 'Much better,' said our Egyptian guide, Aswani. 'Tonight you have a five-million-star hotel.'

We set up camp in a sheltered desert valley inland from the airport at Sharm el Sheik. The night before it was Gatwick and now we are sleeping under the stars. While we clean our faces and wonder about the toilet arrangements, the Egyptian drivers are building a bonfire and making the first of a thousand cups of tea. The smell of roasting chicken soon follows, and we gather around the flames for a briefing from the British tour leader, Tamsin Clegg. This needs to be done before the stars emerge, as three people in the group are deaf and it's hard to read sign language in the dark.

Rachel Mapson, of the Royal National Institute for Deaf People, is the group's interpreter and will soon be signing Tamsin's instructions, her face as expressive as her gestures as she copes with the signs for snakes and scorpions, the problems of dehydration, camels and suntan cream, and explaining the toilet arrangements. A desert journey is down to earth in more ways than one. Ladies to the left, gents to the right, find yourself a handy rock, bury the waste and discreetly dispose of the paper in the rubbish bags provided. Later I ask Rachel what's the most difficult thing she's ever had to interpret. 'A pantomime,' she says. 'Can you imagine having to sign "zip-a-dee-doo-dah"?'

The group is more concerned about what might pop up in the desert at night, but Tamsin soon puts our minds at rest. 'There are a few creepy-crawlies around,' she says and Rachel signs, 'but they won't harm you. There's the odd snake or scorpion but it's unlikely you'll see one, though it's best not to unroll your sleeping bag before you want to go to bed, just in case something takes a fancy to crawling into it.'

There is a particular reason why this mixed group of deaf and hearing people has come to the Sinai, besides its stunning scenery and the chance to camel trek for a few days accompanied by the local Bedouin from the Mezaina tribe. This tribe suffers from congential deafness, worsened by its tradition of intermarrying. 'It is on the increase too,' Aswani tells me. 'Deafness has always been common in the Bedouin because they intermarry. But lately it has been getting worse so that now it is common to have two deaf children in a family of seven or eight children. But here it is not seen as a disability. They are just different.'

Deafness is so common that almost everyone knows some sign language for talking to friends and relatives. Although sign languages vary from country to country, there's enough in common to make communication between deaf visitors and the Bedouin much easier than between people who share no language at all.

'Deaf people are used to thinking visually and in symbols,' Rachel tells me, 'so that also makes communication easier. Most cultures do have many symbols in common. For example, to gesture behind you is to indicate the past, and in front of you indicates the future, except for some North American Indian signing systems where the past is in front of you, because you can see it, and the future behind you.' What was in front of us was four days of trekking through the lands of the Mezaina tribe, once we had been given the permission of Sheikh Hamid to do so.

'Sheikh Hamid is the ruler of one family within the tribe,' explains Tamsin, 'and he's a very good man. The sheikh is responsible for the whole group and must look after their welfare, which he does, making sure that, for example, the camel trekking is divided up fairly between all the men in the tribe in turn. It's the men who look after the camels, the women and girls have always

traditionally looked after the sheep and goats. The women are a very important part of the Bedu life. Men and women have different responsibilities but
each is vital and therefore respect is mutual. The women are lively and funny,
and I've had some entertaining evenings with them when it's been women
only. The women have great parties together.'

We collect our camels from Sheikh Hamid and set off into the desert, all
12 of us, with the elderly Sabali and half a dozen young Bedu men to guide,
cook and help us get on and off the camels. Being tall I'm given a large camel,
a handsome white one called Abden, who is good-tempered by camel
standards and doesn't even react when, one day, another camel bites him on
the bum. It could have been nasty if Abden had decided to race off into the
desert.

We plod through the sand past sculpted sandstone rocks. It's the ultimate
Lawrence of Arabia fantasy and we see no one but each other and a few
Bedouin encampments for the next four days. The sun blazes down with a
blowtorch heat. The apparently limited palate of the desert has infinite variety.

Only someone who has never been there could call the desert landscape
boring. We head for what seems to be a solid rockface, only to find that a
narrow crack leads into a secret zigzag red-rock canyon, through which the
camels tread single file, ripping at the occasional acacia tree with their
rasping tongues.

When the sun is at its highest we seek shade beneath overhanging rocks,
or beside some trees, and picnic on chickpeas, humous, feta cheese, olives,
halva and, always, freshly baked bread.

The Bedu boys produce flour and water, a plastic bowl to mix them in, a
flat stone and an old jar to roll out the dough, and the top of an oil drum to
heat in the flames and cook the bread on. If time allows, and there's enough
wood, they build up a fiercer heat and bake a thick bread under the fire in
the charcoal ashes. After lunch, while the camels graze, we sit around and
talk, sleep or sign. The biggest of the boys is Mohamed. 'Were you born
deaf?' Rachel asks him, using the graphic sign for someone being born, a
gesture that Mohamed understands. 'Yes,' he nods. He is 17, will get married
in three years and has three sisters and five brothers, one of whom is also
deaf.

'I feel I've got to know Mohamed quite well,' says Christine, one of the
deaf travellers. When sorting out the camels, Mohamed immediately took
two of the deaf visitors and put them on his two camels, so he could walk
beside them.

'Its easy to sign on a camel when Mohamed's walking alongside,'
Christine explains, 'and he's told me a lot about his family and his life. He was
very interested in my hearing aid. He said to me that sometimes he shouts to
me and I turn round, and sometimes I don't. I told him that I don't always
have my hearing aid switched on. He tried it but it was just a jumble of noise
to him. He doesn't need one here, because everybody signs.'

Everybody signs to such an extent that, one day, Mohamed was signing with two of his friends and when he walked away to do something, the friends carried on signing instead of reverting to speech.

It was speech, though, that conveyed to me the immensity of this experience for everyone. It was one of the most enjoyable weeks of my life. And as we scrambled up a mountain side, to look at a cave high up in the rock face, seeing more and more of the vast desert panorama as we climbed, Louise paused to get her breath and turned to Tamsin who was helping her struggle up. 'I think I must be dreaming,' she said. 'I just can't believe I'm here. I'm so happy.'

ZAMBIA: THE SAUSAGE TREE ROMEOS

This article by Andrew Eames, about Kawaza village in Zambia, first appeared in the *Evening Standard* on 5 January 2001.

The lads and I were talking about sex. Or rather, the lads were doing the talking and I was doing the listening. We'd started the morning at a 'beer' party, knocking back a maize-based concoction with a kick like a mule, and now they were filling me in on the mistress situation. It seems there was a surfeit of women in the village and dances such as the one we had had the previous night were happy hunting grounds for married men interested in acquiring a 'spare wheel'.

Size most definitely mattered in keeping one's spare wheels turning, Constantini was suggesting, and all the local males worked hard to achieve suitable manhood dimensions, eating select powdered roots and choosing huge fruits from the sausage tree to give themselves something to aim for. And what, he politely enquired, did we do to make our willies grown larger in England? Morning-after-the-night-before conversations such as this take place all over the world, although the hair of the dog is unlikely to be quite so hairy as sorghum beer fermented with battery acid. But then Kawaza village is hardly Basildon, stuck as it is in the navel of Zambia, a huge nation sprawled across the groin of Africa.

We don't hear much about Zambia in this country. This silence actually betrays an economic and political stability all too rare in Africa, but it also conceals Zambia's good, if small, wildlife tourism industry in which walking safaris and night drives are a speciality. And now Zambia also has Kawaza, an ordinary rural village which has decided to throw open its mud huts to foreigners interested in local culture.

Kawaza sits on flat elephant-rich land surrounded by papaya and mango trees next to South Luangwa National Park. With the help of Robin Pope Safaris, a big employer hereabouts, the villagers have built a summer house, long-drop loos and several *rondavels* – thatched huts – for visitor accommodation.

The guests can choose to work in the fields, help at the school, visit the chief or just hang out in the meeting room. A kitchen produces three meals a day, all based on the staple *ncima*, a bland mealie meal goo that makes semolina seem interesting. But you don't come here for the cuisine: it's the people that make it rich.

The gangling Constantini, who styles himself the project's entertainments manager, has a dramatic family history. His fisherman father was killed by a hippo which had been 'witched', he said, by other fishermen jealous of his skills. His brother, a truck driver, had also died from black magic, in this case in the form of a cloud of smoke which appeared from nowhere, wrapped itself around his windscreen and caused him to crash.

But the most colourful of all the characters was Fanny the faith healer, a graceful septuagenarian with a photograph of golfer Colin Montgomery stuck to the wall of her consulting room. Why Montgomery? Why not Nick Faldo, who at least had a caddy called Fanny?

But it was the wrong time to ask, because in the half-light the healer had turned in to a sort of voodoo Florence Nightingale, dressed in crucifix-covered white robes and clutching a Bible. She began to snort and groan as the benevolent spirit of Hetina took occupation of her body.

I'd heard that Fanny/Hetina was inclined to ascribe everything to sex, so it came as no surprise to find her pressing my groin as she began a rambling discourse which provoked ululations of laughter from a mob of ladies who'd gathered outside. Some of the words sounded disturbingly familiar.

Apparently, I was 'washout weaky in my power jonny, my ya-du-du-du was norty-norty' and it sounded as if my 'bugger-power-you' was never going to achieve full capacity.

I feared the worst, but when Constantini translated it turned out my norty-norty power jonny was in perfect working order. Instead, something had disturbed my ribs long ago and this had caused pain at the base of my spine (quite right – I have three displaced discs). The cure lay in a couple of roots which I was to grind to powder, mix with lotion, and rub into my anus.

The roots still languish in the corner of my office, in their Sainsbury's plastic bag. I promised Fanny I would apply them, and I do intend to do so – just as soon as I have sorted out a good cover story in the event of a sudden trip to casualty.

THAILAND: LIFE'S A BEACH

This article of mine originally appeared in *Wanderlust* in February 2000, just before the film of *The Beach* was released. It contrasts a 'local' village beach with Alex Garland's fantasy paradise and the reality of tourist resorts such as Ko Phi Phi. The visit was organized by the Thai organization REST. (For information about *Wanderlust*, call 01753-620 426 or visit www.wanderlust.co.uk.)

Ko Yao Noi means Little Long Island. It sits in the middle of Phang Nga Bay in southern Thailand, an hour's boat ride from the neon lights and crowds of Phuket, one of Thailand's biggest tourist resorts. Phang Nga Bay is one of Thailand's natural wonders, with coral reefs, rainforests, mangrove swamps and postcard-perfect white-sand beaches. What gives the area its special beauty, though, is the karst limestone geology. The limestone is eroded into huge cliffs, dramatic pillars and other bizarre formations, pitted with canyons, caves and sinkholes. Phang Nga Bay is studded with hundreds of jungle-topped islands – some no bigger than football pitches – which rise like sheer-walled fortresses from the shimmering blue water.

In the middle of the bay, on Ko Yao Noi, I sat and looked out of Dang's window. I could see the dirt road that passes in front of his house, red and muddy from the afternoon's rain. It had rained every afternoon that week, although November was supposed to be the start of the dry season. Across the road, behind a thin curtain of trees, was the beach. It wasn't quite postcard-perfect, this beach. Instead, it was scattered with discarded plastic and torn bits of fishing net, and assorted wood and flotsam from the sea. A dozen long-tail fishing boats bobbed up and down in the water, their extended rudders protruding like the tails of exotic birds. A fisherman, dressed in a sarong, sat in one of the boats and smoked a cigarette as he untangled his net. Beneath the house, which was built on stilts, I could hear Dang's geese and ducks quacking. A goat bleated. An overfed rabbit hopped around and a cat sat idly by as a hen fussed over her brood of tiny chicks. Behind me, Dang's wife Ma sat cross-legged on the floor and cut up vegetables for our dinner.

A beach in Thailand. Inevitably, my thoughts turned to Alex Garland's novel, which I'd just finished reading and which was just about to be released as a film. In Garland's story, a bunch of backpackers discover the 'perfect' beach: an untouched, uninhabited tropical paradise hidden away on a small island in a Thai national park.

The novel reflects the seemingly endless quest of the modern traveller. Like Arthurian knights in tie-dye trousers, backpackers roam the tropics, searching for the Holy Backpacker Grail – the 'undiscovered' beach. From Phuket and Ko Phi Phi to Ko Samui and Ko Pha Ngan on the opposite coast, Thailand is full of once-undiscovered islands and beaches that have now become tourist honeypots.

Dang didn't want Ko Yao Noi to become just another beach on the backpacker trail. Like most men on Ko Yao Noi, he'd been a fisherman all his life and didn't want to become a tour guide or beach hustler. Yet he now invited small groups of *farangs* (the Thai word for foreigner) into his home, as part of an alternative tourism scheme run by a Thai development agency called REST (Responsible, Ecological and Social Tourism). The idea, though, was to offer visitors a look at everyday life in rural southern Thailand, rather than a pretend escape to a non-existent 'paradise'.

We'd arrived on the island two days before, after a one-hour boat ride from Phuket. While the tour boats raced past on day trips to 'James Bond Island' (the beach location in *The Man With The Golden Gun*) and other famous spots in the bay, we'd been fishing with another fisherman, Mhak. We'd seen cliffs which daring climbers scaled to retrieve the highly prized swifts' nests used by the Chinese to make birds nest soup. According to Noi, our guide and the manager of REST, a kilogramme of these nests sold for $1,500. In a country where the average annual income is $2,500, it's hardly surprising that people will risk their lives to get them.

We'd visited a rubber plantation and watched the tree trunk being cut to draw the sticky white sap to the surface, then collected and squeezed through a press into sheets that looked like car footmats. We'd visited a floating fish farm. We'd toured the island on motorbikes, passing coconut plantations and villagers at work in the paddy fields, children playing football and flying kites and a man taking a monkey for a walk tied to a piece of string. The monkey, Noi told us, was trained to climb trees and throw down coconuts.

Everything was lightened by the Thai concept of *sanuk* – or fun – which Thais believe should be applied to every activity in life. The fishing trip, for instance, involved dropping out a few hundred metres of net, then heading off to a nearby island for a swim and lunch on a sandy beach. Mhak showed us a small cave in the limestone cliff-face. Swimming through the narrow opening, we emerged in a hidden lagoon surrounded by towering jungle-coated cliffs. After lunch, we returned to the nets. As Mhak hauled them in, pausing for photographs whenever he pulled up a particularly large fish, we tried to guess what would appear next. A crab, perhaps? A shrimp, or a squid, or any number of tropical fish.

That evening, we sampled the day's catch, with a feast of fried fish and crabs. (During our three-day stay, we must have eaten about six crabs.) The next morning, we went to the market for breakfast, investigating a range of delicious Thai sweets such as sticky rice steamed in banana leaves with coconut milk. The food was mouthwateringly good – Thailand is a country where even the humblest market vendor can be guaranteed to produce something delicious.

On our first night, we'd discussed tourism with Dang, Mhak and a dozen other islanders, with Noi as interpreter. In fact, we learned, the catalyst for the tourism project on Ko Yao Noi was nothing to do with tourism. About six years ago, commercial boats from Phuket, Malaysia and Singapore had begun illegally fishing for anchovy off Ko Yao Noi. Their indiscriminate overfishing had greatly depleted local fishing stocks and today catches were a fraction of what they were a decade ago. The threat to their livelihood prompted the islanders to set up a community organization to fight the anchovy boats.

As part of this fight, the islanders decided to take in tourists – middle-class Thais from Bangkok as well as *farangs*. They plan to use the income to buy a motor for a patrol boat to guard the coast, and to use tourism to tell outsiders about their struggle. But, if the anchovy boats keep coming and fish stocks around the island don't recover, tourism may also have to replace some of the income that once came from fishing.

Looking out of Dang's window, beyond the beach and the bobbing fishing boats, I could make out the faint silhouette of Ko Pi Phi on the horizon. The twin islands of Phi Phi Don and Phi Phi Leh are the most beautiful in the bay, and large chunks are designated as national park. Maya Beach on Phi Phi Leh was the location for the filming of Garland's novel.

Yet Ko Phi Phi is a lesson in what happens if tourism is allowed to develop uncontrolled. When the first intrepid backpackers arrived, they must have found beaches as perfect as that in the book. Yet today, tourist bungalows, hotels, restaurants and bars sprawl along the beaches of Phi Phi Don. Rubbish lies rotting on the ground. Rock music and the unrelenting drone of generators and outboard motors disturb the tropical tranquillity while the once-brilliant coral reefs are being destroyed by anchors of tour boats and pollution from the onshore tourist development.

From Dang's house I could see three Beaches: in my mind I pictured the virgin sands of Garland's fantasy, devoid of human footprints. On the horizon across the water lay Ko Phi Phi and the reality of what that fantasy can become once tourists arrive. The Traveller's Quest has become a depressing and self-defeating one – no sooner is a beach 'discovered' than it falls victim to the sort of unregulated development that can be seen in Phuket, Ko Phi Phi, Ko Samui and dozens of other once-pristine destinations.

And then there was peaceful Ko Yao Noi and the beach right in front of Dang's house. With the odd discarded bottle and bits of old fishing net, it may not be as perfect as Ko Phi Phi once was, but – for precisely that reason – it is unlikely to suffer the same fate. Instead it is just what is has always been. An ordinary beach in southern Thailand, home to ordinary people. As I listened to the clucking of Dang's chickens and ducks and his goats bleating, I knew which beach I'd rather be on.

LESOTHO: PONY TREKKING

This article by Lisa Sykes was first published in *The Sunday Times* on 28 January 2001. Lisa travelled to **Malealea Lodge** with **Tribes Travel**.

I am not a big giver to charity. A standing order to WaterAid salves my conscience, and at least it is doing something tangible – a water pipe here, a well there. But the idea that going on holiday can actually help people in poorer parts of the world, without so much as a mention of the word charity, really appealed.

Depending on who you talk to, it's called community, or ethical, or fair-trade tourism. The concept is straightforward: your holiday is run by, and for, local people; most (or all) of the profits are reinvested in the local community; and you have a guilt-free good time.

Following these fine principles, I found myself perched (slightly uneasily) on an African horse as it carried me (slightly unsteadily) down the steep-sided gorge of the River Makhaleng. I had booked this pony trek from Malealea Lodge, in the spectacular mountains of Lesotho through Tribes, a UK-based company that has been voted Most Responsible Tour Operator by the campaign group Tourism Concern. By going, I would be supporting a pony-trekking association set up and run by a committee of the Basotho people, who live in the Maluti Mountains.

The committee organises a rota of local guides and horses for hire, and rents *rondavels* (round thatched huts), equipped with gas stoves, basic pots and pans, mattresses and a bucket of clean water, from villages en route. Half the fee for hiring the huts is paid to the owner, usually the headman, and half is kept to buy and replace equipment. A proportion of the income from trekking is set aside in a fund for saddles, bridles and blankets.

Malealea's pony-trekking association began taking tourists in 1991 and is thriving. Some guides have earned enough money to build their own houses, and all are careful to keep their horses well fed and healthy, to ensure that they don't miss a lucrative trekking party.

Our guide was Vincent. In Harlem he'd have been a hustler, in London a wide boy. Here in Lesotho, he lived with his father, mother, grandfather, grandmother, three sisters and two brothers in a hut in a village called Ha Moleffe, a few miles from Malealea Lodge. His equivalent of a flash lime-green convertible was his old but willing horse. He had led 20 or so pony-trekking trips already and made good money. He spoke patchy English and wore fake Caterpillar boots, denim jeans and a baseball cap. He tried hard to be a man of the bush – 'The rains are coming,' he told us – but it was more from hope than intuition.

Trekking guides have to speak some English, though don't expect long, enlightening conversations on the economic situation in Lesotho – you probably won't get much more than the names of villages, headmen and mountain peaks. A guide is essential, however; there are no route markers, no good maps, no nice little log cabins. It wasn't a luxurious trip, but it was an adventure – albeit a safe, 'We'll be back for a hot shower and a beer in three days' – type adventure.

The tricky descent to the Makhaleng made for a demanding start. The ponies placed their feet on steady rocks and looked for the path, half-feeling their way as we leant right back in the saddles, legs akimbo. Sisal plants like triffids marked the way, throwing out huge stems with flower heads. The blossoms along the trails formed hedgerows, perfumed with yellow mimosa flowers and wormwood, which smelled like lavender – it's used as a decongestant. Vincent helpfully told us it was a 'peaches tree', although, frankly, his botany was worse than his English.

At one village, a party was going on. There was some interesting role reversal; a man was knitting a straw hat while an old woman sat drinking home-made beer. People were flocking to the action from all directions, scrambling up the steep slopes. Everyone wore a thick, patterned blanket wrapped intricately around them. These blankets, which I coveted throughout the trip, were originally woven by English mills to a series of unique Basotho designs. I bought one back at Malealea's trading store for £35 – nobody could say I wasn't supporting the local economy, and it looks good with Ikea furniture.

When we dismounted at the village of Ribaneng, after six hours in the saddle, a volunteer guide was waiting to escort us to the Ribaneng Falls. We were tired and stiff after our first day's riding, but when I told him we'd skip the falls, he looked so crestfallen (well, there were tips to be had – the price of a couple of beers) that we quickly changed our minds. This supporting-local-people business can be hard work; it was an hour's walk each way, up and down the slopes, but the falls were pretty and they gave off a refreshing cool spray.

At 5am the next day, a crowing cockerel woke me up to the smell of damp earth from rain during the night. I sat outside in my sleeping bag during the slow, electricity-free dawn, watching the villages dotted around the head of the valley wake up. Most people here have never left the mountains, never mind been into surrounding South Africa or beyond. Vincent broke into my reverie when he arrived with the horses – he sang all the time, a deep, throaty African song that we caught the tune of and began to hum too.

There are times on a trip, especially a trek, when you are cold, tired, wet or hungry. On the second day, we were all of these. It rained all day – every minute. As we left Ribaneng and climbed up into the Maluti Mountains proper, my horse, Msabe, panted with the effort of dragging my 11st uphill. We rode through a high pass where the landscape opened out: red-hot pokers lined the way, and the exposed rocks had a layered, petal-like look to them where extremes of temperature had peeled off the outer strips.

As we finally approached the village of Ha Hlalele, the clouds lifted. We guess which was our hut – they were always conveniently near the tell-tale tiny corrugated-iron shed that was the toilet. Most of the villagers don't use it, but the pony-trekking association insists that when a village builds a hut for tourists, they have to build a long-drop toilet, too.

We staggered off the horses and into our hut. It was definitely not five-star. There was a big hole in the windowpane, so we dragged a spare mattress across it, frankly too tired to care. But the bright spot was Georgina, the English-speaking *de facto* head of the village, now her husband was drinking himself to an even earlier grave. She brought us a pot for cooking, fresh water from the village tap and a little paraffin stove that was ineffectual but cheering. A sheep appeared on the hill outside and looked in at the window, bleating forlornly… and in vain. While I don't mind roughing it a bit, sharing my hut with a sheep is where I draw the line.

In the morning sunshine, Ha Hlalele was a different place. The deep voices of the villagers echoed over the mountains, and what the previous night had looked like a bleak, desolate place became a friendly gaggle of people, children, dogs, sheep, goats and cattle. Philip, Georgina's seven-year-old grandson, took us to the magnificent Ketane Falls, a tremendous drop into a canyon that sheers up from the river. Anywhere else, it would be a big draw for tourists: here, it was just us and a child shepherd, waving from his tiny hut across the gorge.

Now our opinion of Ha Hlalele had changed, we were reluctant to leave. I played for time, encouraging Georgina to talk to us in shy but fluent English. She invited us into her second hut, which turned out to be her private bedroom, and shattered all my preconceptions about how these mountain people lived. Inside was a Victorian three-piece bedroom suite crafted from dark varnished wood. On the dressing table, like any good grandma, she had jars of sweets for her grandchildren. On the wall was a pinboard with photographs of pony-trekkers; I was the 856th to stay with her since she built the tourist hut 15 years ago, and she has a spidery handwritten record of every one in her visitors' book.

Finally, we said our goodbyes and trekked down a river valley full of rock pools and robust tussock grasses. Desert rats scurried away from the horses at the last minute. There were more red-hot pokers, aromatic alpines that infused the air with menthol, and yellow celandines poking through burnt, acrid grasses. Vincent was chanting those African songs again. It reminded me of those tapes you buy in foreign markets, the ones that sound so atmospheric until you play them in your living room. Bouncing off the hills, his baritone was perfect – my own personal Walkman.

We spent our third night in Ha Sekoting, the village of headman Puli – 'Chief Goats,' said Vincent, our willing mine of information. Chief Puli, hands dripping blood from killing lambs for dinner, showed us our hut. It was an estate agent's dream: 'A very impressive period of dwelling with Georgian-style windows, raised architraves, a tidy thatch and traditional mud walls.'

We cooked pasta for dinner – for all Puli's hospitality, the Basotho are not a gourmet people – then settled outside our *des res* to watch the village go to bed. The herds were coming in from all directions. The chief's shepherd was trying to get a lamb to suckle, a crippled sheep struggled up the hill to join a flock, safe in a *kraal* for the night. The chickens queued and cackled, heaving their plump bodies into the air for the short hop onto the peaches tree, where they flustered until they finally fluffed and roosted. Cooking pots steamed, and there was an unintelligible buzz of family chatter. It's not a communal way of living – more together, but separate. The *rondavels* have distinct plots, and are arranged in such a way that each family retains some privacy. It's a neighbourly, rather than a tribal, lifestyle.

Children ran home, and the last bundle of firewood was carried up the hill. The doors of the huts began to close as darkness fell fast. Among it all, we sat and watched, unnoticed. Nobody spoke to us, nobody made any attempt to tell us what they were doing. We observed quietly, fascinated as people went about their business. We were absorbed by the contrast to our own lives. For them it was simply – life.

CUBA: DANCE YOURSELF DIZZY

This article by Jan Fairley appeared in *Being There*, a magazine published by Tourism Concern, in July 2001. It describes a Spanish language and dance holiday in Cuba run by **Caledonia Languages Abroad**.

'Uno-dos-tres', one-two-three, and it's definitely not a slow waltz I am learning. It's 10am and with a group of 12 other Brits I'm on the old stage of the Teatro Oriente in Santiago de Cuba starting a salsa dance class. Sixto, a member of the Grupo Folklorico Cutumba, is guiding me with a deft touch as we move forward for eight, back for eight. There's an hour of *son*, the grand-daddy of salsa, followed by an hour of salsa itself. Outside it's hot; inside it's cool, but the sweat is soon pouring off as we snatch swigs at bottles of water while Sergio and Michi, the group's leading dancers, take us repeatedly through our paces.

We each have a member of the company as partner. Natasha from Glasgow is already a great dancer, while Maureen from Leicester has also obviously danced before. Most of the others, including all the men, are first-timers. I may have been dancing salsa for more than ten years, but I soon realize I've got a lot to learn in terms of disciplined moves Cutumba-style. Any fantasies about being discovered as the first lady of salsa are soon dispelled.

But where better to learn the Latin moves of the moment than in the country that gave birth to the rumba, the mambo and the cha-cha-cha? Within days we are all moving well, although the fast salsa variations Michi has in store for us keep the mind as busy as the body.

By the second week, we are hurtling round learning the *rueda*. We form a circle of couples and the men pass the women around, all the while clapping our hands and performing complex moves such as twirls and double twirls. Despite jokily sexist calls like 'don't like this one, pass me another' and 'give me two, give me three', it's addictive. Adrenaline whooshes around as you respond to each shout within a second.

Santiago is a beautiful old town on the eastern edge of Cuba, close to Haiti and the Dominican Republic. Not for us the detachment of hotel rooms – we are lodging with a local family through a homestay programme. My host, one of the heads of the region's electricity board, and her mother, are very welcoming. My room, large with a small veranda onto the roof, has air-conditioning and typical slatted wooden windows. I share the bathroom with Christina, another holiday-maker.

Every day after breakfast we set off, me to practise my dance, Christina to her Spanish lesson. Spanish classes on our trip (they've been changed slightly since) tend to stress grammar and many of us opt for individual conversation with teachers in their homes.

On the way to our various lessons, we often fit in trips to places such as the vegetable market and the famous Moncada Barracks, the site of a failed attack by Fidel Castro and others in the early 1950s that is nevertheless deemed to have marked the start of the revolution. One morning, we visit a local primary school where the children recite the words of national poet José Marti instead of prayers before class. Evening meals are generally soup, followed by roast chicken or pork or tasty fish, with fried plantain, rice and salad, then fruit. Watching TV with the family, while drinking some of their delicious home-made wine, offers insights into such things as why Cubans prefer Brazilian to Colombian soap operas and the impact of the Pope's visit to Cuba.

Anyone holidaying in Cuba becomes aware of the economic limbo the people live in. With a dual economy, tourists pay for everything in dollars while Cubans use the peso. But there are many things you can only buy with dollars, which means that if you invite a Cuban for a beer in exchange for a few dances, most will accept. Not surprisingly, Cubans are politely keen to make friends with foreigners.

We spend the days chilling out by the pool of a city hotel and soon get the hang of Santiago's vibrant night life (from 10pm until past 3am). One evening, we catch the grand *Son de Santiago* concert involving most of the musical groups in the city. With the award-winning Los Jubilados, colleagues of the Buena Vista oldies, playing at the town's Casa de la Trova (musicians' club) each evening, life is sweet. Most clubs hire professional dancers to partner tourists as they take to the floor to practise their steps.

Throughout our stay, there are full- and half-day trips, the most memorable being a short climb to the top of the Gran Piedra, a huge rock with views over the Sierra Maestra mountains. We also join a countryside *asado* hosted by a local family who roast a young pig over a charcoal pit outside their wooden house – their garden full of sugar cane and banana trees. There's also a palm from whose coconuts we drink.

One evening, we were invited to a *bembé*, the most accessible form of Afro-Cuban religious worship, which takes the form of a party for a specific god. Held in the house owned by one of the Cutumba dancers, this is a real eye-opener. On a home-made altar on the floor, offerings of honey, perfume, flowers, herbs, rum and cake are laid out to Elegga, the god of the pathways. Singers lead a sequence of calls for different *orishas* (gods) of Santería with everyone responding and swaying on the spot. The joyful response is as infectious as their *orisha* songs, and a drumming pattern soon emerges. Here, as in so much of Cuban life, people are inspired by music and dance. Without these rhythms, Cuba wouldn't be what it is.

SECTION TWO

HOLIDAY DIRECTORY

OUTBOUND OPERATORS

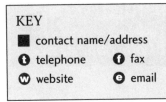
This directory features responsible tourism companies and organizations in the UK, Europe, the US and Australia that include local community tourism projects on their tours. Contact details for these operators are updated on Tourism Concern's website at www.tourismconcern.org.uk. If you work with local community tourism projects and wish to be listed in this directory in future, email: info@tourismconcern.org.uk

UK-BASED TOUR OPERATORS

International dialing code +44.

Bear Print International
Tours to Native American lands and communities run with tribal leaders and Native American educators and cultural representatives. Tours aim to give a real insight into the history and lives of Native Americans, rather than the tourist stereotypes. Trips to different regions and tribes including the Navajo, Lakota (Sioux), Cheyenne and Blackfeet. Bear Print also publishes The Trail of Many Spirits by Serle Chapman, about the history and contemporary culture of Native America.

■ PO Box 1, Wakefield, West Yorkshire WF4 4YB

☎ 01924 840 111

ⓔ bearprint@bun.com

Caledonia Languages Abroad
Language courses in Spain, Italy, France, Portugal, Peru, Mexico, Ecuador, Costa Rica, Russia, etc. They also run two-week holidays to Cuba and Argentina, combining Spanish with classes in Cuban dance or tango, and can organize volunteer work placements in Latin America.

■ The Clockhouse, Bonnington Mill, 72 Newhaven Road, Edinburgh EH6 5QG

☎ + ☎ 0131 621 7721/2 ☎ 0131 621 7723

ⓦ www.caledonialanguages.co.uk ⓔ info@caledonialanguages.co.uk

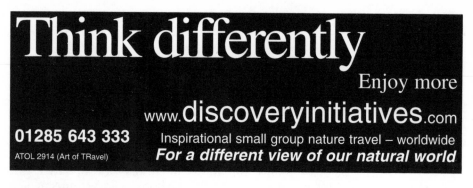

Discovery Initiatives

Small-group and tailor-made wildlife trips run in partnership with conservation organizations in destination countries, featuring wildlife lodges and safaris, trekking, horse trekking and rainforest tours. Destinations include southern and east Africa, India, China, Mongolia, Borneo, Australia, Canada, Hawaii, Peru and Ecuador and the Galapagos. 10 per cent of revenue goes to the local conservation organization. ATOL bonded.

■ 51 Castle St, Cirencester, Gloucestershire, GL7 1QD

❶ 01285 643 333 ❶ 01285 885 888

Ⓦ www.discoveryinitiatives.com Ⓔ enquiry@discoveryinitiatives.com

Dragoman

An adventure holiday operator that incorporates visits to locally-run and community-based tourism projects into many of its trips. Brochure available. ATOL bonded.

■ Camp Green, Debenham, Stowmarket, Suffolk IP14 6LA

❶ 01728 861 133 ❶ 01728 861 127

Ⓦ www.dragoman.co.uk

Earthwatch Institute (Europe)

Paying volunteer holidays with conservation research projects. Their focus is mainly conservation, archaeology and wildlife, but a few projects involve communities.

■ 57 Woodstock Road, Oxford OX2 6HJ

❶ 01865 318 838 ❶ 01865 311 383

Ⓦ www.earthwatch.org.uk Ⓔ info@earthwatch.org.uk

Exodus   TOUR
A well-established UK adventure tour operator. Their 15-day Ghana trip features a 5-day village stay where guests live with a local family and participate in daily life.

■ 9 Weir Road, London SW12 0LT

☎ 020 8675 5550 ✆ 020 8673 0779

 www.exodus.co.uk

Full Moon Night Trekking
Walking holidays to Baltistan in northern Pakistan, with great scenery and trekking among the Karakoram and Himalayan mountains.

■ 9a Avonmore Mansions, Avonmore Road, London W14 8RN

☎ 020 7603 9893

Ⓦ www.fmntrekking.com ℮ info@fmntrekking.com

IntoAfrica

'Fair traded' adventure treks, wildlife safaris and mountain climbing in Kenya and Tanzania. This is the UK partner of an African company (See Local tours: Kenya and Tanzania). The emphasis is on insights into local life, environment and cultures as well as seeing the wildlife and famous national parks.

■ Chris Morris: 59 Langdon Street, Sheffield S11 8BH

❶ 0114 255 5610

Ⓦ www.intoafrica.co.uk Ⓔ enquiry@intoafrica.co.uk

Karamba Ltd

Music and dance holidays to Cuba and Senegal.

■ Gary Newland: Ollands Lodge, Heydon, Norwich, Norfolk NR11 6RB

❶ + ❶ 01603 872 402

Ⓦ www.karamba.co.uk Ⓔ karamba@gn.apc.org

Make a Difference Aid Adventure

Small-group adventure tours to northern India, with 20 per cent of income donated to local charities.

■ Darren Odell: Waters Edge, Bridge Street, Andersey Island, Abingdon, Oxfordshire OX14 3HY

❶ 01235 527 401 ❶ 01235 536 381

Ⓦ www.madaid.com Ⓔ info@madaid.com

Muir's Tours

A non-profit tour operator offering trekking, mountain biking, rafting, skiing and climbing holidays in Nepal and the US West in particular, plus Bhutan, Ladakh, Mongolia, India, Tibet, Thailand, Peru and Ecuador. Profits go to various charities and development projects. Set up by a UK charity called the Nepal Kingdom Foundation.

■ Maurice Adshead: 97a Swansea Road, Reading RG1 8HA

❶ 0118 950 2281 ❶ 0118 950 2301

Ⓦ www.nkf-mt.org.uk Ⓔ info@nkf-mt.org.uk

The Nepal Trust

A Scottish charity that works with communities in Nepal to develop health, education and other community projects. It runs treks that combine hiking with volunteer work on these projects.

■ 4 Marina Quay, Lossiemouth, Moray IV31 6TJ, Scotland

❶ 01343 810 358 ❶ 01343 810 359

Ⓦ www.nepaltrust.org Ⓔ admin@nepaltrust.org

North South Travel

A non-profit flight agency that offers competitive discount flights with profits going to community projects in developing nations, including Children of the Andes, Tulsi Trust, Wells for India, Joliba Trust and others.

■ Brenda Skinner: Moulsham Mill, Parkway, Chelmsford, Essex CM2 7PX

❶ + ❶ 01245 608 291

Ⓦ www.northsouthtravel.co.uk Ⓔ brenda@northsouthtravel.co.uk

Rainbow Tours

Tours and tailor-made self-drive itineraries to South and southern Africa and Madagascar featuring wildlife parks, undeveloped Indian Ocean beaches and visits to communities. Rainbow works with many community-based lodges, hotels and tours. ATOL bonded. Brochure available.

■ Roger Diski: Canon Collins House, 64 Essex Rd, London N1 8LR

❶ 020 7226 1004 ❶ 020 7226 2621

Ⓦ www.rainbowtours.co.uk Ⓔ info@rainbowtours.co.uk

Responsible Travel.com

A website featuring a selection of holidays from sustainable and 'responsible' tour operators.

■ www.responsibletravel.com

Safari Njema

Trips to northern Tanzania and Zanzibar combining wildlife (Ngorongoro, Serengeti) with an insight into local life, including visits to community projects.

■ Simon McGowan

❶ 0115 929 8785; 07733 021769

Ⓦ www.safarinjema.com Ⓔ simon@safarinjema.com

Tailor-made tours off the beaten track. Development projects, cultural tourism, remote tourist sites. Your chance to see the real Tanzania.

Simply Tanzania Tour Company

54 Cotesbach Road, London E5 9QJ. Tel/fax: 020-8986 0615
enquiries@simplytanzania.co.uk
www.simplytanzania.co.uk

Simply Tanzania
Tailor-made 4WD tours run by an ex-VSO field director for Tanzania, combining wildlife safaris with visits to communities and off-the-beaten-track destinations. Also trips to the less-visited south, including the superb Selous game reserve and the Iringa/Mheya mountains.

■ Tony Janes: 54 Cotesbach Road, Clapton, London E5 9QJ

❶ + ❶ 020 8986 0615

Ⓦ www.simplytanzania.co.uk ❷ enquiries@simplytanzania.co.uk

Specialist Trekking
Trekking holidays in Nepal. Also trips to Bhutan and Tibet. ATOL bonded. Brochure available.

■ Chapel House, Low Cotehill, Carlisle, Cumbria CA4 0EL

❶ 01228 562 358 ❶ 01228 562 368

Ⓦ www.specialisttrekking.com ❷ trekstc@aol.com

Sunvil Discovery
One of the more responsible mainstream operators. Their southern Africa programme features projects listed in the Local tours directory in Namibia, Botswana and Zambia. ATOL bonded. Brochure available.

■ Sunvil House, Upper Square, Old Isleworth, Middlesex TW7 7BJ

❶ 020 8232 9777 ❶ 020 8568 8330

Ⓦ www.sunvil.co.uk ❷ africa@sunvil.co.uk

Symbiosis Expedition Planning
A tour operator specializing in small-group tours and customized itineraries to South-East Asia, including community-based projects in Thailand, Indonesia, Malaysia and the Philippines.

■ 113 Bolingbroke Grove, London SW11 1DA

📞 020 7924 5906   📠 020 7924 5907

🌐 www.symbiosis-travel.com   ✉ info@symbiosis-travel.com

Travel Friends International
Travel Friends don't organize trips, but act as an information source for local projects including FESTU (Sri Lanka), the Green Hotel (India), Mitra Bali Foundation, (Indonesia) and Kololi Inn and Paradise Inn (The Gambia), plus organizations in Bulgaria, Poland, Greece and Slovakia.

■ Ted Finch: St Clare, The Street, Pakenham, Bury St Edmunds, Suffolk IP31 2JU

📞 + 📠 01359 232 385

✉ finch-travelfriends@talk21.com

Tribes Travel
Small-group and tailor-made cultural tours and wildlife journeys (including rainforest trips and safaris) incorporating community tourism projects. Destinations include Botswana, Ecuador, Egypt, The Gambia, India, Jordan, Morocco, Namibia, Nepal, Peru, South Africa, Lesotho, Tanzania, Zambia and Zimbabwe. Bond Plus protection.

■ Amanda Marks: 12 The Business Centre, Earl Soham, Woodbridge, Suffolk IP13 7SA

☎ 01728 685 971 **✆** 01728 685 973

ⓦ www.tribes.co.uk **ⓔ** ctg@tribes.co.uk

Wind, Sand & Stars

Holidays in the Sinai with Bedouin guides and communities. Trips include camel treks and desert hiking in the Sinai's mountainous interior. Also customized itineraries plus trips for schools, a student summer expedition and special interest tours (biblical, wildlife, etc). Helps fund local educational and health projects. British Airways Tourism for Tomorrow Awards, highly commended 1996.

■ Emma Loveridge/Liz Dempsey: 2 Arkwright Road, London NW3 6AD

☎ 020 7433 3684 **✆** 020 7431 3247

ⓦ www.windsandstars.co.uk **ⓔ** office@windsandstars.co.uk

Zanzibar Travel

A UK-based tour operator that uses locally-owned hotels and operators and includes village tours, meals with families, etc.

■ Michael Sweeney: Reynards House, Selkirk Gardens, Cheltenham, Gloucestershire GL52 5LY

☎ + **✆** 01242 222 027

ⓦ www.zanzibartravel.co.uk **ⓔ** info@zanzibartravel.co.uk

US-BASED TOUR OPERATORS

International dialing code +1.

Conservation International

An environmental agency promoting conservation through community development, including a number of tourism projects.

■ 1919 M Street NW, Suite 600, Washington DC

☎ 202 912 1000 ext 421 **✆** 912 1044

ⓦ www.ecotour.org **ⓔ** g.ryan@conservation.org

Cross-Cultural Solutions

Three-week (and longer) volunteer placements with NGOs in India, Ghana, Peru, China and Russia. Typical costs: $1950 for a three-week placement. Roles include English teaching, healthcare, arts, computing, working with disabled children, women's groups, etc. Also cultural tours to Cuba, Peru, Ghana and India, including one focusing on Indian women's issues.

■ 47 Potter Avenue, New Rochelle, NY 10801

☎ 914 632 0022; 1-800 380 4777 📠 914 632 8494

🌐 www.crossculturalsolutions.org ✉ info@crossculturalsolutions.org

Dreamweaver Travel

Adventure travel to Cameroon, Niger and Togo. Activities range from camel treks in Niger to whale watching in Togo, plus homestays and opportunities to participate in West African village life. The company contributes to community development projects in the host communities.

■ Dudley Parkinson: 1185 River Drive, River Falls, WI 54022

☎ 715 425 1037 📠 715 426 0829

🌐 www.dreamweavertravel.net ✉ dudley@dreamweavertravel.net

Global Exchange

Non-profit organization that runs 'reality tours' (which they also call 'people to people' tourism). Trips feature meetings with community leaders and activists. Destinations include Brazil, Costa Rica, Cuba, Guatemala, Haiti, India, Iran, Mexico, Ireland, Israel, Nicaragua, Palestine, South Africa, Zimbabwe and Vietnam.

■ 2017 Mission Street, Suite 303, San Francisco, CA 94110

☎ 415 255 7296 📠 415 255 7498

🌐 www.globalexchange.org/tours ✉ realitytours@globalexchange.org

IVEX (International Volunteer Expeditions)

Short-term volunteer holidays on sustainable development projects (environment, organic agriculture, rainforest, recycling, community-based tourism), with an emphasis on the Americas and the Caribbean.

■ 2001 Vallejo Way, Sacramento, California 95818

🌐 www.espwa.org/ivex.htm ✉ ivexinformation@espwa.org

Mesoamerican Ecotourism Alliance / RARE

An alliance of local organizations developing ecotourism projects in Mexico, Honduras, Guatemala and Belize, supported by the US conservation organization RARE.

■ James Dion: 1840 Wilson Blvd, Suite 402, Arlington, VA 22201-3000

☎ 703 522 5070 📠 703 522 5027

🌐 www.rarecenter.org or www.ecotourismalliance.org ✉ jdion@rarecenter.org

The Nature Conservancy (TNC)

The largest conservation group in the US offers 'conservation journeys' to TNC projects in Latin America and Asia, many of which are run in partnership with local community-based conservation organizations.

■ Andy Drumm, Ecotourism Director: Suite 100, 4245 North Fairfax Drive, Arlington, VA 22203-1606

ⓦ www.nature.org/ecotourism ⓔ ecotourism@tnc.org

Tread Lightly

Small-group ecotours run with local conservation organizations using local guides and staff. Destinations include Belize, Borneo, Brazil, Chile, Ecuador, The Falklands, Guatemala, Honduras, Panama, Venezuela, etc.

■ Jim and Audrey Patterson: 37 Juniper Meadow Road, Washington Depot, CT06794

ⓣ 207 853 2632; 1-800 643 0060 ⓕ 860 868 1718 *or* 207 853 2367

ⓦ www.treadlightly.com ⓔ info@treadlightly.com

Wilderness Travel

An ecotour operator that offers trekking, wildlife safaris, cultural tours, sea kayaking, sailing, etc, including some community-based projects.

■ 1102 Ninth St, Berkeley, CA 94710-1211

ⓣ 510 558 2488; 1-800 368 2794 ⓕ 510 558 2489

ⓦ www.wildernesstravel.com ⓔ info@wildernesstravel.com

Wildland Adventures

Ecotours to Latin America and Africa, including some community tours.

■ Kurt Kutay: 3516 NE 155th Street, Seattle, WA 98155

ⓣ 1-800 345 4453 ⓕ 206 363 6615

ⓦ www.wildland.com ⓔ kurt@wildland.com

EUROPE-BASED TOUR OPERATORS

Associazione RAM

An Italian NGO working for fair trade and responsible tourism. They also run trips to Thailand, Vietnam, Sri Lanka, Sikkim, Nepal and India.

■ Renzo Garrone: via Mortola 15 I-16030, San Rocco di Camogli (GE), Italy *or* via Figari 76-16030, Ruta di Camogli (GE), Italy

ⓣ + ⓕ +39 (0)185 77 3061/6028

ⓦ www.associazioneram.it ⓔ orzonero@hotmail.com

Multatuli Travel

Dutch responsible tourism company running trips to Indonesia (with Bina Swadaya, see Local tours: Indonesia), the Philippines, Ecuador, Tanzania, Nepal and South Africa.

■ Freek ten Broeke: Max Euweplein 24, 1017MB, Amsterdam, The Netherlands

✆ +31 (0)20 627 7707 ☏ +31 (0)20 627 4886

🅦 www.multatuli.com ✉ travel@multatuli.nl

AUSTRALIAN-BASED TOUR OPERATORS

International dialing code +61.

Oxfam Community Aid Abroad Tours

The tour agency of Oxfam Community Aid Abroad. Tours feature visits to development projects, meetings with progressive and indigenous organizations and stays with communities, as well as conventional tourist sights and activities. Destinations include Aboriginal Australia, Cuba, Guatemala, India, Laos, Madagascar, Solomon Islands, Tibet, Vietnam, Zambia and Malawi. Brochure available. Trips of one to three weeks. IATA accredited.

■ Brian Witty: PO Box 34, Rundle Mall, South Australia 5000

✆ 08 8232 2727; 1-800 814 848 ☏ 08 8232 2808

🅦 www.caa.org.au/travel/ ✉ info@tours.caa.org.au

Ecotour Travel

'Green' travel agents who also book some Aboriginal tours and overseas community projects.

■ Janet Southern: PO Box 153, Moffat Beach, Queensland 4551

✆ 07 5437 2811 ☏ 07 5437 2911

✉ ecotour@optusnet.com.au

LOCAL TOUR OPERATORS BY COUNTRY

This directory lists locally-based tours, lodges, guesthouses and organizations in destination countries. Updated contact details for these projects are posted on Tourism Concern's website at www.tourismconcern.org.uk.

KEY

■ contact name/address ❶ telephone ❶ fax Ⓦ website ❸ email

ACCOM	accommodation only (camping, guesthouse, lodge, etc)
ACCOM+	accommodation plus activities (cultural displays, etc)
AGRI	'agritourism' – ie learning about local farming methods and lifestyles
BUDGET	no-frills, backpacker-style facilities
CENTRE	visitor centre or museum
DAY	day (or shorter) tours
RAINFOREST	rainforest lodges, tours
LUXURY	upmarket, luxurious
ORG	NGO (non-governmental organization), marketing organization, trade association, etc: sources of more information about local community tourism
SAFARI	wildlife tours, lodges
SAFARI+	wildlife tours, lodges, which also feature cultural tours
SCHOOL	language, music, horseriding, etc, lessons
TOUR	multi-day hikes, usually guided
VOL	volunteer work placements
WEBSITE	website containing useful information

Cost

A cost per *day* indicates an all-inclusive price including accommodation, food and tours. A cost per *night* indicates accommodation only. Prices are per person, usually based on sharing a double room. All prices are approximate, subject to change and for guidance only: contact each tour/project for exact prices. All dollar prices refer to US$ unless indicated.

TELEPHONE CODES

When calling internationally, dial the international network access code for the country you are in, followed by the international dialling code of the country you are calling. Then dial the number listed, dropping the initial zero. For example, to call 061 226 979 in Namibia, dial +264 61 226 979, where the '+' symbol represents the international network access code (in the UK, for example, this would be 00).

WEBSITES

Website addresses change. If the website address we list doesn't work, try entering the project name into a search engine such as www.google.com.

ENGLISH-SPEAKING?

Some Latin American tours are Spanish-speaking only. Check with the tour operator. Unless specified, tours in other countries are in English, or provide English-speaking guides.

HELP US UPDATE

If you know of similar community tourism projects or changes to these listings, please email Tourism Concern at info@tourismconcern.org.uk – subject: community tourism.

AUSTRALIA – ABORIGINAL TOURS

International dialing code +61. Prices are in Australian dollars.

Aboriginal imagery – painting, boomerangs, didgeridoos, rock art, 'Dreamtime' myths, etc – features heavily in Australia's tourism marketing, but few Aboriginal people benefit from tourism. Indeed, Aboriginal Australians endure some of the worst living conditions in the world. In many Aboriginal communities, health and education facilities are almost non-existent and the life expectancy of Aboriginal Australians is 25 years less than for white Australians.

There are a few Aboriginal tours in Australia's cities and along the eastern seaboard, but most are found in the vast central deserts of the Outback or in the tropical north, including Arnhemland and the Kimberley. It's here that you'll find the most 'traditional' Aboriginal culture. Although none are unaffected by white Australia, there are communities where people still speak their own language and gather food from the bush.

Aboriginal culture and spirituality is deeply connected to the land. For this reason, Aboriginal tours are different from standard nature tours. Aboriginal society is one of the most conservation-minded in the world, and learning about the Aboriginal attitude to the environment is a lesson in what it means to truly respect nature.

Aboriginal tours typically feature gentle bushwalks to learn about Aboriginal use of plants for food and medicine ('bushtucker'), plus explanations of Aboriginal culture, spiritual beliefs and 'Dreamtime' stories. There's usually a chance to buy paintings and crafts. All projects listed below are Aboriginal owned and run unless stated. Tours in northern Australia (the 'Top End' of the Northern Territory, Arnhemland, Tiwi Islands, the Kimberley, northern Queensland) generally run in the winter/dry season only (roughly April to November).

There are more Aboriginal tours and cultural centres than we have room to list here. For more information, visit the Aboriginal-owned websites Aboriginal Tour Operators (www.aboriginaltouroperators.com) and Aboriginal Australia (www.aboriginalaustralia.com), or contact Aboriginal Tourism Australia (tel: 03 9620 4533; www.ataust.org.au; ataust@ataust.org.au).

Aboriginal Arts and Cultural Centre   CENTRE/TOUR
ToDo! Award winner
Art gallery, cultural centre and didjeridoo school in Alice Springs, plus tours (bushtucker, nature walks, Aboriginal history and culture) of up to five days. Day tour $121; five days from $595.

■ 86 Todd St, Alice Springs, NT 0870

✆ 08 8952 3408 ✆ 08 8953 2678

Ⓦ www.aboriginalart.com.au Ⓔ aborart@ozemail.com.au

Abtrade.com   WEBSITE
A website featuring Aborginal tour guides and attractions in New South Wales.

Ⓦ www.abtrade.com.au/tourism.htm

Anangu Tours/Uluru Cultural Centre   CENTRE/DAY
Short (two hours or half-day) Aboriginal guided walks near Uluru (Ayer's Rock), explaining bushtucker, medicinal plants, Dreamtime stories.

■ Ayers Rock Resort, NT

✆ 08 8956 2123 ✆ 08 8956 3136

Ⓦ www.anangutours.com.au Ⓔ lbanangu@anangutours.com.au

Australian National Tourism Office   ORG
Has a department developing Aboriginal tourism. Their website describes various Aboriginal tours, including some listed here.

■ Special Interest Tourism Products Team, Sport and Tourism Division, Department of Industry, Science and Resources, PO Box 9839, Canberra ACT, 2600

✆ 02 6213 7014 ✆ 02 6213 7096

Ⓦ www.tourism.gov.au/publications/talent/start.html Ⓔ info.tourism@isr.gov.au

Camp Coorong   ACCOM+
A Ngarrindjeri community with dorms, cabins and camping plus cultural tours, two hours south east of Adelaide (10km south of Meningie). Dreamtime stories, bush tucker, cultural museum, discussions of contemporary issues, ecology. Dorms $14, cabins $45.

■ PO Box 126, Meningie SA 5264

❶ 08 8575 1557 ❶ 08 8575 1448

◉ nlpa@lm.net.au

Darngku Heritage Tours/Darlngunaya Backpackers DAY/ACCOM/BUDGET
Darlngunaya Backpackers is an attractive hostel in a historic building in Fitzroy
Crossing in the Kimberley, while Darngku Heritage Tours run half-day boat
trips to nearby Geikie Gorge.

■ Darngku Heritage Tours

❶ 08 9191 5355 ❶ 08 9191 5085

■ Darlngunaya Backpackers: PO Box 81, Fitzroy Crossing, WA 6765

❶ 08 9191 5140

Desert Tracks   TOUR
Excellent tours to a Pitjantjatjara community. Trips depart from Yulara (Ayer's
Rock resort) and include 'Dreaming' tracks, learning about Outback ecology
and bush tucker, visiting rock art sites, memorable Outback scenery and the
chance to see contemporary Aboriginal central desert life. Two to eight days.
Seven days from $2400.

■ Jim Montgomery: Box 345, Somers, Victoria 3927

❶ 03 5983 2818; 0410 644 480 ❶ 03 5983 2807

Ⓦ www.desert-tracks.com.au ◉ deserttk@alphalink.com.au

Dharawal Aboriginal Tours   DAY
Day tours and overnight camping trips ($45 and $90) from Sydney's Bondi
Beach to Botany Bay and the Royal National Park, exploring Sydney's little-
known Aboriginal heritage. The Dharawal are the traditional inhabitants of the
south Sydney region.

■ Rodney Mason: Dharawal Education Centre, 15 Murrong Place, La Perouse, NSW
2036

❶ 02 9661 1226

Dreamtime Cultural Centre   CENTRE
Aboriginal cultural centre in Rockhampton, with crafts and cultural shows.

■ PO Box 6182, Rockhampton, Queensland 4702

❶ 079 36 1655 ❶ 079 36 1671

Ecotour Travel   ORG
'Green' travel agents that also books some Aboriginal tours.

■ Janet Southern: PO Box 153, Moffat Beach, Queensland 4551

☎ 07 5437 2811 ℻ 07 5437 2911

✉ southern@acon.com.au *or* ecotour@optusnet.com.au

Guluyambi River Trips   DAY
Two-hour boat cruises on the scenic East Alligator River in Kakadu National
Park, near Border Store and the famous rock art site of Ubirr. $30.

☎ 08 8979 2411 ℻ 08 8979 2303

✉ kakair@kakair.com.au

Kimberley Dreamtime   DAY/TOUR
Day and customized tours including fishing, rock art, bushtucker, bush
medicine, Aboriginal culture and spectacular Kimberley scenery.

■ PO Box 214, Wyndham, WA, 6740

☎ 08 9161 1288; 0419 922 015 ℻ 08 9161 1408

🌐 www.ibizwa.com/kimberleydreamtime ✉ kimberleydreamtime@bigpond.com

Kooljaman   ACCOM+
Camping and cabins owned by the Djarindhjin and One Arm Point communities, 220km north of Broome on the remote Dampier Peninsula. Fishing,
swimming, snorkelling plus beautiful deserted beaches and Outback scenery.
4WD or air access only, no pets, booking essential.

■ PMB 8, Cape Leveque via Broome, WA 6725

☎ 08 9192 4970 ℻ 08 9192 4978

🌐 www.kooljaman.com.au ✉ leveque@bigpond.com.au

Lombadina   ACCOM+
Community-run camping and cabins on the remote and beautiful Dampier
Peninsula coast north of Broome. Crafts, mudcrabbing, guided bushwalks,
deserted beaches, boat tours, fishing trips, birdwatching and wildlife. Access by
air or 4WD. Cabins from $38.50 per night.

■ PO Box 372, Broome, WA 6725

☎ + ℻ 08 9192 4936; 08 9192 4116

🌐 www.ibizwa.com/lombadina ✉ lombo@comswest.net.au

Manyallaluk TOUR
Award-winning tours near Katherine Gorge, featuring Aboriginal culture, rock art, swimming holes, explanations of bush tucker, etc. Day tours from $99. Camping available.

■ Steve Fletcher: PO Box 1480, Katherine NT 0851

📞 08 8975 4727 📠 08 8975 4724

Mimbi Caves DAY
Day trips to newly-opened limestone caves near Fitzroy Crossing in the Kimberley.

■ Fitzroy Crossing Tourist Bureau

📞 0891 915 355 📠 0891 915 085

📧 fitzroytb@bigpond.com

Minjungbal Cultural Centre CENTRE
An Aboriginal cultural centre at South Tweed Heads in northern NSW. Museum, dance performances, short walks, crafts.

■ Kirkwood Rd, South Tweed Heads, NSW 2486

📞 07 5524 2109 📠 07 5523 1411

Peppimenarti TOUR
Two- or three-day tours from Darwin to a Ngangikuranggur community on the Daly River south-west of Darwin. Remote Top End scenery, Aboriginal culture, waterfalls, billabongs and wildlife. Two days $500.

■ Aussie Adventure Holidays: PO Box 2023, Darwin, NT 0801

📞 08 8924 1111 📠 08 8924 1122

📧 aussieadventure@attglobal.net

Sydney Aboriginal Discoveries DAY
Day tours exploring Sydney's Aboriginal history and culture, including a two-hour harbour cruise, a bus tour and a walking tour around Circular Quay and the Botanic Gardens.

■ PO Box 584, Leichhardt, NSW 2040, Sydney

📞 02 9568 6880 📠 02 9568 5203

🌐 www.sydneyaboriginal.com.au *or* www.aboriginaldiscoveries.com.au

📧 abtours@abtrade.com.au

Tiwi Tours TOUR
Tours to the Tiwi Islands via light aircraft from Darwin. History and culture of the Tiwi plus bushwalks, Aboriginal art, etc. Day trip $298; two-day camping trip $564.

◼ PO Box 2023, Darwin, NT 0801

🕻 08 8924 1115 🕿 08 8924 1122

◼ Aussie Adventure Holidays: PO Box 2023, Darwin, NT 0801

🕻 08 8924 1111 🕿 08 8924 1122

🄴 aussieadventure@attglobal.net

Tjiapukai Aboriginal Cultural Park CENTRE
Cultural centre in Cairns with art gallery, dance performances and hi-tech cultural shows.

◼ PO Box 816, Smithfield, Cairns, Queensland 4878

🕻 07 4042 9900 🕿 07 4042 9990

🅦 www.tjapukai.com.au 🄴 tjapukai@tjapukai.com.au

Umbarra CENTRE/DAY
An Aboriginal cultural centre and day tours at Wallaga Lake, near Narooma on the southern New South Wales coast.

◼ Francine Greetham

🕻 02 4473 7232 🕿 02 4473 7169

🄴 umbarra@acr.net.au

Umorrduk Aboriginal Safaris TOUR
Tours to a Gummulkbun community in Arnhemland, 365km north-east of Darwin, in beautiful wilderness rich in rock art. From $475 per day.

◼ Brookes Australia Tours: Brian Rooke: PO Box 41086, Casuarina, NT 0811

🕻 08 8948 1306 🕿 03 8660 2143

🅦 www.tourism.gov.au/publications/talent/umorraduk.html

Wreck Bay Walkabouts DAY
Bushtucker and cultural tours run by the Wreck Bay Aboriginal community in Jervis Bay National Park, south of Sydney. The community also co-manage the nearby **Booderee Botanical Gardens** (www.booderee.NP.gov.au).

🕻 02 442 1166

Wundargoodie Aboriginal Safaris TOUR
Aboriginal cultural tours around Broome and Purnululu (the Bungle Bungles) in the Kimberley.

■ Colin/Maria Morgan: 38 Taiji Road (PO Box 5476), Cable Beach, Broome, WA 6726

☎ 08 9192 8088 ✆ 08 9192 5558

BELIZE

International dialing code +501.

Culturally, tiny Belize is more part of the Caribbean than Central America, with a laid-back atmosphere and an English-speaking black majority. However, Hispanic immigrants from Guatemala are slowly bringing the country closer to its Latin neighbours. In tourist terms, Belize is very much an ecotourism destination. A string of islands and the world's second-largest Barrier Reef are the main attractions, and islands such as Ambergris Caye can be quite touristy. The mainland coast is prone to hurricanes and less developed, with long stretches of mangrove swamps rather than beach. Inland, tracts of lush rainforest hide rivers, waterfalls, caves and Mayan ruins.

Information about visiting projects listed here and other ecotourism ventures can be found in *The Rough Guide to Belize*.

Belize Audubon Society ORG
Conservation organization that helps develop some community ecotourism projects.

■ 12 Fort St (PO Box 1001), Belize City

☎ 02 35004; 02 34987 ✆ 02 34985

Ⓦ www.belizeaudubon.org ✉ base@btl.net

Bermudian Landing Community Baboon Sanctuary DAY
A conservation and tourism project 30km inland from Belize City, sponsored by the Worldwide Fund for Nature (WWF) and the Belize Audubon Society. Birdwatching, wildlife (the 'baboons' are actually howler monkeys), guided hikes, canoe trips and homestays.

Cockscomb Basin Wildlife Sanctuary RAINFOREST
A protected area containing jaguar, tapir, armadillo, anteaters, howler monkeys, eagles, scarlet macaws, toucans, boa constrictors, etc, on the rainforested slopes of Mt Victoria, south of Dangriga. Local guides can be hired in the nearby village of Mayan Center (see *The Rough Guide to Belize* for visiting details).

SPEAR (Society for the Promotion of Education and Research)   TOUR
An environmental NGO running ten-day educational tours of Belize. Mayan ruins, snorkelling, beaches, birdwatching and rainforest plus visits to community projects, village stays and exploration of contemporary issues. Ten-day tour $1800. Profits go towards SPEAR's development work. Tours include Mountain Pine Ridge, Lamanai, Altan Ha, the Community Baboon Sanctuary, Calabash Caye, Belize Zoo.

■ PO Box 1766, Belize City

☎ 02 33967 ☏ 02 32367

🌐 www.spear.org.bz ✉ SpearTours@btl.net

Toledo Ecotourism Association (TEA)/Toldedo Institute of Development and Environment (TIDE)/Toledo Visitors Information Centre (TVIC)   ORG/TOUR
ToDo! Award winner
Toledo, an off-the-beaten track area in the far south of Belize, contains some of the country's best rainforest, plus Mayan ruins, caves, wildlife (jaguars, iguanas, howler monkeys, toucans, etc) and offshore cayes and coral reef. Three organizations in Punta Gorda, the tiny local capital, are involved in community tourism. The Toledo Ecotourism Association (TEA), which won a 1997 ToDo! Award, offers trails and village stays in Mopan or Kekchi Mayan and Garifuna villages – visits to local attractions, horseriding, arts and crafts, fishing, storytelling, medicinal plants, etc. From $42.50 per day. TIDE, a local NGO supported by The Nature Conservancy, runs other ecotours including a one-week tour for $540, plus fishing and kayaking trips. The TVIC also runs a homestay programme in Mayan villages where guests participate in village work.

■ TEA: Reyes Chun: 5 Front St (PO Box 157), Punta Gorda

☎ 07 22096 ☏ 07 22929

🌐 www.belizehome.com/toledomaya *or* www.plenty.org/TEA/index.htm

✉ ttea@btl.net *or* plenty1@usit.net *or* plentybz@btl.net)

■ TIDE: Wil Maheia: PO Box 150, Punta Gorda

☎ 07 22129; 07 22274

🌐 www.belizeecotours.org ✉ tidetours@btl.net

■ TVIC

☎ 07 22470

BOLIVIA

International dialing code +591.

Bolivia is sometimes called the Tibet of the Americas: the western half of this poor, landlocked country is an arid high-altitude plateau called the *altiplano*. Here, Quechua and Aymara campesinos live in one of the toughest inhabited environments on earth. The landscape can be dramatic, from shimmering Lake Titicaca and the 6000m-plus peaks of the Cordillera Real to the surreal Salar de Uyuni salt lake and the 'coloured lakes' of the south. La Paz, the world's highest capital, is dramatically situated inside a vast canyon surrounded by snowcapped peaks. Further south, Potosi and Sucre are historic colonial cities.

The country offers magnificent trekking, especially around Coroico and Sorata in the Cordillera Real. The east – accessible by air or by some of the world's most hair-raising bus-rides (I describe one such trip in my book, *The Gringo Trail* [Summersdale, 2001]) – is Amazonian rainforest. Backpackers take jungle tours from Rurrenabaque, while the remote Noel Kempff Mercado and Madidi national parks offer even more pristine – but more expensive – wilderness experiences.

Bolivia is both the poorest and most indigenous of South American nations but, as with other countries in the region, tourism is controlled almost entirely by the Latino or mestizo minority.

Chalalan Lodge/Madidi National Park   RAINFOREST

Madidi is a remote, pristine park in primary Amazon rainforest, accessible by light aircraft, with over 300 types of bird, 1200 butterfly species and monkeys, capibara, jaguar, tapir, caiman, etc. Chalalan Lodge was set up in the park by the American organization Conservation International in partnership with the local Quechua-Tecana community of San Jose de Uchiapiomaoas, with guides drawn from the local community.

■ In the UK: Discovery Initiatives (see Outbound operators)

■ In the US: Conservation International (see Outbound operators)

Villa Amboro Ecotourism Project   TOUR

Tours run by two campesino communities in Amboro National Park, a park of volcanic ridges and tropical forest near Santa Cruz. Guests stay in simple camps, with guided rainforest walks, wildlife, medicinal plants, birdwatching (700 species). Supported by a local NGO, Probioma, with help from SNV and Christian Aid Abroad.

■ Probioma: Equipetrol Calle Córdoba 7E 29

❶ 03 431332 ❶ 03 432098

Ⓦ www.probioma.es.vg *or* www.probioecotur.es.vg Ⓔ probioma@roble.scz.entelnet.bo

BOTSWANA

International dialing code +267.

Botswana, to the north of South Africa, is the size of France with a population of 1.3 million. Its most famous attraction is the vast Okavango Delta in the west, a huge wetlands wilderness with thousands of tree-fringed islands and superb wildlife viewing. Travel in the delta is by dugout canoe along narrow reed-lined waterways.

To the south of the Okavango is the vast Kalahari Desert, traditional home of the San Bushmen. Their culture is one of the oldest on earth, with an intimate knowledge of the harsh desert environment. There are roughly 50,000 Bushmen in Botswana (and a similar number in Namibia). Although a few still live semi-traditionally in the Central Kalahari Reserve, most Bushmen have now been resettled into camps and now form the country's most disadvantaged group.

In addition to the projects below, there are community-run campsites at **Kavimba** in the Chobe Enclave between Kasane and Maun; in **Mmatshumo** at the edge of the Makgadikgadi Pans (guided tours of **Kubu Island**); 25km south of **Sankuyo** on the road to Moremi reserve (with a 'traditional village').

The *Bradt Guide to Botswana*, by Chris McIntyre, is a good source of further information.

Dqãe Qare Game Farm   ACCOM+

A campsite and guesthouse in a Bushman community between D'kar and Ghanzi with guided walks, 4WD wildlife trips (wildebeest, giraffe, zebra, springbok and gemsbok) horseriding, dancing, storytelling.

■ PO Box 219, Ghanzi

❶ + ❶ 596574

❷ dqae@info.bw

■ Kuru Development Trust: PO Box 219, Ghanzi

❶ 596 285

❷ kuru@info.bw

HELP US UPDATE

If you know of similar community tourism projects or changes to these listings, please email Tourism Concern at info@tourismconcern.org.uk – subject: community tourism.

Kalahari Sunset Safaris   TOUR
Customized small-group trips (three to six days) with San Kalahari Bushmen.
Food-gathering walks, tracking, food preparation, herbal medicines, dances,
music (eg mouth bows, thumb pianos), crafts and tool-making, storytelling.
$250 per day ($156 self-catering).

■ Andrea Hardbattle: PO Box 651, Ghanzi

❶ + ❺ 596 959; 07166 2265

Ⓦ www.kalaharisunset.com ⓔ Kornials@hotmail.com

■ In the UK: Karl Kennaugh

❶ +44 (0)7949 921 808

Nata Sanctuary/Kalahari Conservation Society   SAFARI
A wilderness reserve 170km north of Francistown, set up by the local Nata
community with help from the Kalahari Conservation Society. It includes part
of the Makgadikgadi salt pans. Campsites, guided walks, birdwatching, wildlife.
British Airways Tourism for Tomorrow Awards, Southern region winner 1993.

■ Kalahari Conservation Society: PO Box 859, Gabarone

❶ + ❺ 374 557

Nqwaa Khobee Xeya Trust/Thusano Lefatsheng   SAFARI+
The Trust represents the !Xoo Bushman/Bakgalagadi settlements of Ukhwi,
Ngwatle and Ncaang in the beautiful Kalahari desert wilderness of south-west
Botswana (near the new Kgalagadi Transfrontier Park), which all have
campsites. Bushwalks, dancing, storytelling, crafts plus upmarket hunting and
photographic safaris run by Safaris Botswana Bound (tel: 663 055). Assisted by
SNV (see below) and a local NGO, Thusano Lefatsheng.

■ Nqwaa Khobee Xeya Trust: PO Box 122, Hukuntsi.

■ Thusano Lefatsheng: Private Bag 00251, Gaborone

❶ 399 170 ❺ 399 171

Okavango Polers Trust   TOUR/SAFARI
A campsite in Seronga, on the east side of the Okavango's panhandle, with
mokoro (canoe) safaris into the Delta – one of the few ways left for budget
travellers to visit the Okavango. To reach Seronga, take a small ferry from 'the
Swamp Stop' in Sepupa. Alternatively, fly-in trips can be arranged via safari
companies in Maun, including Island Safari Lodge (tel: 660 300; fax: 662 932;
island@info.bw). Superb wildlife.

❶ + ❺ 267 676861

SNV/IUCN Community Based Natural Resources Management Programme
ORG
Joint programme of Dutch development agency SNV and the World Conservation Union (IUCN) to promote rural community development, including community ecotourism.
■ PO Box 611, Gaborone
✆ 352 413 ✆ 314 123
ⓦ www.cbnrm.bw ✉ information@cbnrm.bw

Vumbura Camp/Little Vumbura/Duba Plains   SAFARI/LUXURY
A trio of luxury tented safari camps in the northern Okavango Delta, developed by South African operator Wilderness Safaris and the Okavango Community Trust, which represents local villages. Dugout canoe, 4WD and walking wildlife excursions. From $285 per night.
■ Wilderness Safaris (see South Africa)
ⓦ www.wilderness-safaris.com
In the UK: Sunvil Discovery and Tribes Travel (see Outbound operators)

/Xai /Xai/Cgaecgae Tlhabololo Trust   TOUR
One to seven days cultural tours in the /Xai /Xai area near the Namibian border west of Maun, to a /Xai /Xai (Bushman) community, with bow-and-arrow hunting, gathering veld foods, traditional dancing, singing and story telling, exploring Gcwihaba (Drotsky's) Caves and horseback riding. Visits can be arranged by Uncharted Africa (tel: 212 277; www.unchartedafrica.com).
■ Cgaecgae Tlhabololo Trust: Private Bag 235, Maun.
■ In the UK: Sunvil Discovery (see Outbound operators)

BRAZIL

International dialing code +55.

Brazil is a vast, rich country with a vibrant and celebratory culture and one of the most unequal distributions of land ownership, wealth and income on earth. Such inequality has had an environmental impact, too, as poverty-stricken settlers, denied access to land elsewhere, move into and cut down vast swathes of the Amazon rainforest – threatening one of planet's great 'lungs' and the cultural survival of the Amazon's indigenous peoples.

The Amazon is Brazil's big ecotourism destination. But there are also the wildlife-rich plains of the Pantanal and mighty Iguassu waterfall (the world's largest) on the border with Argentina, plus historic colonial towns and mountain regions with good hiking, such as the Caparaó National Park in Minas Gerais or Itatiaia National Park near Rio. And, of course, there is Rio itself, with its great beaches and fabulous setting.

The North-East is one of Brazil's most enticing regions, with strongly African music and cultural traditions, colonial cities such as Salvador and Recife, and superb beaches. Direct charter flights from Europe to Recife began in 2001, opening up the region for major tourism development, although the inequality of Brazilian society means the benefits are unlikely to be shared by all.

Aldeia dos Lagos/ASPAC/Silves Island   RAINFOREST
Silves Island is an island at the junction of the Urubu River and Canacari Lake in the Amazon rainforest, 300km downriver from Manaus. The area has many lakes and islands and rich aquatic wildlife. With the support of WWF Brazil, local people have formed an environmental organization, **ASPAC (Silves Association for Environmental and Cultural Preservation)** and opened the **Aldeia dos Lagos** jungle lodge. A Manaus tour agency runs tours (four to six days) to the lodge from $368. Rainforest walks, canoe trips, visits to local communities.

■ ASPAC

❶ + ❶ 092 528 2124

❸ aldeiadoslagos@terra.com.br *or* tiberio@internext.com.br

■ Viverde Tourismo: Rua dos Cardeiros 26-Cj, Acariquara Coroado III (PO Box 2224, CEP 69061-970), Manaus

❶ 092 248 9988; 092 9983 3206

Ⓦ www.viverde.com.br/aldeia.html ❸ amazon@viverde.com.br

Favelatour   DAY
Half-day trips to the favelas (shanty towns) of Rio de Janeiro, where many of the city's poorest inhabitants live, offering an insight into a side of the city that most tourists don't see.

■ Marcelo Armstrong: Estrada das Canoas 722/bloco II, apt 125, São Conrado, Rio de Janeiro, CEP: 22610-210

❶ 021 3322 2727; 021 9772 1133

Ⓦ www.favelatour.com.br ❸ info@favelatour.com.br

Prainha do Canto Verde   ACCOM+
ToDo! Award winner
A fishing village 126km south of Fortaleza in North-East Brazil. Residents are fighting plans for large-scale commercial tourism and developing their own

community-run tourism. The village has an excellent beach, guesthouses and restaurants serving fresh seafood. Boat trips, fishing, guided nature walks to sand dunes, mangroves and lagoons, Portuguese lessons. The nearby villages of **Ponta Grossa, Icapuí, Tatajuba, Camocim, Balbino, Cascavel** are also developing community tourism projects and fighting commercial development.

■ René Scharer, Amigos da Prainha do Canto Verde: Caixa Postal 52722, 60151-970, Fortaleza, Ceará

❶ + ❶ 88 413 1426; 85 943 0119

Ⓦ www.fortalnet.com.br/~fishnet Ⓔ fishnet@fortalnet.com.br

Tataquara Lodge/Amazon Coop   RAINFOREST
Tataquara Lodge is a small, eco-friendly rainforest lodge on an island in the Xingu River, four hours by boat from Altamira (an hour's flight from Belem). Forest walks, canoeing, swimming, fishing, wildlife, birdwatching, medicinal plants. Three-day tours from $450. English-speaking local guides. The lodge is owned by **Amazon Coop**, a cooperative of nine indigenous tribes including the Assurini, Kararao and Araro, and all staff are cooperative members. Profits fund local health and education and conservation projects.

■ Amazon Coop

Ⓦ www.amazoncoop.org Ⓔ coopamazon@aol.com

■ In the UK: Journey Latin America

❶ +44 (0)20 8747 8315

Ⓦ www.journeylatinamerica.co.uk

Uakari Lodge/Mamiraua Sustainable Development Reserve   RAINFOREST
A floating rainforest lodge in a flooded forest reserve near Tefé in Amazonas (an hour's flight from Manaus), run by an NGO called **Sociedade Civil Mamirauá**. Wildlife includes dolphin, sloths, monkeys, 400 bird species and 300 types of fish. Three-day packages $260. Profits to conservation of the reserve and local community projects.

■ Aline da Rin/Nelissa Peralta: Sociedade Civil Mamirauá, Av Brasil 197 (Caixa Postal 38), Juruá. Tefe-Amazonas 69-470-000

❶ 092 343 4160 + ❶ 091 249 6369

Ⓦ www.mamiraua.org.br *or* www.pop-tefe.rnp.br *or* www.cnpq.br/mamiraua/

Ⓔ ecomami@pop-tefe.rnp.br *or* ecoturismo@mamiraua.org.br

CANADA – FIRST NATIONS TOURISM

International dialing code +1. Prices are in Canadian dollars.

While nine out of ten Canadians live within 100km of the US border, the vast northern reaches of the country remains one of the world's great wildernesses, a vast expanse of mountains, marshes, lakes, forests, rivers and tundra. There are First Nations communities far to the north, many with tourism ventures that offer amazing wilderness experiences. In fact, there is said to be close to 1500 Aboriginal (sometimes called First Nations) tourism businesses in Canada. Because there are so many, we have organized this section slightly differently, as a set of provincial and territorial entries. In each, the listed tours are merely a selection: for more information, contact the regional Aboriginal tourism offices listed below or **Aboriginal Tourism Team Canada** (Suite 820, 275 Slater Street, Ottawa, Ontario K1P 5H9; tel: 613 235 2067; 1-800 724 7872; fax: 613 235 0396; www.attc.ca;, admino@attc.ca).

British Columbia
British Columbia's magnificent mountains, forests and coast are an outdoor paradise with superb skiing, hiking, mountain biking, sailing, sea kayaking, climbing and wildlife (including whales, dolphin, bears, eagles, caribou). The coastal region is the main centre of aboriginal culture. **Quw'utsun Cultural & Conference Centre** in Duncan on Vancouver Island (tel: 250 746 8119; www.quwutsun.ca), **Ksan Historical Village and Museum** in Hazelton (tel: 250 842 5544; 1-877 842 5518; www.ksan.org) and **Secwepemc Museum and Heritage Park** in Kamloops (tel: 250 828 9801; www.secwepemc.org) provide introductions to local aboriginal culture and history. In Clinton, **Echo Valley Ranch Resort** has horse riding, hiking, white water rafting and falcon training (tel: 250 459 2386; 1-800 253 8831; www.evranch.com; $735 for three nights). On Little Shuswap Lake, near Salmon Arm, **Quaaout Lodge Resort** (tel: 250 679 3090; 1-800 663 4303; fax: 250 679 3039) is run by the Little Shuswap Indian Band. Near Tofino on Vancouver Island's scenic west coast, **Tin Wis Resort Lodge** (tel: 250 725 4445; 1-800 661 9995; www.tinwis.com) has accommodation, while **Walk the Wild Side** (tel: 250 670 9586) runs day tours on Flores Island in nearby Clayoquot Sound. **Wilp Sy'oon Wilderness Lodge** (tel: 250 633 2552; 1-800 596 2226; www.wilpsyoon.com) is a floating fishing lodge on the far north coast that also offers whale watching, photography tours. **Hiwus Feasthouse** (tel: 250 337 5167; www.krentz.com) offers three-day traditional culture packages. **G Cook Tours** (tel: 250 974 5055; www.alertbay.com/cooktour) runs four- to six-day boat trips (May–September) in Alert Bay combining aboriginal culture with nature and wildlife.

■ **Aboriginal Tourism Association of British Columbia (AtBC):** Suite 563, 1959 Marine Drive, North Vancouver, BC, V7P 3G1

☏ 604 924 3322; 1-877 266 2822 **⊕** 604 924 3695

ⓦ www.atbc.bc.ca **ⓔ** director@atbc.bc.ca

Manitoba

On the shore of Lake Katherine in Riding Mountain National Park, the *ToDo!* *Award* winning **Shawenequanape Kipichewin Anishinabe Village** (tel: 204 925 2030; 204 848 2815; www.mbata.ca; May–September) has a cultural centre/museum, camping and tipis, plus horseriding and cultural tours (herbal medicine, beadwork, spiritual practices, etc). In northern Manitoba, **Norway House Riverside Outdoor Adventures** has seven-day canoe trips (tel: 204 359 4444; 1-877 778 4447; www.norwayhouseriver.com; $1795 flying in from Winnipeg), plus shorter lodge-based packages. Also in the north, **Boreal Wilderness Guides** (tel: 204 348 7739; 1-800 362 7185; www.bwg.mb.ca; eight-day tour £1600) and **Northwest Wilderness Adventures** (tel: 204 356 2251; 1-888 225 5694; www.cancom.net/~goldsand/) both offer a year-round range of outdoor adventure trips.

■ Manitoba Aboriginal Tourism Association (MATA): 36 Roslyn Road Winnipeg MB, R3L 0G6

☏ 204 925 2036 **⊕** 204 925 2027

ⓔ mbata@mts.net

Nunavut

In Canada's far north, Nunavut's vast arctic tundra, home to 28 Inuit communities, became a self-governing Inuit territory on 1 April 1999. It contains wild arctic coastline, the spectacular mountains and fiords of Baffin's Auyuittuq National Park, and the rugged marshes of the Hudson Bay lowlands. There is hiking in the high arctic oasis of Ellesmere Island, dog sledding, sport fishing, wildlife – including polar bears, muskoxen, seals and whales (whale watching in August and September) – and Inuit culture. **Inns North** (tel: 204 633 7154; 1-888 866 6784; fax: 204 697 1880; www.arctic-travel.com/INNSN/ innsnorth.html) books 22 hotels throughout Nunavut and the far north and also offers ecotours. **Toonoonik Sahoonik Outfitters** (tel: 867 899 8366; www.pondtours.ca) runs seven- to nine-day dog sledding and whale watching trips around Pond Inlet on Baffin Island. **Pikaluyak Outfitting** (tel: 867 927 8390; www.arctic-travel.com/PIKALUYAK/index.html) also offer dog sledding (spring) and boat trips (summer) on Broughton Island, where visitors can build and sleep in an igloo. In Sanikiluaq, **Nunavut Adventure Travel** (tel: 867 266 8623; fax: 867 266 8903; qikiqtait@hotmail.com) organize Inuit cultural tours (summer and winter) and boat trips on the wildlife-rich Belcher Islands. Many tours in Nunavut only run from March to September. Access to the region is by air only.

■ **Nunavut Tourism**: PO Box 1450, Iqaluit, NU X0C OG0

🟠 867 979 6551 🟠 867 979 1261

🆆 www.nunavuttourism.com ⓔ info@NunavutTourism.com

■ **Nunavut Handbook**

🆆 www.arctic-travel.com

Ontario

As well as Canada's main city (Toronto) and its capital (Ottowa), Ontario stretches up to the Hudson Bay and contains expanses of rivers, lakes and forests. The **Iroquois Six Nations** (www.sixnationstourism.com) on the Grand River near Brantford is the largest First Nations community in Canada, with lodging, a cultural centre and day tours of the reserve. **Chiasibi Mandow Agency** (tel: 819 855 3373; www.mandow.ca) runs Cree tours around James Bay, including photography, skidoos, scuba diving and crafts. Amongst old-growth pine forest on Bear Island in Lake Temagami, **Temagami Anishnabai Tipi Camp** (tel: 705 237 8876; www.venturenorth.com/temagtipi/) offers canoeing, walking, healing and spiritual retreats. At Golden Lake, **Anishinabe Experience** (tel: 613 625 2519; www.anishexp.com) also offers stays in tipis plus dancing, storytelling, crafts and explanations of medicinal plants. On Ottawa's Victoria Island, **Turtle Island Tourism Company** (tel: 613 564 9494; 1-877 811 3233; www.aboriginalexperiences.com) runs a cultural centre and wilderness trips.

■ **Northern Ontario Native Tourism Association (NONTA):** Site 7, Comp 154, RR4 Mission Rd, Thunder Bay ON, P7C 4Z2

🟠 807 623 0497 🟠 807 623 0498

ⓔ nonta@norlink.net

■ **Aboriginal Tourism Association of Southern Ontario (ATASO):** 5M8 Floor (Box 244), 180 Greenwich Street, 2nd Brantford ON N3T

🟠 519 751 1127; 1-877 746 5658 🟠 519 751 1148

ⓔ tourismataso@on.aibn.com

Quebec Aboriginal Tourism Corporation (STAQ)/Tours Innu

Tours Innu is an Aboriginal tour agency that works closely with STAQ to promote Aboriginal tourism in Quebec, with tour packages featuring cultural stays, wildlife, whale watching, dog sledding, hiking and canoe trips. In James Bay in northern Quebec, **Kanio Kashee Lodge** (tel: 819 895 2005; fax: 819 895 2008) can arrange tours of the local Cree community and stays with local people. **Qimutsik Eco-Tours** (tel: 514 694 8264; 1-888 297 3467; www.qimut-siktours.com; $4500 from Montreal) runs an Inuit culture and dogsledding trip in arctic Ingava Bay in winter and polar bear boat safaris in summer. **Nuuhchimi**

Wiinuu Cultural Tours (tel: 418 745 3212; fax: 418 745 3500) in the **Ouje-Bougoumou Cree Nation** (tel: 418 745 3905; www.ouje.ca) offers cross-country skiing, snowshoe hiking, snowmobiles, fishing, hiking and canoeing. The United Nations listed this settlement, a mix of traditional and hi-tech, among 'the world's 50 most outstanding communities'.

■ **STAQ/Tours Innu**: 50 Boulevard Bastien, Bureau 110, Wendake, Quebec
   GOA 4V0

❶ 418 843 5151; 5030 ❶ 418 843 7164

Ⓦ www.staq.net Ⓔ info@toursinnu.com *or* staq@oricom.ca

Yukon

North of British Columbia and east of Alaska, the Yukon contains magnificent mountains and far-north wilderness. On the Yukon River itself, **Ancient Voices Wilderness Camp** (tel: 867 993 5605; fax: 867 993 6532; www.yukon.net/avwcamp; from $250 per day) has rustic cabins and tents, with winter and summer packages featuring traditional medicine, drumming, hikes, snowshoeing and dog mushing. **Fishwheel Charter Services** (tel: 867 993 6237; fax: 867 993 6271; www.yukonweb.com/tourism/fishwheel/) offers year-round wilderness guiding and tours. **Kruda Che Guiding and Outfitting** (tel: 867 634 2378; fax: 867 634 2378) runs three- to ten-day canoe and photography trips on the Kluane, Donjek White and Yukon Rivers.

■ **Yukon First Nations Tourism Association (YFNTA)**: 1-1109 1st Avenue
   Whitehorse, Yukon, Y1A 5G4

❶ 867 667 7698 ❶ 867 667 7527

Ⓦ www.yfnta.org Ⓔ yfnta@yknet.yk.ca

COSTA RICA

International dialing code +506.

Costa Rica, along with Guatemala, is one of the most visited countries in Central America. But whereas Guatemala's big attraction is a large indigenous population, most *Ticos* (as Costa Ricans call themselves) are of mixed or Spanish descent – the indigenous population has been almost entirely wiped out. Nor does Costa Rica have Guatemala's great archaeological sites. Instead, the country enjoys a reputation as a nature lover's paradise, with 10 per cent of the country designated as national park. These parks protect tropical beaches, coral reefs, active volcanoes and tropical forest and contain more birds, animals and plant species than the whole of North America. And the Pacific coast has some of the best beaches in Latin America.

Costa Rica is the 'Switzerland of Central America': a stable and peaceful country in a region not always known for these qualities. It abolished its army in 1948 and has been governed democratically for most of its history. Away from the national parks, Costa Rica is a predominantly rural, agricultural land whose main income comes from coffee and bananas.

Asociación ANAI/ASACODE   ACCOM+/TOUR
Asociación ANAI works with communities operating lodges in the Talamanca region on the Caribbean coast. Tropical forests, birdwatching, medicinal plants, birdwatching, horseriding, crafts. Also tours to the village of **Yorkín**, in a rainforest ecological reserve. **ASACODE** is a campesino conservation organization that manages a lodge in the community of San Miguel, in the coastal rainforest of the La Amistad Biosphere Reserve in southern Talamanca, with five-day study trips for small groups looking at uses of forest plants, conservation and community development.

■ Asociacíon ANAI: Sam Mardell: Apartado 170-2070, Sabanilla

❶ 224 3570 ❶ 253 7524

ℯ anaicr@racsa.co.cr *or* anaicr@sol.racsa.co.cr

■ ASACODE

❶ + ❶ 754 2261; 751 0076; 256-4416

Ⓦ www.asacode.or.cr ℯ info@asacode.or.cr

ATEC (Asociacion Talamanquena de Ecoturismo y Conservacion)   ORG
A community-run tourism association based in Puerto Viejo on the Caribbean coast. The area includes a mix of Latin, Afro-Caribbean and indigenous BriBri people, and has great beaches and tropical forest. On the Panamanian border just south of Puerto Viejo, the Gandoca-Manzanillo National Park protects coral reefs, beaches and rainforest. ATEC can arrange stays in nature lodges or community-based projects plus diving, kayaking, hiking and rainforest tours.

■ ATEC, Puerto Viejo de Talamanca Limon

❶ + ❶ 750 0191; 750 0398

Ⓦ www.greencoast.com/atec.htm ℯ atecmail@sol.racsa.co.cr

CODECE/San Antonio de Escazú   DAY/AGRI
Tours to a village in the mountains west of San Jose on the slopes of Cerro Pico Blanco, offering an experience of rural life, with visits to farms, music, storytelling. Run by a local NGO, CODECE. Day tours $15; two days $50.

■ CODECE: Felipe Mecoya: PO Box 1080-1250, Escuzú

❶ 228 0183; 211 320 ❶ 228 5695

ℯ codececr@rasca.co.cr

COOPRENA (National Eco-Agricultural Cooperative Network of Costa Rica) AGRI/ORG/VOL
COOPRENA comprises 11 small rural cooperatives and offers stays in a rural Tico community, plus opportunities for conservation and organic farming volunteer work. The region includes rainforest, beaches, mangrove swamps and dairy farms.

■ Aptdo Postal 6939-1000

☎ 506 286 4203 ✆ 226 6027

Ⓦ www.agroecoturismo.net ⓔ cooprena@racsa.co.cr

Finca La Flor de Paraíso AGRI/SCHOOL/VOL
Organic farm and ecolodge offering courses in Spanish and sustainable development, plus (WWOOF-ing) volunteer work, visits to local villages and attractions (Irazu volcano, Tapanti National Park). Run by a local non-profit group, **ASODECAH**. $180 for a five-day course.

■ Aptdo 966-7050, Cartago

☎ 534 8003 ✆ 534 8003

Ⓦ www.la-flor.org ⓔ asodecah@racsa.co.cr

Matapalo Foundation (FUNDEECO) ACCOM+
Community-run guesthouses, camping and a visitor centre in Matapalo and San Andres villages, near Quepos on the central Pacific Coast. Horseriding, hiking, birdwatching, cloudforest, mangroves, tropical beaches, youth camps and survival training.

■ Constantijn De Witte: San Andres de Aguirre (Apto 338, Quepos), Provincia de Puntarenas

☎ 779 9215

Ⓦ www.matapalo.com ⓔ info@matapalo.com *or* fundeeco@racsa.co.cr

---

HELP US UPDATE

If you know of similar community tourism projects or changes to these listings, please email Tourism Concern at info@tourismconcern.org.uk – subject: community tourism.

CUBA

International dialing code +53.

Cuba bursts with complexities and contradictions, from socialism to salsa and Santeria. It's a poverty-stricken nation with one of the best health and education systems in the world. The largest island in the Caribbean, it has beautiful beaches and scenery, as well as the exuberant nightlife and faded grandeur of the capital Havana, now being beautifully restored. It is also a powerhouse of Afro-Caribbean culture and music, the home of *son* and *salsa.*

Tourism has been an economic lifeline for Cuba, since the collapse of its Eastern European Socialist trading partners threw the country into chaos and made the US embargo even more keenly felt. But there are other imaginative developments besides tourism, such as the urban organic cooperatives that are springing up all over Havana, squeezed between Soviet-style highrises and colonial mansions.

The beach resort of Varadero has been the main focus of tourist development. While the beaches are beautiful, development here is 'international' in style and gives little feel for everyday life in the rest of the country. The tours we list here take you to different parts of the country and use music – the heartbeat of Cuban culture – as a 'way in' to the island's idiosyncratic magic.

Cubans can now register to let rooms to foreigners, although many people cannot afford a licence and can only covertly approach tourists on the streets. Hustlers usually ask a commission for finding you a homestay but it is still a cheap option and a great way to get to meet Cubans.

Caledonia Languages Abroad   TOUR

Two-week holidays in Santiago de Cuba in February, April, July and November which combine Spanish lessons and Cuban dance tuition (son, rumba and salsa) classes. The holiday is run with the Conjunto Folklorico Cutumba, one of the country's best-known dance and music companies. Accommodation is with local families. The trip includes tours in Santiago and the surrounding countryside and evening outings to dance and music events. £650, excluding flights. Individual Spanish language courses (all levels) with homestays are also available all year round.

■ In the UK: The Clockhouse, Bonnington Mill, 72 Newhaven Road, Edinburgh EH6 5QG

❶ + ❶ +44 (0)131 621 7721/2 ❶ +44 (0)131 621 7723

Ⓦ www.caledonialanguages.co.uk Ⓔ info@caledonialanguages.co.uk

---

Language holidays worldwide

Spanish in Spain, Cuba, Costa Rica, Argentina, Peru, Ecuador and Mexico. **French, German, Italian, Russian** and **Portuguese** in Europe. **Spanish** and **Tango** in Argentina. **Spanish** and **Walking** in the Pyrenees. **Italian** and **Gastronomy** in Tuscany. **French** and **German** plus skiing. French and watersports. All levels, all ages, all year round. Accommodation and cultural activities included.

Caledonia Languages Abroad
The Clockhouse, Bonnington Mill, 72 Newhaven Road, Edinburgh EH6 5QG
Tel: 0131 621 7721/2. Fax: 0131 621 7723
info@caledonialanguages.co.uk
www.caledonialanguages.co.uk

Càlédöñiâ
LANGUAGES ABROAD

Casa del Caribe, Santiago de Cuba   ACCOM/ORG
The Promotor Cultural in the Casa del Caribe can arrange homestays. Santiago is Cuba's second city and one of the cultural and musical centres of the country.
■ 154 Calle 13 y Calle 5, Visa Alegre
❶ 04 2285 ❶ 04 2387

Karamba Ltd   TOUR/SCHOOL
Two-week music and dance holidays in Guantanamo, a little-visited town in the south-east of Cuba. Run with UNEAC (National Union of Cuban Artists and Writers) and Danza Libre, a group of musicians and dancers who mix traditional and modern styles. Holidays include percussion and/or dance lessons plus local culture, nightlife and countryside. £745 for two weeks, excluding flights.
■ In the UK: Gary Newland: Ollands Lodge, Heydon, Norwich, Norfolk NR11 6RB
❶ + ❶ +44 (0)1603 872402
Ⓦ www.karamba.co.uk Ⓔ karamba@gn.apc.org

Las Terrazas/Moka Ecolodge   ACCOM+
Las Terrazas, about 50km west of Havana in the Sierra del Rosario, is a village built as part of a government reforestation project in the 1960s. The comfortable **Moka Ecolodge** has been developed to create employment in the village. Pine forests, horseriding, hiking trails, crafts workshops, fishing. $72 a double room. There is also a campsite nearby.
■ Moka Ecolodge, Las Terrazas, Pinar del Río
❶ 085 2921/96; 33 3814 ❶ 33 5516

DOMINICAN REPUBLIC

International dialing code +1809.

The vast majority of visitors to the Dominican Republic (including 98 per cent of UK tourists) come on all-inclusive packages. Much of the tourism industry is owned by foreign companies and local people have little control over its development, while local restaurants and shops are largely excluded from a share of the tourist dollar.

Most tourists come for the obvious Caribbean attractions of sandy beaches, turquoise seas and tropical sun. But the interior of the country has much to offer too, with rugged mountains (the highest in the Caribbean) and dense forests providing excellent walking and mountain-biking opportunities. There's great whale watching in season around Samaná Bay, plus good diving, snorkelling and windsurfing. The lively capital, Santo Domingo, the oldest European city in the Americas, contains a wealth of colonial architecture, as well as hosting two annual carnivals plus separate merengue and Latin music festivals.

Center for the Conservation of Samaná Bay (CEBSE)   TOUR
The Samaná peninsula in the north-east of the country is one of Dominican Republic's best ecotourism destinations, with whale watching (humpbacks between January and March), snorkelling, diving, waterfalls, horseriding, hiking and caving. CEBSE work with local communities to organize guided tours of the region.

■ Patricia Lamelas: Calle Julio Lavandier/Esq Santa Bárbara de Samaná, Apdo 132, Samaná

❶ 538 2042 ❶ 538 2792

Ⓦ www.samana.org.do Ⓔ lamelasp@usa.net *or* cebse@aacr.net

Cruz Verde Foundation   DAY/TOUR
A non-profit organization in Cruz Verde, a small village in the Monte Plata region that offers day and two-day tours ($59/$89). Organic farms, local homes, crafts, medicinal plants. Income goes to local community projects.

■ Mauricio Fabian

❶ 560 5348

Ⓔ Mauricio_Fabian@yahoo.com

Fundacion Ciencia y Arte   ORG
An organization promoting discussion of ecotourism and social development.

❶ 535 9350/5890 ❶ 535 5020

Ⓔ fund.ciencia@codetel.net.do

Fundacion Loma Quita Espuela   DAY
An NGO that manages a cloudforest reserve in the Northern Cordillera near San Francisco de Macorís. Half- to two-day tours into the reserve with local guides.

■ Av Libertad 44 (Aptdo Postal 236), San Francisco de Macorís

❶ 588 4156 ❶ 588 6008

Ⓦ www.flqe.org ⓔ flqe@codetel.net.do

Kiskeya Alternative   WEBSITE
Kiskeya is a Taino Indian name for the island of Hispaniola, which is now divided into the Dominican Republic and Haiti. This website is devoted to sustainable and community-based tourism on both parts of the island.

■ PO Box 109-Z, Zona Colonial, Santo Domingo

❶ 537 8977 ❶ 221 4219

Ⓦ www.kiskeya-alternative.org ⓔ kad@kiskeya-alternative.org

ECUADOR

International dialing code +593.

Ecuador's famous Galapagos Islands are a naturalist's paradise. But so is mainland Ecuador, with an incredible variety of scenery, species and ecosystems in a relatively small area. In two or three weeks you can see cloudforest, high moorland (called *paramo*) and snowcapped volcanoes in the Andean highlands, Pacific Ocean beaches and the Amazonian rainforest of the Oriente. Agencies in the historic capital, Quito, offer whitewater rafting, kayaking, mountain-biking, horseriding, hiking, climbing and diving.

About half of Ecuadoreans are indigenous, with colourful Andean markets such as Otavalo. In the Oriente, indigenous groups include Cofans, Siecoya, Siona, Huaorani, Shuar, Achuar and Quichua.

Community tourism focuses on two regions. North-west of Quito, the **Choco corridor** aims to link a string of private reserves inlcuding Maquipicuna, Bellavista and Golondrinas into a single protected corridor from the Andes to the Pacific.

The other key area is the **Oriente** – one of the planet's biodiversity hotspots. New roads have opened up this once-inaccessible corner of the Amazon and oil exploration, logging, tourism and colonization (by landless peasants from other parts of Ecuador) threatens the forest, its wildlife and its indigenous communities.

The high rainforest around Tena is most affected by colonization, although it is still predominantly forest with remote valleys, dramatic waterfalls and smoking volcanoes. To see much wildlife, however, you must travel east into the Amazon basin, to such places as Cuyabeno National Park, Zabalo or Kapawi. These trips cost more because they require light aircraft or motorized canoe trips. Lodges and commercial operators (such as Tropic) provide English-speaking guides, but entirely community-run ventures are usually in Spanish.

Ecuador is generally safe, but the emergence of a strong indigenous political movement has lead to occasional tensions. Spillover trouble from the US 'Plan Colombia' may also affect the northern Oriente: check before travelling.

Defending our Rainforest: A Guide to Community-Based Ecotourism in the Ecuadorian Amazon by Wesche and Drumm (1999, Accion Amazonia: Sarmiento N39-198, Quito, Ecuador; tel: 022 259 498; 022 250 659; tel/fax: 022 459 417; acciona@ecnet.ec) includes further details of many tours listed below, plus others. In the US, it is available from Island Press or The International Ecotourism Society (see Resources directory).

The South American Explorers' Club in Quito is another useful resource – the clubhouse is at 311 Washington (PO Box 17-21-431), Quito; tel: 022 225 228; www.saexplorers.org.

Amarongachi Jungle Trips   RAINFOREST

Trips (from one to five days) staying in cabins on the Jatun-Yacu and Anzu rivers in rainforest near Tena. Run by Quichua families.

■ Av 15 de Noviembre 438 (PO Box 154), Tena (or ask at Restaurant Cositas Ricas *or* Hotel Travellers Lodging, Tena)

❶ + ❶ 06 886 372

ⓔ amatours55@hotmail.com

Apturc/Pavacachi   RAINFOREST

Acangau Pavacachi Turismo Comunitario (APTURC) runs tours to the Shuar/Quichua community of **Pavacachi** in the Yasuni National Park – a remote area of pristine rainforest with good bird and wildlife, an hour's flight from Shell. Culture plus jungle walks and canoe trips. Book through **Tropic** for English-speaking guides.

■ Raúl Tapuy: Av 27 de Febrero y Bolivar, Puyo, Pastaza

❶ + ❶ 03 885 285; 0993 86555

ⓔ tamia212000@yahoo.com

■ c/o Pascual Kunchicuy

❶ + ❶ 09 386 555

ⓔ ikiamp21@hotmail.com

■ Tropic Ecological Adventures (see below)

ATACAPI Tours RAINFOREST
Jungle tours run by an agency set up by OPIP, a local indigenous organization. Most tours are in a settled area of the Oriente near **Puyo**. This easily accessible region is high rainforest with valleys, waterfalls, good hiking and birdwatching. Other tours (three to five days) head east to a remote region where the wildlife and forest is less affected by settlement. These visit **Llanchamococha** and **Jandiayacu** (the last two villages of the Zaparo people) or **Curaray**, a Quichua village on the edge of the Yasuni National Park. $30/60 per day. All these communities have simple tourist cabins.

🔳 27 Febrero y Sucre, Pastaza

☎ + 🖷 03 883 875

📧 papangu@ecua.net.ec

Bellavista Reserve ACCOM+
A private cloudforest reserve near Mindo, north-west of Quito, which is developing community-based study tours and a research centre. Birdwatching.

🔳 Richard Parsons: Jorge Washington E7-23 y 6 de Diciembre (Aptdo Aereo 17-12-103), Quito

☎ + 🖷 022 232 313; 022 901 536; 022 903 165/6

🌐 www.ecuadorexplorer.com/bellavista *or* www.alink.net/~jimd/bellavista.html

📧 bellavista@ecuadorexplorer.com *or* aecie3@ecnet.ec

Casa Mojanda ACCOM
A hosteria and farm near Otavalo, with organic and vegetarian food, horseriding, hiking and mountain views. The owners support local community projects including an environmental association, a rural clinic and kindergarten.

🔳 Casilla 160, Otavalo

☎ + 🖷 09 731 737; 09 720 890 🖷 09 731 737

🌐 www.casamojanda.com 📧 mojanda@uio.telconet.net

Cofan Dureno BUDGET/RAINFOREST
This community, near the first oil well in the Oriente, has been hard hit by oil exploration, but the forest behind their village is intact and they run budget four-day jungle tours. (I describe a visit in my book *The Gringo Trail* (Summersdale, 2001).) It's a two-hour bus ride from Lago Agrio: the driver drops you at a footpath to the river. Shout loudly and someone will row across to collect you! In the village, ask for Delfin or Laureano.

Cuyacocha Ecological Reserve   RAINFOREST
A rainforest conservation project in the southern Oriente on the Rio Pindo Yacu, an area of primary forest, reached by a 40-minute light aircraft flight from Shell. Stay with families in the Quichua community of Cuyacocha.

Bartolomé Mashiant: Casilla 16-01-849, Shell, Pastaza

❶ 03 795 219

Ⓦ http://cuyacocha.iwarp.com **Ⓔ** cuyacocha@aol.com

Fundacion Golondrinas   TREK/VOL
Treks (two to four days) through a private reserve, with income going to community conservation projects. The reserve includes high paramo, cloudforest and subtropical forest. Plus volunteer and research opportunities. Golondrinas is part of the **Choco Corridor** plan.

La Casa de Eliza hostel, Calle Isabel La Catolica 1559, La Floresta, Quito

❶ 06 648 679; 022 226 602 **❶** 022 222 390

Ⓦ www.ecuadorexplorer.com/golondrinas

Ⓔ manteca@uio.satnet.net or fundaciongolondrinas@latinmail.com

In the UK: Tribes Travel (see Outbound operators)

Huacamayos/Cabañas Llaucana Cocha   RAINFOREST
A tourism network of 11 Quichua communities in high rainforest in the Huacamayos Cordillera near Tena. Rainforest walks, waterfalls, canyons, canoeing, pottery and local crafts. There are also many petroglyphs (ancient rock carvings) in the area.

Benito Nantipa: Union Huacamayos, c/o FION, Calle Augusto Rueda 242, Tena, Napo

❶ 06 886 288/826

In Quito: Probona

❶ 022 466 622/3

In the UK: Tribes Travel (see Outbound operators)

Junin   ACCOM+
Community-run cabanas in the Choco cloudforest near Garcia Moreno, northwest of Otavalo. Good birdwatching, wildlife (jaguars, ocelots, monkeys, spectacled bears), orchids. An NGO called **DECOIN (Defensa y Conservacion Ecologica de Intag)** is helping the community to fight construction of a copper mine in the forest, and to develop tourism as an alternative.

DECOIN: PO Box 144, Otavalo, Imbabura

❶ + ❶ 06 648 593

Ⓦ www.decoin.org **Ⓔ** decoin@hoy.net

110

Kapawi LUXURY/RAINFOREST

A luxury lodge deep in the rainforest, which pays the local Achuar community a monthly rent plus a percentage of the profits. The lodge will be handed over to the Achuar in 2011. Superb wildlife and forest. $160–180 per day, plus $150 return flight from Quito. English-speaking guides. British Airways Tourism for Tomorrow Awards, highly commended 1998.

■ Canodros SA: Luis Urdaneta: 1418 y Av de Ejercito, Guayaquil

❶ 042 285 711 ❶ 042 287 651

Ⓦ www.kapawi.com or www.canodros.com Ⓔ eco-tourism@canodros.com.ec

■ In the UK: Penelope Kellie

❶ +44 (0)1962 779 317

Ⓔ pkellie@pkworldwide.com

Maquipucuna ACCOM+

A private cloudforest reserve and lodge in the Choco corridor, two hours north-west of Quito. **Fundacion Maquipucuna** works with local communities in ecotourism and sustainable farming, supported by UK-based NGO **Rainforest Concern**. Excellent birdwatching. At **Yunguilla**, a nearby campesino community, there is mountain biking in the Pululahua volcanic crater, agricultural/forestry tours and hiking to Maquipucuna (contact via Fundacion Maquipucuna).

■ Fundacion Maquipucuna: Mauricio Caviedes Baquerizo E9-153 y Tamayo, PO Box 17-12-167, Quito

❶ 022 507 200/2 ❶ 022 507 201

Ⓔ ecotourism@maquipucuna.org

■ In the US

Ⓔ usa@maquipucuna.org

■ In the UK: Rainforest Concern, 27 Lansdowne Crescent, London W11 2NS

❶ +44 (0)20 7229 2093

Oyacachi ACCOM+

A Quichua community in the Cayambe-Coca Ecological Reserve north-east of Quito, accessible by road from Cayambe. Single or multiday guided hikes in rugged mountain, paramo and cloudforest, with lakes, waterfalls, hot springs, horseriding. Assisted by a conservation NGO called **Ecociencia**.

■ Ecociencia: Saskia Flores: Calle el Sol 39-270 y Gaspar de Villarroel, Quito

❶ 022 921 710/4 ❶ 022 921 715

Ⓦ www.ecociencia.org Ⓔ osos@ecociencia.org

Piraña Tour RAINFOREST
This Siecoya community, but different guides, features in the Being There chapter. Four-day stays in the community's guest cabin learning about Siecoya culture, traditional uses of the rainforest, etc, and an eight-day canoeing and hiking trip to remote Rio Lagartococha on the Peruvian border. $65/75 per day, including transport from Lago Agrio, plus $50 per day for an English-speaking guide, booked through Tropic. Guides: Cesar Angulo and Gilberto Piaguaje. Cesar also guides trips to **Limoncocha**, a Quichua community near Coca. $30 per day.

■ Manuel Silva: Casa de la Cultura, Colombia y 18 de Noviembre, Lago Agrio, Sucumbios

❶ 06 830 624 ❶ 06 831 311

■ Cesar Angulo: cce-ns@ecuanex.net.ec

■ Tropic Ecological Adventures (see below)

Playa de Oro Lodge ORG
A simple ecolodge on Ecuador's northern coast, a half-day's boat ride from Esmeraldas in the Choco rainforest on the edge of the Cotacachi-Cayapas Reserve. It is run by the local African-Ecuadorean community with help from the NGO **Ecociencia** (www.ecociencia.org). Excellent birdwatching, rainforest, African-Ecuadorean culture. Four- to five-day tours from $370.

■ Angermeyers Enchanted Expeditions: Foch 726 y Amazonas (PO Box 17-1200599), Quito

❶ 022 569 960; 022 221 305 ❶ 022 569 956

Ⓦ www.angermeyer.com.ec ❸ angermeyer@accessinternet.net

■ In the UK: Tribes Travel (see Outbound operators)

RICANCIE (Red Indigena de Comunidades del ORG/RAINFOREST
Alto Napo para la Convivencia Intercultural y Ecoturismo)
An organization in Tena representing nearby Quichua communities, including **Capirona** (one of Ecuador's first community-run tourism projects) **Chuva Urcu, Cuya Loma, Huasila Talag, Las Galeras, Machacuyacu, Rio Blanco, Runa Huasi, Salazar Aitaca** and **Union Venecia**. All have lodges or cabins and RICANCIE runs tours (three to six days). Rainforest, waterfalls and caves, crafts, medicinal plants, shamanic rituals, participation in communal 'minga' work, farming techniques, etc. $45 per day.

■ Emilio Grefa *or* Luis Yumbo: Av 15 de Noviembre 772 (Apto 243), Tena

❶ + ❶ 06 887 953/072

Ⓦ http://ricancie.nativeweb.org ❸ ricancie@ecuanex.net.ec

ECUADOR'S LEADING ECOTOURISM OPERATOR
Nature Lodges * Community Programs*
Birdwatching * Diving

AMAZON * GALAPAGOS * ANDES

Winner of the 1997
ToDo! Award for
Socially Responsible
Tourism

tropic@uio.satnet.net
www.tropiceco.com

SionaTour   RAINFOREST
The tour agency of the Siona organization ONISE. It is developing tours to the Siona communities of **Orahueaya, Biana** and **Puerto Bolivar**. The latter is close to the Lagunas Grande in the Cuyabeno reserve, one of the prime wildlife destinations in the Oriente.

■ Sionatour (FEPP): 12 de Febrero 267 y 10 de Agosto, Lago Agrio, Sucumbios (*or* Casilla 17-110-5202, Quito)

❶ 06 831 875 ❶ 06 830 232

Tropic Ecological Adventures   RAINFOREST/TOUR
ToDo! Award winner
A tour operator that runs excellent rainforest tours in partnership with indigenous communities. One trip visits the Cofan community of **Zabalo** (superb wildlife, locally-resident US guide Randy Borman is an exceptional nature guide: Freddy Espinoza; cofan@ibm.net). Other tours visit the Huaorani communities of **Wentaro** and **Quehueri'ono** with guide Moi Enomenga – the main character in Joe Kane's brilliant book *Savages* (Pan, 1997). Plus **Piraña Tour** and **Kapawi, Maquipucuna** and **Yachana** lodges (see separate entries) and Quichua communities. Trips of four to ten days; $50/100 per day. Also Galapagos cruises and customized highlands itineraries.

■ Aptdo 1a, Edificio Taurus, Av Republica E7-320 y Diego de Almagro, Quito

❶ 022 234 594; 022 225 907 ❶ 022 560 756

Ⓦ www.tropiceco.com Ⓔ tropic@uio.satnet.net

■ In the UK: Discovery Initiatives (see Outbound operators)

HELP US UPDATE

If you know of similar community tourism projects or changes to these listings, please email Tourism Concern at info@tourismconcern.org.uk – subject: community tourism.

Tsanta Tours RAINFOREST
Jungle trips run by an English-speaking Shuar guide, Sebastian Moya. Profits from tours contribute to an indigenous cultural foundation – Yawa Lee – that trains young Shuar to be shamans. $50 per day.

■ Oriente y Eloy Alfaro (Casilla 18-02-1930), Baños

❶ 03 740 957 ❶ 03 740 717

ⓔ yawalee@tu.cordavi.org.ec

Yachana Lodge RAINFOREST
A rainforest lodge near Coca on the Rio Napo, run by an NGO called FUNEDESIN. Profits go to local community projects. Guests can visit these projects, which include health, food production (chocolate and jam) and rainforest conservation, as well as the local Quichua communities and a traditional healer (shaman). Four-day package: $340, including transport from Quito.

■ FUNEDESIN: Francisco Andrade Marin 188 y Almagro (PO Box 17-17-185), Quito

❶ 022 237 278/133

Ⓦ www.yachana.com ⓔ info@yachana.com

EGYPT

International dialing code +20.

Egypt is one of the birthplaces of world civilization. Cairo is a fascinating historic city (as well as an overcrowded modern one) with an atmospheric mediaeval market, one of the world's great museums and, of course, the Pyramids. The Valley of the Kings near Luxor is another of the world's great archaeological sites.

Few river trips match the romance of the Nile – if you don't mind roughing it a bit and want your money to go into the local economy, then go to Aswan or Luxor and book locally on a *felucca*. These traditional sailing boats are cheap and evocative, and you'll probably get to meet the captain's family too.

The Sinai peninsula has dramatic mountainous desert and coral reefs. The diving in Red Sea resorts such as Sharm el Sheikh is breathtaking, although perhaps overcrowded. Many Bedouin in the Sinai are involved informally in tourism (running cafés, guesthouses, selling clothes and handicrafts) especially in Dahab, which has become a backpacker hangout, although whether tourism in either Dahab or Sharm is sustainable and beneficial is debatable.

Basata   ACCOM

Small, eco-friendly resort on the Sinai coast north of Nuweiba.

◼ Sherif El-Ghamrawy: Nuweiba-Taba Road, Sinai

☏ 062 500 481; 062 530 481

Ⓦ www.basata.com Ⓔ basata@basata.com

Wind, Sand & Stars   TOUR

A UK company that run tours to the Sinai with local Bedouin communities. Trips include camel treks and desert hiking in the Sinai's mountainous interior. Plus customized itineraries, trips for schools, a student Summer Expedition and special interest tours (eg biblical, wildlife). Helps fund local educational and health projects. British Airways Tourism for Tomorrow Awards, highly commended 1996.

◼ In the UK: Emma Loveridge/Liz Dempsey: 2 Arkwright Road, London NW3 6AD

☏ +44 (0)20 7433 3684 ☎ +44 (0)20 7431 3247

Ⓦ www.windsandstars.co.uk Ⓔ office@windsandstars.co.uk

FIJI

International dialing code +679.

A stop on the trans-Pacific air route, with white-sand beaches and coral reefs, Fiji is one of the most popular South Pacific destinations. But few visitors venture far from the palm-fringed beaches and thatched cocktail bars of the all-inclusive resorts that line the coast of Vitu Levu, the main island. Yet the island's volcanic, hilly interior is well worth a look, even if sugar plantations have replaced much of the original forest. Due to an unusually enlightened British colonial regime, Fiji has a more intact indigenous culture than many other South Pacific nations. The British also imported Indian labourers to work the sugar plantations; today Indians make up half of Fiji's population – at times leading to tension between indigenous Fijians and Indians.

Fiji's other islands are quieter and more 'traditional', with pristine reefs. Connected to Vitu Levu by flights or once or twice-weekly ferries, they see few visitors, but if you have time they are well worth the effort.

Abaca   ACCOM+

A village 16km from Lautoka on Vitu Levu, with good hiking around nearby Mt Koroyanitu, the only region of the highlands never to have been logged, and the opportunity to participate in daily activities. The villagers have built a 12-bed self-catering lodge ($10 per night, home-cooked meals $3) and also offer homestays ($15).

■ Mr Semi Lotawa: PO Box 6729, Lautoka
❶ 0651 168; 666 644 (dial 1234 after the tone) ❶ 0651 168

Navala ACCOM
Traditional *bure* (thatched house) accommodation in a village in the hilly interior of Vitu Levu. Navala is one of the few villages to still consist mainly of bures and offers the chance to see Fijian life away from the resorts. No organized tour, but you are free to wander around the village and surroundings. It's hard to arrange a visit in advance – you may have to simply turn up. Access by bus from Ba on the north coast. $20 per night. Stays are also possible in the nearby village of **Bukuya** (fax: 679 700 801).

THE GAMBIA

International dialing code +220.

English-speaking Gambia is a tiny finger of a country poking into francophone Senegal in West Africa. It consists of little more than a narrow strip of land on either side of the Gambia River. In recent years, the short Gambian coastline has become a popular package tour destination, with cheap charter flights and winter sun. Inland, however, the country is little affected by tourism. Visitors who do make the effort will find ordinary rural African life, as well as interesting animal and birdlife along the banks of the Gambia.

Gambia Tourism Support (www.gambiatourismsupport.com) is a useful site about responsible travel in The Gambia. The dry season is November to May.

ASSET/Gambia Tourism Concern ORG
Gambia Tourism Concern produces a magazine sold by 'bumsters' – young beach hustlers – on Gambia's beaches, and has collaborated with Tourism Concern on an in-flight video designed to introduce incoming tourists to Gambian life and sensitivities. It has set up **ASSET (The Association of Small-Scale Enterprises in Tourism)** to represent small-scale and community enterprises in a country whose tourism industry is dominated by foreign companies and all-inclusives. ASSET's members include **Tumani Tenda** (see below), Tendeba Nature Camp (tel: 541 024), **Bulaba Nature Camp** (tel/fax in the UK: +44 (0)1366 501 377; fax in The Gambia: 486 026), **Maksasutu Lodge** (PO Box 2309, Serrekunda), **Tanje Village Museum** (PO Box 172, Banjul; tel: 371 007; http://huizen.dds.nl/~tanje/) and Bigolou Monkey Park.

■ Gambia Tourism Concern: Adama Bah: Bakadaji Hotel (PO Box 4587), Bakau
❶ 462 057 ❶ 466 180

ⓦ www.gambiatourismconcern.com ⓔ bahs@qanet.gm

◼ ASSET

ⓦ http://go.to/asset

Tumani Tenda Ecotourism Camp   ACCOM+

ToDo! Award winner

Community-owned riverside accommodation in local-style houses in a Jola village south of Banjul. Boat trips, forest walks, workshops in batik making and other local crafts, dance and music performances. Nearby Brikama is known for its kora musicians. $15 per day, including meals. Excursions: $3/8 per group per hour.

◼ Sulayman Sonko: PO Box 4587, Bakau (bookings can also be made via ASSET – see above)

❶ + ❶ 462 057; 466 180

ⓔ tumanitenda@hotmail.com

◼ In the UK: Tribes Travel (see Outbound operators)

GHANA

International dialing code +233.

For centuries a key centre of the brutal slave trade, Ghana was the first black African nation to win independence in 1957, under Kwame Nkrumah. Today, not yet 'discovered' by tourists, Ghana is one of West Africa's friendliest and safest countries. Accra is one of the more enjoyable African capitals, a bustling seaside city with great nightlife and markets and a real African feel. The coast west of Accra has good beaches, surf and seafood, fishing villages and a string of European forts, many dating from the 17th century when the colonial powers were competing for control of the slave trade.

Inland, the main cultural centre is the town of Kumasi, capital of the once-powerful Ashanti kingdom and still home to the Ashanti royal family. The surrounding Ashanti villages are known for their arts and crafts. West Africa may not have the extensive savannahs of southern and east Africa, but the Kujani Game Reserve/Digya National Park, Kakum National Park (see below) and Mole Game Reserve contain hippo, elephants, lions, antelope, monkeys and over 300 bird species.

The *Bradt Guide to Ghana* by Philip Briggs has more information on community tourism, as does the Nature Conservation Research Centre website (see below).

Academy of African Music & Arts SCHOOL
A drumming school and hotel in Kokrobite, west of Accra, run by a local master drummer. Private or group lessons. Take a *tro-tro* (bush taxi) from Accra to the Kokrobite turnoff, then walk or hitch the remaining 8km.

Bowiri village/Lackham Lodge ACCOM+
A village 22km north of Hohoe in the Volta region, with simple accommodation and camping. Hiking, birdwatching, rural life.
■ Lackham Lodge, PO Box 537, Hohoe, Volta Region
■ In the UK: Julie Sherman: sherman_julie@hotmail.com

Exodus TOUR
A well-established UK adventure tour operator. Their 15-day Ghana trip features a 5-day village stay where guests live with a local family and participate in daily life.
■ In the UK: 9 Weir Road, London SW12 0LT
❶ +44 (0)20 8675 5550 ❺ +44 (0)20 8673 0779
Ⓦ www.exodus.co.uk

Kakum National Park RAINFOREST
A hanging treetop-level 'canopy walkway' in the rainforest of Kakum National Park, 20km inland from Cape Coast, developed with **Conservation International**. Good birdwatching, wildlife, accommodation nearby.
■ In the US: Conservation International (see Outbound operators)

Kasapa Centre ACCOM+/TOUR
ToDo! Award winner
A resort of thatched roundhouses in the fishing village of Nyanyano, 40km west of Accra, run by a German-Ghanaian couple who pay rent to a community fund. Drumming, dance workshops and tour programmes of up to five days to see markets, music events, birds and villages in the interior, including the old Ashanti royal town of Kumasi.
■ Kofi Acheampong: PO Box KS 125, Kasoa/CR
❶ 021 304 749 ❺ 021 304 749
Ⓦ www.forum-anders-reisen.de/kasapa Ⓔ walther-weltreisen@t-online.de

Nature Conservation Research Centre (NCRC) ORG/DAY/WEBSITE
A conservation organization developing community-run ecotourism projects in villages throughout Ghana. There is attractive hiking in the highlands east of Lake Volta, around Amedzofe (guided walks) and **Adaklu Mountain** (drumming, dancing, *kente* weaving and guided hikes from the village of

be wild

be charmed

be chilled

be still

be thoughtful.

exodus.co.uk

The Different Holiday

be relaxed

be educated

be aware ...

be sizzling

be mobile

be inspired

be tempted

be respectful

be sociable

be stretched

Leaders in small group Walking & Trekking,
Discovery & Adventure holidays, Biking Adventures,
European Destinations, Overland Journeys and Multi
Activity holidays worldwide.
Tel. 020 8675 5550 for brochure.
e-mail: sales@exodus.co.uk www.exodus.co.uk

Exodus Travels Ltd.
ATOL protected 2582/AITO

Helekpe; guesthouse and homestays $2.50 per night). The community-run **Tafi Atome** monkey sanctuary (plus drumming, dancing and other cultural activities; guesthouse $3 per night) is in the same region. Other projects include the **Wechiau** hippo sanctuary in the north-west (also good birdlife, canoe trips, $10 per day), and **Boabeng-Fiema** monkey sanctuary and the kente-weaving village of **Bonwire** near Kumasi. Plus **Kusanaba**, **Tano Boase** sacred grove and bat caves, **Paga** crocodile ponds, **Liati Wote** and **Wli** waterfalls, **Bobiri** butterfly sanctuary, **Bonsu** arboretum and **Pra** river tour. Most projects have accommodation in village guesthouses or homestays.

■ Mawuko Fumey: PO Box KN925, Kaneshie, Accra

❶ + ❶ 021 231 765

Ⓦ www.ncrc.org.gh Ⓔ ncrc@ghana.com

GRENADA

International dialing code +1 473.

This Caribbean island, just 60km north of Venezuela, has the region's usual attractions of year-round sunshine and fine beaches, plus lush green hills and a variety of tropical forests to explore. St George's, a charming spot with a lovely natural habour, winding 19th-century streets and 18th-century forts, is one of the world's prettiest capitals.

Homestays Grenada   ACCOM+

Visitors can experience ordinary life on the island while spreading income from tourism beyond the resorts and into rural areas. Homestays cost around $40 per night. Also cultural workshops ($10/15 per hour) including steel pan, dance, cookery, drumming, woodcarving and hammock making.

■ Earl and Elisabeth Williams: PO Box 810, St George's

❶ + ❶ 444 5845

Ⓦ www.homestaysgrenada.com Ⓔ grenhome@caribsurf.com

GUATEMALA

International dialing code +502.

Guatemala has the most indigenous population in Central America and is one of the region's cheapest and most scenically diverse countries. This makes it a popular and rewarding destination, now the violence of the 1980s is over. Most tourists visit the cool, rugged, Mayan-populated highlands, with the old colonial capital of Antigua, (famous for its Easter Week parades when residents cover the cobbled streets with huge tableaux of flowers), beautiful Lake Atitlan and the colourful, if touristy, market at Chichicastenango. (For a more 'authentic' market, try the Friday market at San Francisco el Alto, near Quetzaltenango.)

One hour's flight (or 12-hour bus ride) north to Flores and you're in a different Guatemala: the hot Petén rainforest, containing the awe-inspiring ancient Mayan city of Tikal. Logging and farming threaten the forest: community-based ecotourism may be a less harmful alternative.

Guatemala's tiny strip of Caribbean coastline around Livingston is culturally distinct from the rest of the country, with a mainly black, English-speaking population that has more in common with neighbouring Belize.

Guatemala is the heart of the Mundo Maya. This multi-million dollar tourism promotion uses the culture, history and imagery of the Maya to attract tourists to mega-resorts such as Cancún in Mexico, yet it has brought little benefit to the Maya themselves. Few Mayan people are involved in tourism in Guatemala, except as souvenir sellers and porters, etc, and most hotels and tour companies are owned by *latinos*.

Eco-Escuela/Bio-Itza School   SCHOOL

Two community-owned language Spanish schools in the Petén lowlands, set up with help from Conservation International. The **Eco-Escuela**, in the village of San Andres on Lago de Petén Itzá, near Flores, combines Spanish with trips to the Petén rainforest and archaeological sites such as Tikal. The **Bio-Itza School** (www.bioitza.com) in nearby San José has classes in Spanish and Maya and in traditional (medicinal) plant use. One week with homestay and 20 hours tuition costs from $175.

■ Book through EcoMaya (see below)

■ In the US: Conservation International (see Outbound operators)

EcoMaya/Pro-Petén/Caminos Maya   TOUR

Pro-Petén (Calle Central, Flores) is a local development NGO in the lowland Petén region, supported by US-based Conservation International. It runs a travel agency in Flores called **EcoMaya** to market the **Eco-Escuela** and **Bio-Itza School** (see above) and a range of community tours called **Caminos Maya**. These include a rainforest hike to Tikal, visiting the little-known ruin of **El Zotz**, the **Scarlet Macaw Trail** – a two- to three-day jungle tour with wildlife, river trips and more Mayan ruins and **El Mirador**, largest of all the Mayan cities.

■ Armando Castellanos, EcoMaya: Calle 30 de Junio, Ciudad Flores, Peten

● 926 1363/3202; 926 0495 ● 926 3322

● ecomaya@guate.net

Hotel Backpackers ACCOM/BUDGET
A hostel (underneath the bridge on the south side) in Rio Dulce set up by the **Casa Guatemala** (www.casa-guatemala.org) orphanage to create jobs for teenagers from the orphanage. Rio Dulce is on Lago de Izabal, near Livingston.

❶ + ❶ 930 5168/9; 232 5517 **❶** 331 9408

Ⓦ www.mayaparadise.com/backpe.htm **ⓔ** backpackers@casa-guatemala.org

PROCUCH/Bosque Huito/Mirador Piedra Cuache ACCOM+/AGRI
In the Cuchumatanes mountains, the **Proyecto Ecoturisticos de Bosque Huito** (in El Rosario) and **Mirador Piedra Cuache** (in nearby Chiabal) have homestays, guides and camping. Agritourism, crafts, walking trails in forested hills, Mam culture. Horse trips to Laguna Magdalena, a beautifull small lake, and community homestays at Siete Pinos, Paquix. The villages are assisted by PROCUCH, an NGO in Huehuetenango.

■ PROCUCH: Jose Monzon, Coordinador de Ecoturismo

❶ 502 764 4539

ⓔ jmonzon@uvg.edu.gt

Proyecto Eco-Quetzal TOUR/BUDGET
Three-hour hike to Kekchi Maya villages (San Lucas and Chicacnab) close to the Quetzal Reserve near Coban in Alta Verapaz, plus one- to four-day tours into the reserve's cloudforest. Homestays, birdwatching, caves, participation in daily activities of host family. Plus tours to the villages of Rokjá Pomptila and San Marcos in the rainforest north of Coban, near unspoilt Laguna Lachua, with good wildlife and forest. Three-day tours $41.

■ 2 Calle 14-36, Zona 1, Coban

❶ + ❶ 952 1047

ⓔ bidaspeq@guate.net

Spanish schools, Quetzeltenango SCHOOL
Guatamala is a good place to learn Spanish with schools charging $100–150 per week for 20 hours of one-to-one tuition plus full-board homestays with local families. The homestay element is great way to meet local people, practice your Spanish and put money into the local economy. Antigua is the country's most popular centre, although the volume of (English-speaking) students can be a bit self-defeating. Quetzaltenango is an alternative. Many schools here are involved in social development and offer visits to community projects and volunteer opportunities. They include: **Deserollo del Pueblo** (tel/fax: 761 6754; in the UK: Hannah Roberts: +44 (0)1865 552 653), **Centro de Estudios de Espanol Pop Wuj** (tel: 761 8286; http://members.aol.com/popwuj/

index.html), **Utatlán** (tel: 763 0446) and **Casa Xelajú** (tel: 761 5954; www.casaxelaju.com). The **Proyecto Linguistico Quezalteco de Espanol** (tel/fax: 763 1061; www.hermandad.com) also has a school in Todos Santos in the scenic Cuchumatanes mountains.

Totonicapan   DAY/TOUR
Totonicapan is a small Kiche Maya town in the highlands, surrounded by hills and pine forest, 20km east of the Quatro Caminos road junction near Quetzeltenango. The town is not on the tourist circuit but is known for its artisans and craftsmen and busy Tuesday and Saturday markets. The local Casa de la Cultura organizes one- to two-day tours which visit workshops (pottery, masks, musical instruments, costumes, etc) and traditional dance presentations, plus meals in family homes and overnight homestays.

■ Carlos Humberto Molina Gutierrez, Casa de la Cultura, 8a Avenida 2-17 Zona 1, Totonicapan

❶ 766 1309 + ❶ 766 1575

Ⓦ www.larutamayaonline.com/aventura.html Ⓔ kiche78@hotmail.com *or* larutamaya@hotmail.com

HAITI

International dialing code +509.

Unlike other Caribbean countries, few tourists visit francophone Haiti, the poorest nation in the Americas. Roads are appalling, the electricity supply sporadic, the country has a reputation for crime and most people live in dire poverty.

Yet Haiti is also a fascinating place with friendly people, excellent French-influenced cuisine, vibrant Afro-American music and religious traditions such as Vodou, and a strong artistic and literary heritage. Its history includes the 1803 slave rebellion of Jean-Jacques Dessalines that established the first modern black-led republic, as well as the brutal dictatorship of 'Baby Doc' Duvalier in the 1970s.

In the north, the great Citadelle fort is an architectural gem. And, although poverty has led to severe deforestation and desertification, there are impressive mountains, patches of surviving cloudforest, good birdwatching and hiking in the Macaya and La Visite national parks, beautiful undeveloped beaches and excellent snorkelling and diving.

Visitors can combine a visit to Haiti with the Dominican Republic – the two nations share the island of Hispanola.

Beyond Borders/Fondasyon Limye Lavi   TOUR

Beyond Borders is a US Christian organization that runs 'transformational journeys' to Haiti in partnership with a Haitian NGO called **Fondasyon Limye Lavi**. Homestays, cultural exchange, visits to community projects.

■ In the US: Beyond Borders, PO Box 2132, Norristown, PA 19404

❶ +1 610 277 5045

Ⓦ www.beyondborders.net Ⓔ mail@beyondborders.net

Destination Djon Djon   ORG

An organization working to develop 'alternative' and community-based tourism in Haiti. Member projects include homestays on the Isle de la Tortue, bed and breakfast accommodation in Jacmel, 'solidarity tours' of the country and hiking in the mountains at **Camp Perrin** (c/o Syndicat d'Initiative pour un Tourisme Écologique: Fred Chéry, tel: 286 0197/8).

Ⓦ www.kiskeya-alternative.org/djondjon/ Ⓔ afvp@rehred-haiti.net

Kiskeya Alternative   ORG/WEBSITE

Kiskeya is a Taino Indian name for the island of Hispaniola, which is now divided into the Dominican Republic and Haiti. This website is devoted to sustainable and community-based tourism on both parts of the island.

■ PO Box 109-Z, Zona Colonial, Santo Domingo

❶ 537 8977 ❶ 221 4219

Ⓦ www.kiskeya-alternative.org Ⓔ kad@kiskeya-alternative.org

HONDURAS

International dialing code +504.

Honduras's main tourist attractions are the magnificent Mayan ruins of Copan and the coral-fringed Bay Islands on the north coast (which claim to offer the world's cheapest scuba diving). Elsewhere, the Caribbean north coast between Tela and Trujillo is a near-continuous sandy beach. The region is home to the Garifuna people, descendants of escaped slaves and indigenous Caribs, whose culture combines African, indigenous American, English, French and Spanish influences. There are houses to rent in many Garifuna villages. East of Trujillo, the roadless rainforests, savannah and coastal wetlands of the Moskito Coast constitute one of Central America's wildest regions. Inland, near the capital Tegucigalpa or the towns of Catacamas or Santa Rosa de Copan, there are old colonial towns, good hiking and cloudforest.

Cusuco National Park/Fundacion Pastor-Fasquelle   ACCOM+/BUDGET/DAY

A cloudforest reserve two hours from San Pedro Sula on the Atlantic coast. Camping, cabins and guided tours in the park or to coffee farms, etc. Accommodation $12 a night.

■ Clarisa Ramirez, Fundacion Ecologista Pastor Fasquelle: 1 St 7 Av (PO Box 2749), San Pedro Sula

✆ 521 014; 557 6598 ⊕ 557 6620

Ⓦ www.ecofound.org ⊜ hrpf@ecofound.org

El Carbon   ACCOM+/BUDGET/TOUR

A Pech village in forested hills three hours by bus south of Trujillo. The community is developing a tourism project with an NGO called WATA, with two guesthouses, a visitor centre and guided cloudforest hikes. Over 200 bird species, plus spider monkeys, puma, jaguar, waterfalls, Pech culture, medicinal plants.

■ See the Honduras section of the www.planeta.com website

Rio Platano Biosphere Reserve   BUDGET/TOUR

A world heritage-listed rainforest reserve on the Moskito Coast with rich bird and wildlife. Community tourism is being developed by **MOPAWI**, a local non-profit group, with support from the **Partnership for Biodiversity**. There are lodgings and turtle conservation projects in the Miskito and Garifuna coastal villages of Raista, Belén, Plaplaya. You can hire a boat to the Miskito/Pech village of Las Marias, where there are simple hotels and guided rainforest tours, from day walks and canoe trips to three-day hikes. Costs: $8 per day per guide (a group needs 2/3 guides). Dry season: February to May and August to October. Access to the region is by light aircraft to Palacios from Tegucigalpa or La Ceiba.

■ Jorge Salaverre, La Mosquitia Ecoaventuras: PO Box 890, La Ceiba

✆ 0442 0104

⊜ moskitia@tropicohn.com

■ MOPAWI

✆ 235 8659

⊜ mopawi@optinet.hn

■ Arden Anderson (US Bureau of Land Management)

⊜ Arden_Anderson@co.blm.gov

INDIA

International dialing code +91.

Love it or hate it – and many visitors seem to do both in equal measure – India is sure to leave a lasting impression. On its way to becoming the most populous nation on earth (its population broke the one billion barrier in 1999), it is one of the great historic centres of world civilization, shaped and reshaped over thousands of years by numerous invasions and empires. It is the birthplace of Hinduism and Buddhism, a country of *sadhus* and holy men and esoteric and spiritual traditions such as yoga. It is also a modern, materialistic society with a growing middle class. It boasts the world's largest film industry and one of the world's most sophisticated classical musical traditions.

India's towns and cities assault the senses with their chaotic crowds, noise, traffic, pungent smells and vibrant colours. Throughout the country there are ancient cities, temples, shrines, palaces and monuments – Jodhpur, Jaipur, Jaisalmer, Varanasi, Agra and the Taj Mahal, the Hindu temple of Khajuraho, the ruins of Vijayanagar, the 900 Jain temples on Shatrunjay Hill in Gujarat. There are hundreds of festivals, such as the Pushkar Camel Fair or Puri's Rath Yatra chariot festival.

Yet there are also wild expanses, such as the Rajasthan desert or the Himalayan regions of the north – from lush, green Darjeeling to austere, 'Tibetian' Ladakh (and it's worth noting that India still has a lower population density than England).

Parts of the Indian coast – notably Goa and Kerala – are undergoing major tourist development, not always in the interests of local people. So-called 'rave tourism' in Goa has brought attitudes to drugs and sex that some locals find troubling: sensitivity and respect for local values is important here.

Alternative Travels ACCOM+/TOUR
Small group tours exploring rural life in Rajasthan, including homestays. Plus an ecolodge, **Apani Dhani**, in the Shekhawarti region between Delhi and Jaipur, offering hiking in the Arawali hills, horseriding, cycling, wall-paintings, etc.

■ Ramesh C Jangid: Nawalgarh-333042, Shekhawati, Rajasthan

☎ 01594 22239 ✆ 01594 24061

Ⓦ www.apanidhani.com *or* www.alternativetravelsindia.com ℮ rcjangid@yahoo.com

Ananda ACCOM+/SCHOOL
Homestays either in the Kullu valley of Himachal Pradesh or in Goa, with opportunities to learn yoga, cooking, music and tabla playing, crafts, weaving, etc, plus trekking in the Kullu valley.

■ In the UK: Ben Heron: West Hampstead Farm, Cranmore, Isle of Wight PO41 OXX

☏ +44 (0)1983 761177 🖷 +44 (0)1983 761144

🌐 www.anandacrafts.org 📧 benheron@ecosse.net

Billion Star Hotel   TOUR

A camel-trekking cooperative near Jaisalmer in Rajasthan's Thar desert. 500 rupees per day.

■ c/o Mr Nawal, Shree Giriraj Provision Store (near Kalpana Restaurant, Gandhi Chowk), Jaisalmer

☏ + 🖷 2992 51414

🌐 www.billionstarhotel.com 📧 bookings@billionstarhotel.com

Cross-Cultural Solutions   VOL

Three-week to six-month volunteer placements in partnership with Indian NGOs, run by a US-based non-profit organization called **Cross-Cultural Solutions**. Volunteer opportunities include English teaching, healthcare, arts, computing, etc. Cross-Cultural Solutions also run an annual tour of India called Saheli that focuses on women's issues.

■ 47 Potter Avenue, New Rochelle, NY 10801, US

☏ +1 914 632 0022; 1-800 380 4777 🖷 +1 914 632 8494

🌐 www.crossculturalsolutions.org 📧 info@crossculturalsolutions.org

Development Tourism   TOUR

Tailor-made tours of northern India focusing on everyday life, with visits to villages in West Bengal, run by a Calcutta-based NGO called **Mass Education**. Cost: $30/35 per day.

■ Sukumar Singh/Moulik Singh: Mahamayatala, PO Garia, Calcutta 700 084, West Bengal

☏ 033 435 6036; 033 435 5936 🖷 033 477 2010

📧 mass@cal.vsnl.net.in

HELP US UPDATE

If you know of similar community tourism projects or changes to these listings, please email Tourism Concern at info@tourismconcern.org.uk – subject: community tourism.

Dhami Dham Tours   TOUR/TREK
Customized low-impact hiking in the Himalayan region of Uttarkhand.
■ Ramesh Dhami: 592 Dhami Dham, Egipura, PO Viveknagar, Bangalore 560 047
❶ 080 571 3016
Ⓦ www.mahiti.org/dhamidham ⓔ dhamidham@yahoo.com

Equations   ORG
An NGO that campaigns for fair and responsible tourism in India.
■ PO Box 7512, New Thippasandra PO, Bangalore 75
❶ 080 529 2905 + ❶ 080 528 2313
Ⓦ www.equitabletourism.org ⓔ equations1@vsnl.com

Green Hotel, Mysore   ACCOM
A former palace in Mysore (south of Bangalore), beautifully restored and
converted into a small, eco-friendly hotel (solar power, traditional materials,
etc). The hotel was set up with the aid of the **British Charities Advisory Trust**
to generate income for local charities and as a model of sustainable tourism
with good pay, training and conditions for staff. Lovely garden, good library
about Indian history and culture.
■ The Green Hotel, The Chittaranjan Palace, 2270 Vinoba Road, Mysore, 570 012
❶ 0821 51 2536 ❶ 821 51 6139
Ⓦ www.greenhotelindia.com ⓔ grenhotl@sancharnet.in
■ In the UK: Charities Advisory Trust: Radius Works, Back Lane, Hampstead, London
NW3 1HL
❶ +44 (0)20 7794 9835 ❶ +44 (0)20 7431 3739
ⓔ charities.advisory.trust@ukonline.co.uk

Kolam Responsible Tours and Soft Travel   TOUR
Small-group and customized tours exploring contemporary life in India.
Homestays, visits to development projects, etc. Most tours focus on southern
India and Tamilnadu. Kolam also runs trips for Oxfam and Traidcraft.
■ Ranjith Henry: B-22, Bay View Apartments, Parvathy Street, Kalakshetra Colony,
Besant Nagar, Chennai-600 090, South India
❶ 044 491 3404/9872 ❶ 044 490 0939; 044 491 5767
ⓔ kolam@vsnl.com
■ In the UK: Tribes Travel (see Outbound operators)

Make a Difference Aid Adventure   TOUR

Small-group adventure tours to northern India, with 20 per cent of income donated to local charities.

 In the UK: Darren Odell: Waters Edge, Bridge Street, Andersey Island, Abingdon, Oxfordshire OX14 3HY

☎ +44 (0)1235 527 401 **✆** +44 (0)1235 536 381

ⓦ www.madaid.com **ⓔ** info@madaid.com

ROSE (Rural Organization for Social Elevation)   ACCOM+/VOL

A small non-profit group organizing village stays in Kanda in the Himalayan foothills of Uttar Pradesh. Also volunteer organic farming, English teaching, hiking (to glaciers) and joining in village life. Profits to community projects. £4 per night.

▪ Mr Jeevan Lal Verma, ROSE, Village Sonargaon, Kanda, Bageshwar, UP263631

☎ 91 5963 41081

Tashila Tours and Travel   TREK

Trekking trips in partnership with local communities in Sikkim.

▪ 31/A National Highway (PO Box 70), Gangtok 737101, Sikkim

☎ 3592 22979 **✆** 3592 22155

ⓦ www.tashila.com or www.sikkiminfo.com/tashila **ⓔ** tashila7@rediffmail.com or tashilatt@hotmail.com

INDONESIA

International dialing code +62.

Indonesia is the world's fourth most populous country and consists of thousands of islands and diverse cultures, from the devoutly Muslim Aceh province in northern Sumatra to Buddhist Bali to the animist Dayak in Kalimantan. It has orang-utans and Komodo dragons, superb beaches, coral reefs, rainforest and volcanoes, colourful rural life, delicious food and a rich cultural heritage.

Yogyakarta in Java, with its magnificent temples, and the island of Bali are the two most famous historical and cultural destinations. The southern coast of Bali is now a popular package tour destination but much of the island remains relatively untouched by tourism. East of Bali, there are hundreds of islands, including Sulawesi and the Moluccas, which see far fewer tourists. West of Java, Sumatra is one of Indonesia's wild frontiers, with expanses of rainforest.

Indonesia has a dubious human rights record: for instance, in relation to its occupation of East Timor. There is also opposition to Indonesian rule in Irian Jaya from the (mainly non-Indonesian) local population. Environmentally, too, an alarming proportion of Kalimantan's and Sumatra's rainforests have been felled in recent decades, with many of the most harmful logging concessions having associations with the old Suharto dictatorship. In 1998, forest fires in Kalimantan were so bad that the smoke blotted out the sun for months.

The dry season in most of Indonesia is May to September, with some local variations.

Bina Swadaya Tours ORG/TOUR

Owned by the non-profit Bina Swadaya Foundation, Bina Swadaya Tours runs cultural and nature tours combining tourist highlights with visits to community projects and rural villages. Day trips to 26-day tours, from crafts workshops to trekking in the rainforest and whitewater bamboo rafting. Destinations include Ujung Kulon National Park in Java, the ancient temples of Yogyakarta, climbing active volcanoes, seeing orang-utans in Kalimantan and Sumatra, visiting Dayak villages in Kalimantan and much more. Its tours help to fund the foundation's community development projects.

■ Jln. Gunung Sahari III/7, Jakarta Pusat, 10610, (PO Box 1456), Jakarta 10014

❶ 021 420 4422 ❶ 021 425 6540

ⓔ bst@cbn.net.id

Ciptarasa ACCOM+

A Sundanese mountain village on the edge of the Gunung-Halimun National Park in West Java, roughly 150km from Jakata. Visitors stay with local families who will show them around the village. Also guided trips into the mountainous tropical forests of the national park.

■ Yayasan Ekowisata Halimun (YEH): Didik Purwanto: Jl Subadra III No8, Bumi Indraprasta I, Bogor

❶ + ❶ 251 381 677

ⓔ bcn-ni16@indo.net.id

■ c/o INDECON (see below)

■ In the UK: Symbiosis Expedition Planning (see Outbound operators)

INDECON Foundation ORG

Promotes ecotourism in Indonesia.

■ Ary Suhandi/Indriani Setiawati: Jl Jati Padang IA/No 8, Pasar Minggu, Jakarta 12540

❶ + ❶ 021 781 3712 ❶ 021 781 3712

Ⓦ www.ecotourism-indonesia.com ⓔ indecon@cbn.net.id

Kandora Lodge ACCOM+/TREK

Community guesthouse owned by a local NGO, **WALDA**, south of Rantepao in Tana Toraja, southern Sulewesi. Treks of up to four days are available from the lodge, exploring hills, pine forests and local villages with local guides. Lodge $8 per day; treks $12/20 per day.

■ Walda Foundation: Miss Pina Rante: PO Box 68, South Sulawesi 91831

❶ + ❶ 62 423 27344

ⓦ www.toraja.net/walda ⓔ kandora@toraja.net

Mitra Bali Foundation AGRI/ORG/TOUR

A charity that can arrange transport, hotels and village stays on Bali. They also organize visits to community and development projects including organic farms, the famous irrigation systems in the centre of the island, crafts workshops, etc.

■ Agung Alit, 6 Jalan Sulatri I, Kesiman Denpasar 80237, Bali

❶ 0361 229 304

ⓦ www.balix.com/export/mitrabali ⓔ mitrabali@denpasar.wasantara.net.id

■ In the UK: Emily Readett-Bayley

❶ +44 (0)1400 281 563

■ In the UK: Travel Friends International (see Outbound operators)

Sua Bali ACCOM+

ToDo! Award winner

A 'mini-resort' of seven traditional guesthouses in a rural setting south of Ubud. A good base for exploring the island on day trips (tours or car hire can be arranged) or simply to relax. The resort also offers classes in local culture/crafts, including language, cookery, batik, woodcarving and herbal medicine. The owner works with the local village: staff, guides, instructors and most of the handicrafts on sale come from the village and guests pay $1 per night to a village fund. From $35 per night, full board. Also tours to Lombok and Sulawesi.

■ Mrs Ida Ayu Agung Mas: PO Box 155, Gianyar 80500, Bali

❶ 0361 941 050 ❶ 0361 941 035

ⓔ suabali@indosat.net.id

ⓦ www.suabali.co.id

Togean Ecotourism Network ORG

The Togean Islands are a small archipelago off the coast of Sulawesi, renowned for their excellent diving and snorkelling. Local communities have set up eco-sensitive tourism facilities including boardwalks and guided tours. Visitors can stay in a research centre on Malenge Island. Rainforest and good birdwatching. Supported by Conservation International (see Outbound operators). British Airways Tourism for Tomorrow Awards, highly commended 1998.

■ Togean Ecotourism Network: Jl Sisingamangaraja 10c, Palu 94117

❶ + ❶ 0451 424 205

🅔 togean@palu.wasantara.net.id

■ In the UK: Symbiosis Expedition Planning (see Outbound operators)

JAMAICA

International dialing code +1 876.

Most tourists come to Jamaica for its beaches, year-round sunshine, snorkelling, diving and pounding reggae and calypso music, staying in the resort centres of Montego Bay, Ocho Rios or Negril.

Away from the all-inclusives, the Caribbean's largest English-speaking island has a dynamic sporting and artistic culture, undeveloped beaches and fishing villages, and quiet country life. The forested John Crow and Blue Mountains offer fine hiking and there's rugged wilderness among the limestone hillocks, caves and ravines of Cockpit Country. Kingston, the capital, is a vibrant, if sometimes dangerous, city.

Jamaica is also a developing country of great inequalities, struggling with the social (and environmental) problems left by centuries of slavery and brutal colonial rule.

Countrystyle   ACCOM/TOUR

A tour agency offering village-based accommodation, plus tours exploring rural life in Jamaica. Profits help fund the **Sustainable Communities Foundation through Tourism (SCF)**, an NGO developing community tourism throughout the country. From $40 per day.

■ Diana McIntyre-Pike: The Astra Country Inn, 62 Ward Avenue, Mandeville, Manchester, Jamaica

❶ 962 3725/7758 ❶ 962 1461

www.communitytourismcarib.com 🅔 countrystyle@mail.infochan.com

KENYA

International dialing code +254.

Tourists come to Kenya primarily for the wildlife in parks such as Amboseli, Tsavo and Maasai Mara. The country also has good Indian Ocean beaches near Mombasa and Malindi, and most tourists divide a holiday between sea and safari.

The Swahili island of Lamu on the north coast is a backpacker favourite. North of Nairobi, there are lakes with rich birdlife, forested highlands around Mt Kenya and, beyond that, the rugged scenery of the Rift Valley.

The far north desert around Lake Turkana is beyond the reach of most tourists but an adventurous target for hardy travellers. The fertile south-west, around Lake Victoria, is another little-visited area and a good place to see rural Kenyan life away from the tourist zones.

Most of Kenya's parks were created in the 1940s (although Amboseli was set up by Kenya's independent government in 1974) taking land from the Maasai without compensation or a share of tourism revenues. The Maasai argue that, while the government profits from the parks, they get nothing. We list wildlife and safari tours that involve and benefit local communities, including Maasai. As well as wildlife, these tours often allow visitors to meet Maasai people and learn about their life and culture. Many of these community schemes are outside the national parks. But three-quarters of Kenya's wildlife also live outside the parks: in fact, the parks do not protect complete ecosystems and many animals depend upon the surrounding areas for survival. In recent years the **Kenyan Wildlife Service (KWS)**, which runs the national parks, seems to have become more aware of the need to work with communities.

Commercial tours to Maasai Mara often offer visits to Maasai cultural *manyattas* (homesteads) for a fee: typically, most of this fee goes into the tour guide's pocket while the Maasai themselves receive very little.

African Wildlife Foundation (Conservation Services Centre) ORG
Business support to community tourism projects in Kenya and Tanzania.

■ Wangeci Mwai: PO Box 48177 Nairobi

✆ 02 710 367 ☎ 02 710 372

ⓦ www.awf.org ⓔ WMwai@awfke.org *or* africanwildlife@awf.org

Amboseli Community Wildlife Tourism Project ORG/SAFARI
An NGO helping Maasai communities around Amboseli to develop tourism, including Eselenkei (see below) and **Kimana Community Wildlife Sanctuary** (PO Box 30139, Nairobi; fax: 02 332 334). Swiss tour operator **African Safari Club** (www.ascag.net) currently operates **Twiga Luxury Camp** and **Zebra Lodge** at Kimana.

■ PO Box 385, Loitokitok

❶ + ❶ (0)302 22388

■ In the UK: David Lovatt Smith

❶ +44 (0)1323 833 660 ❶ +44 (0)1323 833 608

ⓔ lovattsmith@amboseli.org

Eselenkei Community Wildlife Sanctuary SAFARI

A wildlife reserve near Amboseli National Park owned by a Maasai community with tours run by a company called Porini Ecotourism. Lion, leopard, cheetah and occasional migrating elephants, plus rarer species such as lesser kudu and gerenuk.

■ In the UK: Jake Grieves-Cook, Tropical Places: Freshfield House, Forest Row, Sussex RH18 5ES

❶ +44 (0)1342 825 123 ❶ +44 (0)1342 826 916

ⓦ www.tropicalplaces.co.uk

Il Ngwesi Lodge/Tassia Lodge ACCOM+/SAFARI

Two beautiful safari lodges owned by local communities near Samburu National Reserve, north of Mt Kenya. Developed with the help of the **Lewa Wildlife Conservancy** (which also owns **Lewa Safari Camp**), the lodges look over wooded plains and hills with plentiful wildlife. 4WD and walking safaris led by Samburu and Maasai guides, plus cultural tours. Both lodges only take single-party booking for up to 12 people. British Airways Tourism for Tomorrow Awards, finalist 1997.

■ Lewa Wildlife Conservancy: Private Bag, Isiolo (*or* PO Box 10607, 00100-Nairobi)

❶ + ❶ 0164 31405 (*or* tel: 02 607 893, fax 02 607 197)

ⓦ www.lewa.org ⓔ lewa@swiftkenya.com *or* LEWA1@bushmail.co.za

■ Let's Go Travel: PO Box 60342, Nairobi

❶ 02 441 891 ❶ 02 447 270

ⓦ www.letsgosafari.com ⓔ info@letsgosafari.com

■ In the UK: Discovery Initiatives (see Outbound operators)

IntoAfrica SAFARI/TOUR

A Kenyan company with a UK partner running adventure treks, wildlife safaris and mountain climbing. The emphasis is on insights into local life, environment and cultures as well as wildlife and national parks. Supports community health and education projects and pays agreed fees to local communities Trip prices from £530 for seven days.

■ IntoAfrica Eco-Travel: PO Box 50484, Nairobi, Kenya.

■ Chris Morris: 59 Langdon Street, Sheffield S11 8BH

☎ 0114 255 5610

Ⓦ www.intoafrica.co.uk Ⓔ enquiry@intoafrica.co.uk

Kereto Campsite   ACCOM+

A simple Maasai-owned campsite near the Mara Sopa lodge and Ololaimutiek gate of the Masai Mara national reserve. £8 per night. Plus Maasai culture, dances.

■ PO Box 435, Narok

☎ 072 827 104

Ⓔ davidkereto@hotmail.com

Sarara Camp   SAFARI/LUXURY

A small luxury tented camp in the scenic Mathews range of northern Kenya, run by the local Samburu community in partnership with **Namunyak Wildlife Conservation Trust** and safari operator **Acacia Trails**, with help from **Lewa Wildlife Conservancy** (see above). Good wildlife and scenery plus visits to Samburu communities.

■ Acacia Trails: PO Box 30907, Nairobi

☎ 02 608487; 501853 ☎ 02 608487

Ⓔ acacia@swiftkenya.com

Shompole Ecotourism Project/Maa O'Leng   SAFARI

Shompole, a Maasai group ranch three hours south of Nairobi, is developing a lodge with safari company **Art of Ventures**. (The community's company is called **Maa O'Leng**.) Wildlife safaris, Lake Magadi (known for its pink colours and flamingoes) and Maasai culture. Assisted by the **African Conservation Centre** (www.conservationafrica.org).

■ Joseph ole Munge: PO Box 6, Magadi.

■ Art of Ventures: PO Box 10665, 00100 Nairobi

☎ 02 884 135; 02 883 280 ☎ 02 884 135

Ⓔ art@form-net.com

Taita Discovery Centre/Kasigau Wildlife Corridor   SAFARI+/VOL

Tour operator **Savannah Tours** is working with local group ranches and the **African Wildlife Foundation** (see above) to create the **Tsavo Kasigau Wildlife Corridor** in a region of the Tsavo plains around Mt Kasigau that is rich in wildlife and biodiversity. The project includes environmental education and the creation of sustainable community-based businesses in local villages. On

Taita Ranch, the **Taita Discovery Centre** (TDC) takes study groups of up to 40 people: courses include working on community projects and discussing conservation with local people. Nearby **Galla Camp** is for individuals and smaller research groups. There are also volunteer opportunities: the **Kasigau Bandas** are village-run hostels for volunteers. Another, community-owned, research centre is planned.

■ Savannah Camps: Steve Turner: 11th Floor, Fedha Towers, Standard Street (PO Box 48019), Nairobi

❶ 02 331 684; 335 935 ❶ 02 216 528

Ⓦ www.savannahcamps.com ❷ eaos@africaonline.co.ke

Tawasal Institute   ORG/TOUR/SCHOOL
Mainly academic trips/placements, but can also organize travel for tourist groups seeking grassroots insight into Kenyan life. Visits to Maasai villages and development projects, *dhow* trips, safaris, homestays, lessons in Swahili and in crafts such as beadwork and carving.

■ PO Box 248, Lamu

❶ 0121 33533

❷ tawasal@africaonline.co.ke

■ In the US

❶ 516 733 0153

LAOS

International dialing code +856.

Laos is South-East Asia's least developed country, with a sleepy charm, expanses of wild forest and beautiful landscapes of limestone crags, sparkling rivers and lush paddy fields. Landlocked, mountainous and sparsely populated, it has historically been more of a buffer between more powerful neighbours than a coherent nation. In the Vietnam War, for instance, Laos became the most bombed nation on earth (as the US pounded North Vietnamese routes through Laos's eastern highlands) even though Laos was officially not at war with anyone. Today, more ethnic Lao live in north-east Thailand than in Laos itself (a result of colonial border-drawing) while the mountainous north and east are inhabited mainly by ethnically non-Lao hilltribes who have migrated from China into Laos, Thailand, northern Vietnam and Burma.

Still a communist state, Laos is now open to tourists. Key attractions, such as the old capital of Luang Prabang, have become part of the 'Thailand' backpacker circuit, although the country's lack of coast and beaches will probably keep it off the mass tourism map.

Nam Ha Ecotourism Project   TREK
A UNESCO-sponsored project offering hilltribe trekking and river trips in the buffer zone of the Nam Tha Conservation Area in northern Laos. Treks in rugged forested hills, staying in Khmu, Lanten, Hmong, Red and Black Thai or Yao villages. The project trains local guides and income stays in villages or goes into a community development fund. Three-day trek, $35.

■ PO Box 7, Luang Namtha 03000

❶ + ❻ 086 312 150

Ⓦ www.unescobkk.org/culture/namha Ⓔ khamlays@hotmail.com *or* sschipa@hotmail.com

SUNV Laos   ORG
A partnership of Dutch development agency SNV and the United Nations Volunteers, which is developing community tourism in Savannakhet and Khammouane.

■ UNV: PO Box 345, Vientiane

❶ 021 451551 ❻ 021 451393

Ⓦ www.undp.org Ⓔ thaba.niedzwiecki@undp.org

LESOTHO

International dialing code +266.

Lesotho is a small landlocked independent nation completely surrounded by South Africa. The country is mainly mountainous – high enough to have a winter ski resort – and offers great hiking and pony trekking in beautiful scenery. (Its eastern mountains fall away to become South Africa's Drakensberg range.) Partly due to its rugged terrain, Lesotho avoided colonization by the Boers and English, although it did lose much of its most fertile land to Boer settlers in what is now South Africa's Free State. This loss, and the clearing of almost all the country's trees, has put a great environmental strain on Lesotho's remaining land, most of which is too poor for farming, and soil erosion is a major problem.

HELP US UPDATE

If you know of similar community tourism projects or changes to these listings, please email Tourism Concern at info@tourismconcern.org.uk – subject: community tourism.

Malealea Lodge and Pony Trekking Centre ACCOM/TREK

Superbly situated lodge and rondavels at the foot of the Thaba Putsoa mountains, 85km from Maseru. The lodge arranges pony trekking with local Basotho guides in beautiful mountain scenery (either riding or hiking while using the ponies to carry your pack), staying in local villages on the way.

■ In South Africa: Mick and Di Jones: PO Box 12118, Brandhof, Bloemfontein 9324

❶ + ❶ +27 (0)51 447 3200; 448 3001

Ⓦ www.malealea.co.ls *or* www.malealea.com Ⓔ malealea@mweb.co.za

■ In the UK: Tribes Travel (see Outbound operators)

MADAGASCAR

International dialing code +261.

This mainly tropical country has mountains high enough to see snow in winter, producing a wide range of ecosystems. Cut off from the African mainland, it contains many birds, plants and animals found nowhere else on earth. (Lemurs, chameleons and the thick-trunked baobab tree are the country's most iconic species.) Culturally, the country is a blend of Africa and Asia. Rice paddy fields remind visitors of South-East Asia and Malagasy ancestory mixes South-East Asia and the African mainland: the language closest to Malagasy is found in southern Borneo.

Madagascar has great national parks and coral reefs. In the north, Nosy Be is the country's main resort area and Montagne d'Ambre its most popular national park, with good walking trails and bird and wildlife. In the west, the world heritage-listed limestone pinnacles and rainforest of Tsingy de Bemaraha also contain good wildlife. Further south, there are the sandstone ridges and rock formations of Isolo National Park. Overfarming and deforestation, however, have devastated Madagascar's rainforests and led to serious soil erosion. Ecotourism may be one alternative source of income.

Akany Avoko ORG/DAY

An organization working with destitute children near Antananarivo that offers day tours of the project and local area, including visits to local markets and ruins, traditional dancing and crafts.

Ⓦ www.akanyavoko.com

CCD Namena ACCOM+

An environmental NGO working with Betsileo and Tanala tribal communities in eastern Madagascar. Camping, simple accommodation and tours of the silkworks. Walking trails are being developed.

■ A few kilometres south of Ambalavao on the RN7

☎ 20 75501

Project Ifotaka   ORG/TOUR
Tours to the dry spiny Ifotaka Forest, near Berenty in southern Madagascar, run by a local conservation organization. The area contains ringtail, sifaka, mouse and sportive lemur and many endemic species.

■ In the UK: Rainbow Tours (see Outbound operators)

MALAYSIA

International dialing code +60.

Malaysia has two distinct parts: the peninsula between Thailand and Singapore, and Sarawak and Sabah on the island of Borneo. (Most of the rest of Borneo belongs to Indonesia.)

Peninsula Malaysia is more developed – especially the west coast, with its large and entrepreneurial Chinese population. The eastern side of the peninsula is quieter, more ethnically Malay, with beautiful beaches and islands. In the centre of the peninsula, Taman Negara National Park contains some of the oldest rainforest on earth.

Sarawak and Sabah have huge cave systems, rugged scenery (including Sabah's Mt Kinabalu) and (rapidly shrinking) rainforest. Sarawak is home to the Iban and Dayak peoples. Living in rich rainforest and maintaining fairly traditional lifestyles and animist beliefs, the Iban are a popular draw for 'adventure tourists' and some Iban villages host visitors in traditional communal longhouses.

Ulu Ai   ACCOM+
An Iban village in the rainforest of Sarawak on Borneo that hosts visitors in a longhouse in partnership with a private tour operator. Stays offer a glimpse of Iban life, plus guided walks in the forest to spot wildlife, including orang-utan. British Airways Tourism for Tomorrow Awards, highly commended 1994.

■ Borneo Adventures: 55 Main Bazaar, 93000 Kuching (PO Box 2112, 93741 Kuching), Sarawak

☎ 82 245 175 **❶** 82 422 626

■ In the UK: Symbiosis (see Outbound operators); Magic of the Orient (tel: +44 (0)1293 537 700)

MEXICO

International dialing code +52.

Despite the overbearing presence of its powerful northern neighbour, Mexico retains a strong identity and culture that expresses itself in distinctive architecture, art, films, music, cooking, religion, pottery and weaving. This culture clearly reflects the mixed Spanish and indigenous *mestizo* ancestry of most Mexicans – a mix seen, for instance, in the rich imagery of the 'Day of the Dead' on 1 November.

Mexico has long been a centre of civilization, from the Olmecs, Toltecs and Mayans to the Aztecs. The *conquistadores* marvelled at Tenochtitlán, the Aztec predecessor to Mexico City – a stone city of 300,000 people in the middle of a lake and as magnificent as any city in Europe. The Spanish destroyed the Aztec capital, but Mexico has many other superb archaeological sites, including the Yucatan's Mayan ruins (such as Chichén Itzá), the hilltop city of Monte Alban near Oaxaca and the great pyramids of Teotihuacán outside Mexico City.

Package tourists fly in and out of Acapulco or Cancún, but Mexico has much more to offer. Ecotourists can hike the mighty canyons of the northern Sierras, sea-kayak and see whales in the Baja California, or explore the wild (although shrinking) rainforest of southern Yucatan and Chiapas. Many of the projects below provide fantastic opportunities to discover little-known natural reserves and beauty spots.

Most rural communities in Mexico are officially organized as *ejidos* with elected councils; many of the projects we list are run by these *ejidos*.

Mexico: Adventures in Nature by Ron Mader (Santa Fe: John Muir Publications, 1998) is a useful guide to community and ecotourism in Mexico, as is Ron's excellent *www.planeta.com* website.

Agua Selva Ecotourism Project/Sierra Huimanguillo　　　　ACCOM+
South of Villahermosa, the **Sierra Huimanguillo** has hiking, caves, canyons, waterfalls, wildlife and ruins. There are community-run guesthouses in **Malpasito** (Albergue Ecológico and La Pava) and another, Cabana Raizes Zoque, in **Mujica**, where there are guides. The Cafe Orquidias/Hotel del Carmen in Huimanguillo has information.

■ Hotel del Carmen: Morelos 39, Huimanguillo, Tabasco

❶ + ❶ 0937 50915

Ajagi   TOUR
Trips to Huichol villages in the Sierra Madre north of Guadalajara, run by a local development NGO. Walks, forest, canyons, hot springs, music, Huichol culture. Eight-day tours, $900.
☎ + ✆ 0382 66103
📧 wirrarica@yahoo.com

Bioplaneta   ORG/WEBSITE
A network of community-based crafts and food cooperatives and tourism projects.
☎ 0566 16170/12061
🌐 www.bioplaneta.com 📧 ecoturismo@bioplaneta.com

Chiapas
Chaipas is one of Mexico's most strongly indigenous areas, and one of its most bio-diverse. Pressure to open this resource-rich region to commercial develop-ment is just one issue behind the Zapatista uprising, which began in 1994 – for information on the struggle or visiting Zapatista villages, see the websites of the **EZLN** (www.ezln.org), **Chiapaslink** (www.chiapaslink.ukgateway.net) and **SIPAZ** (www.nonviolence.org/sipaz).

The Lacandón rainforest of Chaipas merges with Guatemala's Petén to form the largest rainforest north of the Amazon. Near the Mayan ruins of Palenque and the spectacular Agua Azul cascades, there are community-run guesthouses in **Agua Clara** (Hotel Sna Ajaw: 0934 50356) and **Misol-Ha** (tel/fax: 0934 51210). The **Monte Azules Biosphere Reserve** has wildlife (howler monkeys, jaguars, scarlet macaws, toucans, crocodiles, etc) and Mayan ruins. Community-based cabañas in the reserve include **Las Guacamayas** in Reforma Agraria, **Escudo Jaguar** in Frontera Corozal (tel: 0934 50356; 520 16441; fax: 0520 16440), nearby **Ara Macao** (tel: 0520 15979/28) and **Lacanjá Chansayab** (tours to nearby Bonampak), plus **Emiliano Zapata** (tel: 0967 80468; fax: 0967 84307; danamex@mail.internet.com.mz) near Lake Miramar. **Ixcan Lodge** and campsite (tel/fax: 0563 13032) is a community project aided by Conservation International.

On the Pacific coast near Guatemala, **San José el Hueyate** (tel: 0962 53940) has cabañas plus beaches, surfing, birdwatching, boat trips and water-sports.

Most accommodation costs around $30 per night; guided tours $5/10 per day.

The NGO **STAACH** works with many of these community projects.Another NGO, **Na Bolom** has a museum about the Lacondón people in San Cristobal and run tours to San Juan Chamula and San Lorenzo Zinacantán.

■ Na Bolom: Avenida Vicente Guerroro 33, CP 29220, San Cristóbal de las Casas, Chaipas

☎ 0967 81418 ☎ 0967 85586

Ⓦ www.ecosur.mx/nabolom Ⓔ nabolom@sclc.ecosur.mx or nbcultur@mundomaya.com.mx

■ STAACH: Lozano Miguel: Periférico Sur Poniente 1020, Tuxtla Gutiérrez, Chiapas CP 29000

☎ + ☎ 0961 11410

Ⓦ www.sic.chiapas.com/staach.html Ⓔ staach@laneta.apc.org or staach@correo.chiapas.com

CICE (Centro Internacional para la Cultura y Ensenanza de la Lengua)   TOUR/SCHOOL

Spanish and Náhuatl tuition in Cuernavaca, one hour from Mexico City, plus homestays and twice-yearly workshops in traditional medicine. Two-week courses, $350. Lodging from $15 per night. Income goes to local health clinics.

■ Estela Roman: Aptdo Postal 1-166, Cuernavaca, Morelos, Mexico CP 62001

☎ 07 312 5090

Ⓔ cice@cuer.laneta.apc.org

■ In the US: Rethinking Tourism Project (see Outbound operators)

Grupo Ecologico Sierra Gorda   ORG/TOUR

A non-profit group promoting conservation in a new UNESCO World Biosphere Reserve of semi-desert, cloudforest and jungle 300km north of Mexico City. Ecotours, walking, biking and swimming in crystal-clear rivers.

■ Laura Patricia Perez-Arce: IAP Arroyo Seco 306, Col Estrella, Queretaro, 76030

☎ + ☎ 0429 60222/42

Ⓔ sierrago@ciateq.mx or sierrago@sparc.ciateq.conacyt.mx

Las Canadas   ACCOM+/TOUR

A private cloudforest reserve in Veracruz that works with local communities. Ecolodge, hiking, organic farming workshops and environmental education, birdwatching.

■ Ricardo Romero: AP 24, Huatusco, Veracruz 94100

☎ + ☎ 02 273 41577

Ⓦ www.bosquedeniebla.com.mx Ⓔ bosquedeniebla@infosel.net.mx

Los Tuxtlas/Selva del Marinero   RAINFOREST/TOUR
A local organization, **Red de Ecoturismo de Los Tuxtlas**, runs one- to four-day ecotours in the **Los Tuxtlas Biosphere Reserve** on the coast east of Veracruz. Rainforest and cloudforest, mangroves, birdwatching, ruins, kayaking. (Four days, $1500: book through **Bioplaneta**, above.) There are campsites and guest-houses in Sontecomapan, Miguel Hidalgo, Las Margaritas and Lopez Mateos (tel: 0515 00405). Another NGO, **Cielo, Tierra y Selva**, runs the **Selva del Marinero** tourism project at López Mateos (hiking, rainforest, volcanoes).

■ Cielo, Tierra y Selva: Luisa Paré

❶ 0281 77148

✉ lpared@yahoo.com

Maruata 2000   ACCOM+/BUDGET
Community-owned cabañas in a Náhuatl village near Aquila on the Michoacán coast south of Colima. Good beach plus nature tours, a turtle/iguana conservation project, fishing. Horses, boats and bicycles for rent. From $5 per night.

■ Ezequiel García Palacios: Caseta Maruata, Aquila, Michoacán

❶ 0332 50368

Oaxaca
As well as the world heritage-listed colonial capital, Oaxaca has mountains, forests, lakes and Pacific coastline, plus the impressive archaeological site of Monte Alban. It is also renowned for traditional crafts. The **Museos Communitarios de Oaxaca (UMCO)** is an association of 15 villages with cultural museums/projects. It runs day or two-day tours exploring rural life and crafts such as cooking, weaving, pottery, etc. Plus cycling, horseriding, hiking, caves, fiestas.

The pine and cloud forests and hills of the Sierra Norte are ideal for outdoors activities such as hiking, mountain biking, fishing, plus Zapotec culture, handicrafts, etc. There are guesthouses, homestays and guides in the villages of Santa María Yavesia (**Proyecto Viajes Ecoturísticos Shoo Ra**: tel. 0955 36042; yashoora@yahoo.com.mx). **Expediciones Sierra Norte** (García Vigil 406, Oaxaca; tel: 0951 48271; www.sierranorte.org.mx; SierraNorte@oaxaca.com), a cooperative of eight villages, and **Ecotours Rua Via** in Ixtlán de Juárez (tel/fax: 0955 36075; ecoixt@hotmail.com) offer tour packages of up to one week.

On the Oaxaca coast, the **Cooperative Ecotúristica La Ventanilla** (tel: 0515 011721; ecosolar@laneta.apc.org) has birdwatching, canoeing in lagoons and mangroves, horseriding, beaches, turtles, iguanas.

The last three are also part of **Bioplaneta** (see above).

The state tourist agency **SEDETUR** has more information and also supports **Tourist Yú'u** – simple village guesthouses with attractive walking and scenery.

There are Tourist Yú'u in Teotitlán del Valle, Tlacolula, Benito Juárez Lachatao (tel: 0954 59994), Hierve El Agua (petrified waterfalls, tel: 0956 20922; 0951 42155) and Santiago Apoala (tel: 0515 19154).

■ UMCO: Teresa Morales/Patricia Ramirez: Tinoco y Palacios 311-12, Col Centro, Oaxaca CP 68000

❶ + ❶ 951 65786

Ⓦ www.umco.org * turismo_comunitario@umco.org *or* info@umco.org

■ SEDETUR: Abdon Vazquez, Alternative Tourism Department: Independencia 607, Oaxaca

❶ 0951 41778; 951 48298 ❶ 951 60984

Ⓦ www.activemexico.com *or* www.oaxaca.gob.mx Ⓔ info@oaxaca.gob.mx *or* sedetur5@oaxaca.gob.mx

Sierra Tarahumara

The rugged Sierra Tarahumara offers bizarre rock formations, lakes, caves, waterfalls, great hiking and mountain biking. Highlights include the huge Copper Canyon (twice as big as the Grand Canyon) and the spectacular *Chihuahua al Pacífico* railway, while Creel is the popular tourist base. The Tarahumara, north America's second-largest indigenous group (after the Navajo), preserve much of their traditional culture. However, plans to develop the region for an influx of US tourists, with roads, lodges and campsites, could threaten this way of life.

Many Tarahumara want little to do with outsiders but one community, **Arareko/San Ignacio** (Tomás Toribio: tel/fax: 145 60126), has cabañas and a hotel ($6 or $25 per night) plus a museum, bicycles and horses for rent and guided walks ($10 for a half-day) into the canyons and Sierra. Near Creel, there are rustic cabins at **Cueva de los Leones** (Rigoberto Yánez: tel: 145 60176), just outside Bocayna village, and **Cusárare** is also developing tourism. Near Uruachi canyon, the community-run **Hostal de Uruachi** ((Fernando Domíngez: tel: 01 1415/9717; $60 per night for a six-bed cabin) can organize horseback trips ($10). Nearby Piedra Volada waterfall in Basaseachi Falls National Park is Mexico's highest. An American guide, Santiago James Barnaby, runs hiking trips in the region with Tarahumara guides organized into **La Cooperativa de Los Guias Alta y Baja Tarahumara** (tel: +1 406 587 3585; www.coppercanyonguide.com). Santiago helps the village of Norogachi organize a special homestay tour during the traditional Tarahumara Easter week festival.

Taselotzin   ACCOM/BUDGET

Cabañas in wooded hills near Cuetzalan village, north of Puebla, run by an indigenous women's craft group, **Maseualsiuame Mosenyolchikauani**. Ruins, walks, forest, caves and waterfalls.

■ Juana María Nicolasa Chepe: Barrio Zacatipan, Cuetzalan, Puebla
☎ 233 10480
✉ maseualsiua@laneta.apc.org

Yucatan

The Yucatan has beaches and coral reefs, Mayan ruins and huge limestone caves. The development of Cancun – from an island of 12 families in 1970 to a resort with 2.6 million visitors a year and a population of 300,000 – has created inevitable environmental problems yet brought little benefit to most of the Yucatan's mainly Mayan population.

Community-run alternatives include **Nohoch-tunich cabañas** near Tulum and horseriding and guiding at **Felipe Carrillo Puerto**. Nearer Merida, there are boat trips from **Rio Lagartos** (Juan Velazco: tel: 0992 60481) into the Rio Celestun Biosphere Reserve to see flamingos and ibis. Near Villahermosa in neighbouring Tabasco, the Chontal community of **Nacajuc** runs an animal sanctuary (manatees, alligators, etc) and farming and crafts demonstrations. South of Cancun, the **Sian Ka'an Biosphere Reserve** has rainforest, mangroves, beaches and coral reef, plus jaguar, howler monkey, tapir, manatee, turtles, crocodiles. **Amigos de Sian Ka'an** (tel: 0984 81618/1593; fax: 0988 06024; sian@cancun.com.mx) organizes trips from **Cabanas de Ana y Jose** (tel: 0988 75469) in Tulum. Beside Bacalar lagoon, inland from Chetumal, there are cabañas at **Botadero San Pastor** (0983 29610; kayaks for hire).

The NGO **Yaxche, Arbol de la Vida** (Carlos Meade: tel: 0987 59095; www.laneta.apc.org/yaxche; akumalik@cancun.com.mx) is helping communities develop tourism in the region.

MOROCCO

International dialing code +212.

At its closest, Morocco is only a few kilometres from Europe. Yet its culture and landscapes can seem a world away. Morocco has a rich cultural heritage, isolated mountain villages, desert oasis communities and historic cities such as Fez and Marrakesh, with their fantastic architecture and enormous markets (*kasbahs*). It has mountains as well as desert: you can ride a camel through the Sahara and then hike or even ski in the Atlas Mountains. Moroccans are a mix of Arabic Muslims and indigenous tribal people, such as the Berbers. Small areas of the country, mainly the northern ports, have a reputation for hassling tourists, but once you travel south you'll find people are friendly and welcoming.

Tizi-Randonnées TOUR
A Berber-owned company offering 'soft adventure' tours throughout Morocco, including trekking in the High Atlas mountains. They work with about 30 different communities around the country and money from their trips goes to community development projects.

■ In the UK: Tribes Travel (see Outbound operators)

NAMIBIA

International dialing code +264.

Namibia has fantastic scenery, clear starry skies, huge tracts of pristine and virtually empty wilderness with stunning wildlife. In vast open areas such as the Namib-Naukluft National Park, you can drive for hours through endless deserts, plains, mountain massifs and spectacular canyons without seeing a soul. Namibia is four times the size of Britain with an ethnically diverse population of 1.5 million (including Himba, San and Damara). The Namib Desert has plants and animals found nowhere else on earth. The Skeleton Coast is the resting place of dozens of shipwrecks. Namibia's wilderness is easy to explore independently – even in Etosha, one of Africa's top parks, driving around is easy – and prices are low for southern Africa.

In 1996, Namibia introduced communal area conservancies, which permit local people to sustainably manage wildlife, agriculture and tourism. Many of the projects below are community conservancies. *Namibia: The Bradt Travel Guide* by Chris McIntyre (Bradt Publications) includes good information on visiting community camps.

Rebel/military action recently made the Caprivi Strip unsafe: check the situation before travelling.

Damaraland Camp ACCOM+/SAFARI
A luxury camp in northern Damaraland developed by **Wilderness Safaris** (see South Africa) with **IRDNC** (see below), WWF and the local Damara community. It features guided nature walks, birdwatching, wildlife and spectacular scenery. From £120 per day.

■ In the UK: Sunvil Discovery (see Outbound operators)

Etendeka Mountain Camp SAFARI
A safari camp on the arid Etendeka plains of northern Damaraland that gives a share of income to local communities. Nature walks, birdwatching, wildlife. From £80 per day.

■ PO Box 21783, Windhoek

❶ 061 226 979 ❶ 061 226 999

■ In the UK: Sunvil Discovery (see Outbound operators)

IRDNC (Integrated Rural Development and Nature Conservation)   ORG
Supports communities in the Caprivi region including Kubunyana Camp, Mashi Craft market at Kongolo and Salambala Community campsite (all NACOTBA members, see below).

■ Margaret Jacobsohn: Box 24050 Windhoek

❶ 061 228 506/9 ❶ 061 228 530

ⓔ irdnc@iafrica.com.na

Kaokohimba Safaris   TOUR
Tours to the remote, rugged desert of Kaokoland in northern Nambia, inland from the Skeleton Coast, featuring walking, wildlife, desert scenery. Kaokohimba also run adventurous donkey-treks of up to 12 days led by Himba guides, and are involved in community development projects with local Himba communities. Two-day tours, £450; six days, £800.

■ Koos Verwey, Kaokohimba Safaris, PO Box 11580, Windhoek

❶ + ❶ 061 222 378

Lianshulu Lodge   ACCOM/DAY
A lodge in Mudumu National Park in eastern Caprivi. Good birdwatching and wildlife (hippos, elephants, crocodiles, etc). A share of income goes to local communities. Nearby **Lizauli Traditional Village** (a NACOBTA member) features local crafts, music, medicine, etc. Lianshulu, £80 per night; Lizauli, £3.

■ PO Box 90391, Windhoek, Namibia

❶ 00 264 61 254317 ❶ 00264 61 254980

Ⓦ www.namibiaweb.com/lianshulu/ ⓔ lianshul@mweb.com.na

■ In the UK: Sunvil Discovery (see below)

NACOBTA (Namibia Community Based Tourism Association)   ORG
An association of community camps and projects. These include, in Damaraland: **Purros (Ngatutunge Pamue)**, 100km north of Sesfontein in a Himba community (walking safaris, medicinal plants walks, visits to Himba villages); **Kunene Village Rest Camp** (tel: 065 273 043; walking, birdwatching, etc) in Opuwo, with bungalows and camping; and **Okarohombo** in the beautiful Marienfluss Valley north of Opuwo. Plus **Ongongo, Anmire Traditional Village** and **Khowarib** (guided walks, camel rides), all near Warmquelle. In the Caprivi Strip, there is **Salambala** (50km south of Katima Mulilo) and Kubunyana, near Kongola (tel: 0677 2108).
Other camps include **Aba Huab** (Elias Aro Xoagub: PO Box 131, Twyfelfontein via Khorixas; tel/fax: 065 712), with guided walks, donkey rides and rock-art; and **Nakambale** near Ondangwa (tel: 065 240 241/536) with local guides and a museum. **Omatako Valley Rest Camp** (PO Box 1391,

Grootfontein, Arnold: Private Bag 2093, Omatako) is run by a !Kung San community between Groofontein and Tsumkwe and has wildlife, horseriding, dancing, 'bush food' and crafts, plus *rondavels*. Near Swakipmund, there is **Okombahe Rest Camp, Spitzkoppe Camp** (tel: 064 530 879; camping and bungalows) and **Brandberg Mountain Guides** (PO Box 159, Uis; tel: 064 504 030; day walks and treks). Camps typically cost £2/4 a night; half-day guided walks £5/10.

■ Theo Ngaujake/Maxi Louis: 18 Lilliencron St, (PO Box 86099), Windhoek

❶ 061 250 558; 061 221 918 ❶ 061 222 647

Ⓦ www.nacobta.com.na ❸ nacobta@iafrica.com.na

Nyae Nyae Conservancy   ORG
A wildlife conservancy in the Kalahari, near Tsumkwe, belonging to local Bushman communities. The **Nyae Nyae Development Foundation** is developing community-based camps and wildlife/cultural tours and aims to open a tourist office in Tsumkwe.

❶ 061 236 327 ❶ 061 225 997

❸ nndfn@iafrica.com.na

Sunvil Discovery   SAFARI+/TOUR
A responsible mainstream British tour operator with a specialist expertise in Namibia. They market **Tsumkwe Lodge, Damaraland Camp, Lianshulu Lodge** and **Etendeka Camp**. Brochure. ATOL-bonded.

■ In the UK: Chris McIntyre: Sunvil Discovery, Sunvil House, Upper Square, Old Isleworth, TW7 7BJ

❶ +44 (0)20 8232 9777 ❶ +44 (0)20 8568 8330

Ⓦ www.sunvil.co.uk ❸ africa@sunvil.co.uk

WIMSA (Working Group of Indigenous Minorities in Southern Africa) ORG
An advocacy group for the San (Bushmen) that helps San communities negotiate with tourist lodges, tour operators, etc. Also helps communities to set up campsites.

■ Joram Useb and Axel Thoma: PO Box 80733, Windhoek

❶ 61 244 909 ❶ 61 272 806

❸ wimsareg@iafrica.com.na

NEPAL

International dialing code +977.

The big draw in Nepal, of course, is trekking in the Himalaya, with the world's highest peaks and Tibetan Buddhist culture. The majority of trekkers head for Everest Base Camp, the Langtang Valley or the Annapurna range north of Pokhara.

Kathmandu is a vibrant, bustling capital that still manages to feel like an overgrown village, while the Kathmandu valley offers a mix of rural life, historic temples and towns. There is whitewater rafting on rivers flowing down from the high mountains. Heading down towards the Indian border there are tropical forests, the wildlife of Chitwan National Park and Lumbini, birthplace of the Buddha.

Trails in the Nepalese Himalaya tend to follow existing local pathways through the valleys. Rather than remote wilderness, you are walking along well-used paths and passing through villages, many of which provide food and lodgings for trekkers. This means you see a lot of local life – one of the pleasures of trekking in Nepal – but tourists need to be aware of their impact on local people and on a fragile environment.

Our own **Himalayan Code**, drawn up with the **Annapurna Conservation Area Project (ACAP)**, offers guidelines for responsible travel. The **International Porter Protection Group (IPPG)** has also produced a code covering the employment of local porters. Every year, porters die because trekkers and tour leaders fail to provide proper medical attention or adequate clothing, while porters suffering from altitude sickness are often sent down the mountain unaccompanied. (See Responsible tourism codes.) ACAP and IPPG are both listed below.

The **Himalayan Explorers Club** (see KEEP, below, for address. Tel: 01 259 275; www.hec.org; members@hec.org) in Kathmandu is a useful source of information for travellers.

**Annapurna Conservation Area Project
(ACAP)/Dhiprang Community Lodge/
Ghalekharka-Sikles Eco-trekking Route**   ACCOM/TOUR/ORG
ACAP (part of the **King Mahendra Trust for Nature Conservation**) uses income from trekking fees for conservation and community development. It has developed the community-owned **Dhiprang Lodge**, plus a four- to seven-day **Ghalekharka-Sikles Eco-trekking Route** (either self-guided or with local guides) from Dhiprang to Pokhara. Accommodation en route is in simple community-run campsites or guesthouses in the Himalayan foothills (900 to 2500 metres). Great views of the Annapurna peaks. ACAP has an information centre on Pokhara's lakeside.
■ PO Box 183, Pokhara
❶ 061 21102/28202 ❶ 061 28203 (Sikles office: 061 29338)
Ⓦ www.kmtnc.org.np Ⓔ acap@mos.com.np

Centre for Community Development and Research (CCODER)   TREK
Treks from four days to several weeks, away from the crowds in the beautiful mid-hills of Nepal (at altitudes of up to 3600 metres), starting from the town of Gorkha. Great mountain views, homestays in villages, learn about Ayurvedic medicine, herbal plants, village life.
■ Babu Ram Bhatta/Martina Mascher: PO Box 5716, Kathmandu
❶ 01 351681
Ⓦ www.ccoder.org Ⓔ info@ccoder.org

Explore Nepal   TOUR
A trekking company committed to good employment and conservation practices. It also donates to community and environmental projects, such as reforestation schemes.
■ In the UK: Tribes Travel (see Outbound operators)

General Travel and Tours   TOUR
Treks and general tours with profits going to a development NGO called
General Welfare Prathisthan.

■ LB Thapa: PO box 3245, Gyaneswor, Kathmandu

☎ 01 422 754; 01 432 206 ✆ 01 417 979

ⓦ www.everestnepal.com/gtt ⓔ gtt@htp.com.np

Himalayan Foundation for Integrated Development   ORG
Helps local communities in the Solu region of Solu Khumbu district to develop
sustainable tourism businesses. The project includes training for local people
and the development of a visitor centre.

■ Solu Khumbu, Sallery, PO Box 4995, Kathmandu

ⓦ www.keepnepal.org/hf ⓔ hf@sallery.wlink.com.np

IPPG (International Porter Protection Group)   ORG
A campaign to improve conditions and safety for trekking porters.

■ Prakash Adhikari: Himalayan Rescue Association, PO Box 4944, Thamel, Kathmandu

ⓔ ippgnepal@mail.com.np

■ Overseas contacts: see Resources directory

KEEP (Kathmandu Environmental Educational Project)   ORG
KEEP provides advice on low-impact trekking and tourism in Nepal to tourists
and local communities. It has a visitor centre in the Thamel district of
Kathmandu, which it shares with the **Himalayan Explorers Club**
(www.hec.org) and the **Keep Green coffee shop**. With a Dutch NGO called
Gift for Aid, Keep has also set up **Gift for Aid Nepal** (tel: 01 259 122;
www.giftforaid.org), which organizes volunteer work with development
projects in Nepal.

■ Pasang Temba Sherpa Kerung: Jyatha Road, Thamel (PO Box 9178), Kathmandu

☎ 01 259567; 01 259275 ✆ 01 256615

ⓦ www.keepnepal.org ⓔ tour@keep.wlink.com.np

HELP US UPDATE

If you know of similar community tourism projects or changes to these listings,
please email Tourism Concern at info@tourismconcern.org.uk – subject:
community tourism.

Muir's Tours TOUR
A non-profit tour operator run from the UK, but set up by the Nepal Kingdom Foundation. Tours are mainly trekking and mountain-based adventure travel. Also cultural tours. Profits go to charities and local development projects.

■ In the UK: Maurice Adshead: 97a Swansea Road, Reading RG1 8HA

☏ +44 (0)118 950 2281 ☏ +44 (0)118 950 2301

ⓦ www.nkf-mt.org.uk ⓔ info@nkf-mt.org.uk

The Nepal Trust ORG/TOUR
A Scottish charity that helps develop health, education and other community projects in Nepal. It runs annual treks that incorporate work on community projects such as building a health clinic or restoring religious sites. The Trust is helping the **Women's Welfare Service** in the Humla region to develop a women's trekking cooperative and guesthouse in Simikot and can arrange study trips in the area looking at local culture, herbal medicine, religion and the environment.

■ In Nepal

☏ 01 429 112 ☏ 01 436 224

ⓔ ntrust@chun.mos.com.np

■ In the UK: 4 Marina Quay, Lossiemouth, Moray IV31 6TJ Scotland

☏ +44 (0)1343 810358 ☏ +44 (0)1343 810359

ⓦ www.thenepaltrust.demon.co.uk ⓔ admin@nepaltrust.org

Sirubari Model Village TOUR
Homestays (two to five days) in a Gurung village south of Pokhara, with views of the Annapurna range. Dance performances, rural Nepali life. Developed with a commercial company called **Nepal Village Resorts**. Two-day tour from Pokhara $160.

■ Nepal Village Resorts: PO Box 9048, Kathmandu

☏ 01 430 187 ☏ 01 435 027

ⓦ www.nepalvillage.com ⓔ village@ecomail.com.np

Specialist Trekking TOUR
Trips to the main trekking areas and lesser-known regions such as Mustang, Dolpo and Kangchenjunga or Makalu base camps, plus Bhutan. Also trekking peaks and school, charity and special interest trips. A share of profits goes to a charity, **Community Action Nepal**, which supports health and education projects in rural villages. From £1400. Brochure available. Passenger Protection bonding.

■ In the UK: Specialist Trekking: Chapel House, Low Cotehill, Carlisle, Cumbria CA4 0EL

☏ +44 (0)1228 562 358 ☏ +44 (0)1228 562 368

🌐 www.specialisttrekking.com ✉ trekstc@aol.com

Sustainable Tourism Network   ORG
An association of organizations developing sustainable and community-based tourism in Nepal. It includes **KEEP, GIFT, CCODER, Sirubari Model Village** (all listed above), SNV (John Hummel: tel: 01 523 444; snv@snv.com.np; jhummel@snv.org.np), WWF Nepal (www.wwfnepal.org.np), **Eco Himal** (www.ecohimal.or.at), **King Mahendra Trust for Nature Conservation** (www.kmtnc.org.np), **The Mountain Institute** (www.mountain.org) and others. The Nepal Tourism Board's **Tourism for Rural Poverty Alleviation Project (TRPAP)** (Ravi Pandey/Brigitte Nitsch: 01-256909; brigitte@ntb.wlink.com.np) is also helping local communities develop tourism facilities in trekking areas throughout Nepal.

■ Julie Webb, Sustainable Tourism Network Coordinator, Nepal Tourism Board: PO Box 11018, Kathmandu Nepal

☏ 01 256 909 extension 143

🌐 www.welcomenepal.com ✉ jwebb@ntb.wlink.com.np

NEW ZEALAND – MAORI TOURISM

International dialing code +64.

Like the Australian Aboriginals or North America's indigenous peoples, New Zealand Maoris suffer serious health, education and employment problems, and Maori life expectancy is markedly lower than for the non-Maori population.

In Rotorua and Kaikoura, Maori tourism is well integrated into the mainstream tourism industry. In Rotarua, it is geared to coach parties and high turnover rather than in-depth cultural insight, with up to 200 people a night for cultural shows. It does, however, generate income for Maori communities and helps to preserve traditional crafts such as woodcarving. Apart from Rotorua and Northland – the top of the North Island – it is hard to find Maori-run tourism ventures.

Main Street Backpackers/Tuku Wairua Centre   ACCOM+/SCHOOL
Kaitaia is the most northerly town in New Zealand, with a large Maori population. Main Street is New Zealand's first Maori-owned backpackers and also organizes marae visits, tours to Cape Reinga and bone-carving lessons. The **Tuku Wairua Centre** (twnt@xtra.co.nz) offers Maori craft workshops and courses.

■ Peter and Kerry Kitchen: 235 Commerce Street, Kaitaia

☎ 09 408 1275/0870 ✆ 09 408 1100

Ⓦ www.tall-tale.co.nz Ⓔ mainstreet@extra.co.nz *or* tall-tale-tours@xtra.co.nz

Rotorua DAY
There are a number of Maori tourist enterprises in this touristy town. They offer short cultural tours, a look inside a *marae, hangii* feasts and dance shows. They cater for a mass market and the cultural experience is superficial, but they are successful Maori-run community enterprises. They include **Whakarewarewa** (incorporating the **National Maori Arts and Crafts Institute**, tel: 07 348 9047), **Magic of Maori** concerts at Taharangi *marae* (tel: 07 349 3949) and Tamaki Tours (tel: 07 346 2823).

Tai Tokerau Maori Tourism Association ORG/WEBSITE
An association of Maori tourism enterprises in the far north around Cape Reinga, Ninety Mile Beach and the Bay of Islands. These include Culture North (Kena Alexander: tel: 09 401 9301), Jake's Horse Trekking (fishing, tramping, horsetreks in Warawara forest, tel: 09 409 5003; jk.dunn@xtra.co.nz) and Waimamaku Maori Homestay in South Hokianga.

Ⓦ www.taitokerau.com Ⓔ twnt@xtra.co.nz

Whale Watch Kaikoura DAY
Maori-run whale watching boat tours from Kaikoura, three hours north of Christchurch. This is one of the best places on earth to see sperm whales, dolphins, seals and other whales. British Airways Tourism for Tomorrow Awards, winner 1994.

■ PO Box 89, Kaikoura, South Island

☎ 03 319 6767 ✆ 03 319 6545

Ⓦ www.whalewatch.co.nz Ⓔ info@whalewatch.co.nz

NICARAGUA

International dialing code +505.

Nicaragua is the largest country in Central America and the least visited. There is little indigenous culture, most of the country is oppressively hot and humid and Managua is a less-than-attractive capital. In the 1980s, idealistic foreigners joined voluntary work brigades in support of the Sandinista regime. Today, a few tourists – mainly backpackers – come to Nicaragua for the crafts market of Masaya, surfing on the Pacific coast, hiking in the lush volcanic highlands near Matagalpa, and the islands in Lago de Nicaragua (see below). For anyone wanting to get off the tourist trail, however, Nicaragua can be a rewarding destination, with vibrant culture and arts, a complex, heroic recent history and exceptionally hospitable and articulate people.

The steamy Caribbean coast is virtually a separate country, never colonized by Spain and cut off from western Nicaragua by a lack of roads. Its inhabitants are mostly indigenous Miskito, Rama or Suma or descendants of black slaves. Music and culture is Caribbean rather than Latin American and most people speak English rather than Spanish.

Finca Esperanza Verde   TOUR

Cultural immersion stays on an organic coffee farm/lodge in San Ramon near Matagalpa, two hours north of Managua. One week $680, including a three-day homestay, plus shorter stays, featuring local life, birdwatching, cloudforest and cultural performances. Income to community projects.

- ☎ 612 5003
- ⓦ www.durham-sanramon.org ⊖ herma@ibw.com.ni
- ■ In the US
- ☎ +1 919 489 1656
- ⊖ info@durham-sanramon.org

Isla de Ometepe   ACCOM/DAY/ORG

An island in Lago de Nicaragua, with two volcanoes linked by a narrow isthmus. Visitors come for the peaceful atmosphere plus horseriding, walking and to climb the volcanoes. A local NGO, Fundación Entre Volcanes, works with a women's group that arranges homestays.

- ■ Fundación Entre Volcanes: Moyogalpa, Isla de Ometepe
- ☎ 459 4118
- ⊖ volcanes@idw.com.ni

Nicaragua Spanish Schools   SCHOOL

A cooperative of three language schools in the historic colonial towns of Leon and Grenada and San Juan del Sur on the south coast (beaches, surfing). From $175 per week, including Spanish tuition plus homestays, cultural activities, excursions and volunteer opportunities. The schools are all involved in non-profit social projects.

- ■ Aptdo SL-145, Managua
- ☎ 244 4512 (in the US: 1-805 687 9941)
- ⊖ http://pages.prodigy.net/nss-pmc or nss-pmc@prodigy.net

SELVA (Somos Ecologistas en Lucha por la Vida y el Ambiente)　　TOUR
A local environmental NGO in the Cosiguina peninsula, 150km from Managua, that has developed ecotours with 10 local villages. They have a guest-house in the town of El Viejo ($10 per night) and offer three tour itineraries around the peninsula. Local attractions include undeveloped Pacific beaches, snorkelling and surfing, hikes to volcanoes, local crafts and agriculture, pony trekking and birdwatching.

■ José Gutiérrez: Aptdo 91, El Viejo, Chinandega

❶ 886 9203; 8849 156 (in English: Julián Guevara, 266 5109)

🅮 codanic@ibw.com.ni

PAKISTAN

International dialing code +92.

For mountain lovers Pakistan's far north – bordered by Ladakh, Kashmir and China – is a jewel, with the greatest concentration of high peaks on earth, including 60 over 7000 metres and four over 8000 metres. There is amazing and uncrowded trekking, plus rare wildlife including the elusive snow leopards and Himalayan bears. Indigenous languages here are related to Tibetan and the region was predominantly Buddhist until the 15th century.

A useful information source and meeting place for travellers in Pakistan is the **Himalayan Explorers Club** (House 14a, Street 63, F-8/4, Islamabad; tel: 51 282146; fax: 51 251221; www.hec.org; hec@trivor.com.pk).

Full Moon Night Trekking　　TOUR
Trekking holidays to the Karakoram and Himalayan mountains of Baltistan in northern Pakistan. Treks in prime snow-leopard habitat with different themes (conservation, nature, culture) and levels of difficulty. All involve staying with local people, using local guides and a strong element of local management. Profits go to local community and conservation projects. Tours start from Skardu, one hour's flight from Islamabad. From £800 for a 10–12-day trek, excluding international flights.

■ In the UK: 9a Avonmore Mansions, Avonmore Road, London W14 8RN

❶ +44 (0)20 7603 9893

🅦 www.fmntrekking.com 🅮 info@fmntrekking.com

PALESTINE

International dialing code +972.

Of the estimated two million people who visit the Holy Land each year – including many Christian pilgrims – less than half visit the West Bank for more than two hours. Most travel on Israeli-run day trips that have little benefit for local people, and few see much of the reality of life for contemporary Palestinians.
Visitors should check the current security situation before travelling.

Guiding Star TOUR
A Palestinian tour agency that can arrange cultural tours throughout the Holy Land, including Bethlehem, Jerusalem and Palestinian villages. Homestays, hiking, Christian tours, desert trips.

■ George Rishmawi: Virgin Mary St, Beit Jala (PO Box 1161), Bethlehem

☎ 02 276 5970 ☏ 02 276 5971

Ⓦ www.guidingstarltd.com Ⓔ george@guidingstar2.com

International Centre of Bethlehem/Abu Gubran guesthouse ACCOM+/TOUR
ToDo! Award winner
A community development organization that also operates a guesthouse in Bethlehem and runs tours offering an insight into life on the West Bank, as well as the historical sights.

■ Dr Mitri Raheb: International Center of Bethlehem: PO Box 162, Bethlehem, West Bank, via Israel

☎ 02 277 0047 ☏ 02 277 0048

Ⓦ www.annadwa.org Ⓔ annadwa@planet.edu

Palestinian Association for Cultural Exchange (PACE) TOUR
Tours in the West Bank, Gaza Strip and Jerusalem exploring Palestinian history, culture and daily life. Also publish a guidebook to the West Bank and Gaza Strip.

■ Al Bireh, Nablus Road, opposite Al Ain Mosque (PO Box 841, Ramallah)

☎ 02 240 4524 ☏ 02 240 7610

Ⓦ www.planet.edu/~pace/ Ⓔ pace@planet.edu

PANAMA

International dialing code +507.

Panama is little-visited: it's relatively expensive and certain parts – notably Colon – have a reputation for robbery and muggings. Crossing the Darien Gap is one of Latin America's great adventures, but may be unsafe due to smuggling activity. Away from these danger spots, however, the country is friendly and safe, with good hiking near the Costa Rican border and Central America's second-largest indigenous population (behind Guatemala). The beautiful San Blas Islands, an archipelago of 365 tropical islands (40 inhabited) off Panama's Caribbean coast, are the semi-autonomous homeland of the Kuna. The *Rough Guide to Central America* has more details on Kuna tourism.

San Blas islands (Kuna Yala)   ACCOM+
The Kuna of the San Blas islands enjoy a degree of self-government that is perhaps unique in Latin America. They own (or at least co-own) and manage all tourist facilities on the islands. The islands' main appeal is their tropical setting: palm-fringed beaches, untamed forest, sun, coral reefs and rich marine life. There are no cultural tours as such, but you will see daily Kuna life all around you. Kuna women are known for their intricately woven blouses, known as *molas*. The following hotels are Kuna-owned and run: **Dolphin Lodge** (tel: 263 3077; fax: 263 3089) on Uaguitupu, **San Blas** (tel: 262 1606/5410) on Nalunega, **Kwadule** (only partially Kuna-owned); **Kuanidup** (tel: 227 5554); **Iskardup, Delfin** near Achutupo, **Anai** (tel: 239 3025) and **Kuna Niskua** (tel: 227 5308) on Wichubhuala, **Kuna Yala** on Isla Raton, **Sugtupu** on Carti Sugtupu and **Ikasa** (tel: 224 8492) on Ailigandi. Panama City travel agents book the larger hotels but, except during holidays, it's cheaper to fly in and book locally. Fly to Porvenir ($54 return) for hotels on Nalunega and Wichubhuala, or to Rio Sidra for Hotels Kuna Yala and Kuanidup. There are also airstrips on Carti Sugtupu and Ailigandi. To visit other islands, you need permission from the village *sahila* (elected elder), who can often arrange guides and homestays. Some islands have become stopovers for cruise ships with some negative impacts. The **Kuna General Congress** publishes a pamphlet entitled *Tourism in Kuna Yala.*

■ Kuna General Congress: Edificio Dominó, Via Espana, El Cangrejo, Panama City

❶ 263 3615

■ Promotion of Ecological and Cultural Tourism in Kuna Yala: Edificio Cermu, 3er piso, oficina 5C, Avenida Cuba, Calle 32, Panama City

❶ 227 5090; 225 5200 ❶ 227 5090

✉ fpci@tutopia.com and inatoy9@hotmail.com

PAPUA NEW GUINEA

International dialing code +675.

Papua New Guinea (PNG) consists of eastern New Guinea (the western half is Indonesia's Irian Jaya) and more than 600 smaller islands. It is one of the most culturally diverse countries on earth, with more than 800 languages in an area the size of France.

New Guinea is the world's largest tropical island, with the world's third-largest tract of tropical rainforest (after the Amazon and the Congo basins). With many endemic plants and animals, 200 species of frog, 740 types of bird (including the colourful birds of paradise), magnificent coral reefs, mangroves and highlands rising to alpine meadows, PNG is one of the planet's bio-diversity hotspots.

Most people live in rural villages and survive by fishing, hunting and small-scale farming. As in other South Pacific countries, the clan system is central – 97 per cent of land is owned communally. In recent years, however, pressure to join the cash economy has led to a gradual decline in communal patterns of resource use and management and has allowed logging and mining companies to gain access to community-owned forests and minerals, threatening the country's natural treasures.

For adventurous travellers, PNG offers superb beaches, diving and snorkelling, endless if undeveloped hiking possibilities in the rugged highlands, great birdwatching, fascinating cultures and colourful *sing sings* (festivals with traditional dances and dress).

Enga Experience   ACCOM+
Village stays near Wabag in Western Highlands province, 150km from Mt Hagen. Orchids, sing-sings, participation in everyday life. Guests collected from Mt Hagen. $50 per day.

■ Adrian/Ben Lokain: Landamanda, Wabag, Enga Province (PO Box 941, Goroka, EHP)

❶ 732 3394

Ⓦ http://homepages.about.com/engaexperience/engaexperience/ *or*
www.geocities.com/nimbinelf/EngaExperience.html Ⓔ engaexperience@msn.com

---

HELP US UPDATE

If you know of similar community tourism projects or changes to these listings, please email Tourism Concern at info@tourismconcern.org.uk – subject: community tourism.

Tubo Lodge   ACCOM

A community-run ecolodge near Moro in the Southern Highlands, overlooking Lake Kutubu in the Kikori conservation area. Primary rainforest, wetlands, grasslands, wildlife (birds of paradise, lizards, butterflies), walking, swimming, fishing, dugout canoeing. From K12 per night, guided tours K20 per day. Supported by WWF.

■ Norman Ba'abi: PO Box 1628, Boroko, National Capital District

☏ 327 3286; 321 3810; 323 9681   ❶ 327 3416

✉ nba_abi@airniugini.com.pg

■ WWF Papua New Guinea (Kikori ICDP Project): PO Box 8280, Boroko, NCD

☏ 325 03224; 323 09855   ❶ 325 3334

✉ wwfpng@dg.com.pg ✉ bnbn@chevron.com

PERU

International dialing code +51.

Since the demise of the Shining Path, Peru has regained its place as one of the most popular destinations in South America. It's a paradise for hikers and climbers, with some of the most accessible big mountains on earth in the Cordillera Blanca near Huaraz. There is superb hiking too, around Cuzco or in the Colca Canyon near Arequipa – often said to be the world's deepest canyon, although in fact nearby Cotahuasi Canyon is deeper.

Peru's monumental heritage rivals Egypt or Greece. Machu Picchu is but one of many Inca archaeological sites near Cuzco, itself one of the most historic towns in the Americas. But there are impressive pre-Inca ruins throughout the country, from the mysterious Nazca Lines on the south coast to the massive Chimu and Moche pyramids and cities near Trujillo and Chiclayo, or around Chachapoyas and the mighty city-fortress of Kuelap in the northern Andes.

Peru's contemporary culture is rich, too, with festivals, markets and colourful dress. For culture and scenery, the central highlands around Huancayo and Ayacucho are a less-visited alternative to Cuzco.

The coastal desert, cloaked in grey (but rainless) cloud for eight months a year, is less obviously appealing but contains a wealth of ancient sites and a few wildlife destinations such as Paracas. Halfway up the coast, Lima is a sprawling metropolis with shanty towns and leafy middle-class suburbs, a historic centre and at least one unmissable museum (the Museo de la Nacion).

In the southern Amazon, Manu and Tambopata rate among the world's top rainforest parks. Iquitos in the north is the other centre for jungle tours.

Agencies in Cuzco offer guided four-day hikes along the Inca Trail to Machu Picchu for as little as $60. To maintain this low price, however, porters are often underpaid and overloaded, not given return transport from Machu Picchu, etc. When booking the Inca Trail (or other trips in Peru) look for companies that belong to the **Peruvian Ecotourism Association (APTAE)** – they guarantee better wages, employment and environmental standards. Similarly, when visiting Manu National Park, look for members of **Eco-tour Manu**, a group of tour operators whose members guarantee good environmental practices and support for conservation projects.

The **South American Explorer's Club** (www.saexplorers.org) has clubhouses in Lima (Av Rep de Portugal 146, Brena (Casilla 3714), Lima 100; tel: 01 425 0142; limaclub@terra.com.pe) and Cuzco (930 Av del Sol (Aptdo 500), Cuzco; tel: 084 223 102; saec@amauta.rcp.net.pe).

Aracari   TOUR
An upmarket tour agency that works with communities on some trips.

■ Marisol Mosquera: Av Pardo 610 suite 802, Miraflores, Lima

❶ 01 242 6673 ❶ 01 242 4856

Ⓦ www.aracari.com Ⓔ postmaster@aracari.com

Casa Machiguenga/Manu Expeditions   RAINFOREST
Manu, east of Cuzco in the high rainforest of Madre de Dios, is one of the world's finest rainforest parks, with fantastic bird and animal life in pristine forest. **Casa Machiguenga** is a jungle lodge built and owned by an indigenous Machiguenga community, with help from a German NGO. **Manu Expeditions**, run by Englishman Barry Walker (who owns the Cross Keys pub) are the Cuzco agents and also manage another lodge, **Manu Wildlife Center**, which is co-owned by a local community.

■ Manu Expeditions (Expediciones Manu): Avenida Pardo 895, Cuzco

❶ 084 226 671 ❶ 084 236 706

Ⓦ www.manuexpeditions.com Ⓔ manuexpedition@terra.com.pe

■ In the UK: Tribes Travel (see Outbound operators)

Eseturpal/Chancas Expeditions   RAINFOREST
Tour operator **Chancas Expeditions** organizes ten-day jungle camping and canoeing trips in the Pacaya Samiria National Reserve in the northern Peruvian Amazon, led by guides from **Eseturpal**, a cooperative in the village of Lagunas. Excellent bird and wildlife. $1050 per person.

■ Chancas Expeditions: Albert Twiss: Jr Rioja 357, Tarapoto

❶ 094 52 2616

Ⓦ www.geocities.com/amazonrainforest Ⓔ chancas@terra.com.pe

Granja Porcon   AGRI
A farming cooperative (**Cooperativa Agraria Atahualpa-Jerusalen**) near Cajamarca in the northern Andes that offers stays, including a three-day programme. Visitors join in with day-to-day farming tasks, crafts, fiestas, etc, as a way of learning about local life. Other activities include horseriding and walking in the surrounding hills and pine forests. Supported by an NGO called **ADEFOR**. This cooperative is one of the few surviving from the land reforms of the 1960s.

■ Santo Chilón Gonzales: Cooperativa Agraria de Trabajadores Atahualpa-Jerusalén, Jr Chanchamayo 1355, Cajamarca

❶ + ❶ 044 825 631

✉ granjaporcon@hotmail.com

■ ADEFOR: Carretera al aeropuerto km3, Fundo Tartar, Cajamarca

❶ + ❶ 044 821 369; 044 823 097

InkaNatura Travel   RAINFOREST
A non-profit travel company set up by two Peruvian NGOs (Peru Verde and Selva Sur). It has helped the indigenous Machiguenga community of **Timpia** build the **Machiguenga Center for Tropical Studies** – a rainforest lodge in the lower Urubamba Valley, close to the dramatic Pongo de Mainique gorge and a macaw salt lick. Four-day tours from Cuzco, $1295. Plus cultural and nature tours throughout Peru and other lodges co-owned by indigenous communities, including **Manu Wildlife Center** and **Pantiacolla Lodge** in Manu National Park, and **Sandoval Lodge** in Tambopata National Park, all with superb rainforest and wildlife.

■ Manuel Bañon 461, San Isidro, Lima

❶ 014 402 022; 014 228 114 ❶ 014 229 225)

ⓦ www.inkanatura.com ✉ travel@inkanatura.com

■ In Cuzco: Avenida Plateros 361

❶ + ❶ 084 251 173

■ In the US: Kit Herring

❶ +1 352 485 2514; 1-888 287 7186 ❶ +1 352 485 1452

✉ kit@inkanatura.com

Llama Trek, Cordillera Blanca   TOUR
A moderate four-day hike on a pre-Incan route through the beautiful Cordillera Blanca mountains from Olleros to Chavin de Huantar, considered by many to be the centre of early Peruvian culture, with guides from the villages of Olleros and Canrey Chico. Llamas are used to carry packs. The trek includes visits to

local communities, music performances. From $150. Dry season: May to September.

■ Jorge Martel Alvarado, Calle Agustin Loli 463, Plazuela de la Soledad, Huaraz

❶ + ❶ 044 721 266

■ Aracari (see above)

Ollantaytambo Heritage Trails/DRIT   DAY
Walking or horseback trails in the mountains around Ollantaytambo, near Cuzco, visiting nearby villages, craftspeople and archaeological sites. Ollantaytambo is at the start of the Inca Trail, with its own impressive Inca ruins above the village. Guides available. Supported by **DRIT (Dirección Regional de Industria y Turismo)** in Cuzco.

■ Asociación CATCCO, Museo de Sitio, Ollantaytambo

❶ 084 204 024

Ⓦ www.cbc.org.pe/rao

■ DRIT: Avenida de la Cultura 734 (3er piso), Cuzco

❶ 084 223 701 ❶ 084 223 761

Posada Amazonas   RAINFOREST
A jungle lodge in Tambopata National Park in southern Peru co-owned by **Rainforest Expeditions** and the indigenous **Ese'Eja** community. Rainbow Expeditions run four- to eight-day tours. Superb birdwatching and rainforest.

■ Rainforest Expeditions: Av Aramburu 166, Dep 4b, Miraflores, Lima 18

❶ 01 421 8347; 01 221 4182 ❶ 01 421 8183

Ⓦ www.perunature.com Ⓔ rforest@perunature.com

■ *or* Calle Triunfo 350, Cuzco

❶ 084 232 772

Ⓔ cusco@rainforest.com.pe

■ In the US

❶ +1 919 401 5598

Ⓔ MLcorvetto@aol.com

PromPeru (The Commission for the Promotion of Peru)   ORG
A government agency promoting Peruvian tourism, including community tourism.

■ Mitinci (13 piso), 50 Calle 1 Oeste, Urbanización Córpac, San Isidro, Lima 27

❶ 01 224 3271/3118 ❶ 01 224 3323

Ⓦ www.peru.org.pe Ⓔ postmaster@promperu.gob.pe

Taquile   ACCOM+/BUDGET

This island community, towards the Puno end of Lake Titicaca, offers homestays. The location is beautiful and peaceful and this is a fine opportunity to sample rural Andean life. Families host tourists on a rota basis. The neighbouring island, **Amananti**, runs a similar scheme.

■ Mision, Lago Titicaca, Casilla 312, Taquile, Puno

☎ 054 367 771 ✆ 054 351 574

🌐 www.incacorp.com/taquile ✉ taquile@incacorp.com

Willoc   TOUR

An Inca village in the Urubamba Valley near Cusco with homestays and walking in attractive mountain scenery.

■ Silvia Uscamaita Otorola, Personal Travel Service: Portal de Panes 123 oficina 109, Cuzco

☎ + ✆ 084 244 036

🌐 www.cbc.org.pe/rao ✉ ititoss@terra.com.pe

Winaymarka/Anapia   ACCOM+/AGRI

Tours to **Anapia** island on Lake Winaymarka, a part of Lake Titicaca. Tours are organized by **All Ways Travel**, a Puno tour agency, and include homestays, sailing on the lake, beautiful setting, insights into rural Andean life and Aymara culture. All Ways Travel can also organize visits to the lakeside village of **Llachon** on the Capachica peninsula. There are boats from Capachica to Taquile and Amantani (see above).

■ All Ways Travel: Eliana Pauca: Jr Tacna 234, Puno

☎ + ✆ 054 355 552 ✆ 054 367 246

✉ awtperu@terra.com.pe *or* elianapauca@hotmail.com

THE PHILIPPINES

International dialing code +63.

The Philippines consists of over 7000 islands, of which Luzon in the north and Mindanao in the south are the largest. (The capital, Manila, is on Luzon.) The country sees less tourists than other South-East Asian nations and is less traditionally 'Asian' – four centuries of Spanish and American rule have resulted in Asia's only Christian (Catholic) country, with a passion for fast food and basketball. Most Filipinos are Malays but there are indigenous tribal communities in northern Luzon, Palawan and Mindoro.

The country offers ample scope for island-hopping, and has thousands of great beaches, superb diving and snorkelling and some of the most diverse wildlife and birdlife in South-East Asia – especially on Palawan. Two famous attractions are the bizarre Chocolate Hills on Bohol and the vast Ifugao rice terraces near Banaue in northern Luzon.

Filipinos love to party, with lively nightlife and fiestas. January's Ati-Atihan festival, in Kalibo on the island of Panay, is the most spectacular; the Moryonan Easer festival on Marinduque a less commerical alternative.

The island of Mindanao has a separatist movement: check the security situation before visiting. As in Thailand, sex tourism is an issue in the Philippines. On Borocay, long a backpacker favourite, outside business interests have moved in and the benefit of tourism for local people has become questionable.

The Philippines is hot and tropical. The dry season is January to June.

Aeta Jungle Environment Survival Tour   DAY/RAINFOREST/TOUR
During the Vietnam War, the indigenous Aeta taught jungle survival to US soldiers from Subic Bay military base. Now they take tourists into the forest instead. Day or overnight trips. November to April.

■ Subic Tourism Department
❶ 047 252 4809/4032/4193/4242

Biyaheng Pinoy/Initiatives for International Dialogue (IID)   TOUR/TREK
Biyaheng Pinoy is a programme of tours with communities in Samal Island, Mt Apo and Maragusan Valley in Mindanao in the southern Philippines, organized by **Initiatives for International Dialogue**, a Filipino NGO. Tours include a five-day trek to Mt Apo, the highest peak in the country; Mt Kitanglad in Bukidnon; an urban tour in Iligan City visiting self-help projects; and a tour to the 'island garden city' of Samal in Davao Gulf, with beaches, caves, coral. Plus homestays, handicrafts, ecology and conservation.

■ Mimi Arquiza/Mary Ann Arnado: 27d Rosario Townhouse, Galaxy Street, GSIS Heights, Matina, Davao City

☎ 082 299 2574 **✆** 082 299 2052

Ⓦ www.skyinet.net/~iiddvo **Ⓔ** biyaheng-pinoy@skyinet.net *or* iid@skyinet.net

Olongo Birds and Seascape Tour   DAY
Day boat trips to two small islands off Mactan Island in Cebu, which are a marine sanctuary and important stopping point for migratory birds. Tours are run by the **Suba/Olango Ecotourism Cooperative** of local villagers, assisted by the **Coastal Resource Management Project.**

■ Samuel Mabitag/Monette Flores

☎ + **✆** 032 495 7951; 032 233 1228

Ⓦ www.oneocean.org **Ⓔ** mamoninaflores@hotmail.com *or* ecotour@oneocean.org

**Philippines Community Based Sustainable Tourism
Association (PHIL-CBSTA)**   ORG
An association promoting community tourism in the Philippines.

■ c/o ASSET, Room 100-E, Philippine Social Science Center (PSSC) Building, Commonwealth Ave, Diliman, 1101 Quezon City

☎ 02 926 9365; 02 922 9621 **✆** 02 924 4220

Ⓔ asset@pacific.net.ph

Philippines Rural Reconstruction Movement (PRRM)   ORG/TOUR
A Manila-based NGO that runs **Ecodev Tours** to provide sustainable incomes for local communities, from day trips to week-long tours. Trips feature homestays, local culture, visits to community projects, beaches, snorkelling, rainforest, hot springs and volcano hikes. Destinations include Marinduque, Camiguin island in northern Mindanao and El Nido in the north of Palawan, with beautiful limestone sea cliffs and caves. There are also tours to the Ifugao villages and world heritage-listed rice terraces of northern Luzon.

■ Gay Miclat Gatbonton/Lilibeth Coronado: 56 Mother Ignacia St (cnr Dr Lazcano), 1101 Quezon City

☎ 02 372 2152; 02 371 2107 **✆** 02 372 4995

Ⓦ www.csi.com.ph/~ecodevfd

Ⓔ ecodevfd@csi.com.ph *or* gay@csi.com.ph

RUSSIA

International dialing code +7.

Russia's potential as a tourist destination has hardly been tapped. Moscow and St Petersburg are rich in culture, while Siberia has grand scenery and a large indigenous population – particularly around Lake Baikal (the world's deepest freshwater lake) and in the volcanic, rugged far east. Elsewhere, the Caucasus, Europe's highest mountains (higher than the Alps) offer superb, but as yet undeveloped, hiking and climbing possibilities.

Eco-Travels/Ecologia Trust ORG
A Scottish charity arranging student, group, GAP year and independent travel to St Petersburg and Moscow, including homestays. Profits help subsidize a children's home in Russia.

■ In the UK: Liza Hollingshead: 66 The Park, Forres, Morayshire IV36 3TZ, Scotland

ⓣ + **ⓕ** +44 (0)1309 690 995

ⓦ www.rmplc.co.uk/eduweb/sites/ecoliza **ⓔ** ecoliza@rmplc.co.uk

SAMOA

International dialing code +685.

The South Pacific Samoan islands are divided between the US territory of American Samoa and independent Samoa (formerly Western Samoa). This section refers to independent Samoa.

Samoa consists of two hilly and volcanic islands, Savai'i and Upolu, plus some offshore islets. The small capital, Apia, is on Upolu. The country retains a more traditionally Polynesian culture than its American counterpart – one of the most traditional in the South Pacific – with an intricate village-based social system.

The islands' have coral reefs, diving and snorkelling, beaches and areas of rainforest. Although the usual catalogue of environmental worries applies – overfishing, deforestation and damage to coral – much of the country is wild and undeveloped and tourism is smaller scale and less resort-based than, for instance, on Fiji. Samoans are exceptionally friendly and visitors are often invited to stay in villages.

HELP US UPDATE

If you know of similar community tourism projects or changes to these listings, please email Tourism Concern at info@tourismconcern.org.uk – subject: community tourism.

EcoTour Samoa   TOUR
Seven-day cultural ecotours visiting five islands and including village stays and local culture.

▣ Funealii Lumaava Sooaemalelagi/Dr Steve Brown: PO Box 4609, Matautu-uta

❶ + ❶ 22144; 25993

Ⓦ www.ecotoursamoa.com Ⓔ tours@ecotoursamoa.com

Samoan Customized Tours   ACCOM+/TOUR
Homestays and cultural tours on Manono Island.

▣ PO Box 4228, Apia

❶ 24204 ❶ 26905

Samoa Visitors Bureau   ORG
Can arrange overnight stays to rural villages. Their website lists various ecotour operators.

▣ Beach Road (PO Box 2272), Apia

❶ 63500; 20878 ❶ 20886

Ⓦ www.visitsamoa.ws Ⓔ samoa@samoa.ws *or* info@samoa.ws

Vaotuua Beach Resort   ACCOM+
Traditional village-based resort in Faleu village on Manono Island, with accommodation in thatched *fales* over the sea. $20 per night. For other village-based fales, contact the Samoa Visitors Bureau (above).

❶ 46077; 22144

Ⓔ vaotuua@ecotoursamoa.com

SENEGAL

International dialing code +221.

Senegal is a Muslim, French-speaking West African country that surrounds The Gambia. The northern half of the country, above The Gambia, is predominantly Wolof. The capital, Dakar, is here, and inland the holy city of Touba is one of the great religious centres of West Africa.

The southern part of Senegal, south of The Gambia, is the Casamance. The village *campements* are all in this region, which is closer to Banjul in The Gambia than to Dakar. The lush and tropical Casamance is unlike dry northern Senegal and consists of a blend of forests, rivers and rice fields. Inland, the Niokolo Koa National Park is one of West Africa's best national parks.

The people of the Casamance are largely non-Muslim Jola. Since 1990 there has been a separatist struggle in the region and the number of visitors has fallen greatly. It is usually safe to travel but check the current situation.

Senegal is renowned for its music and has produced such international stars as Youssou N'dour and Baaba Maal.

Campement Villageois   ACCOM+
Community-run village guesthouses in the Lower Casamance in southern Senegal. There are *campements* at **Baila**, **Koubalan**, **Enampore**, **Affiniam**, **Kafountine**, **Dioher**, **Thionck-Essyl**, **Oussouye**, **Elinkine** and **Abené**, all within reach of Ziguinchor, the regional capital. Attractions include village tours and rural life, hiking, birdwatching, canoeing trips and crafts. Most villages are inland on rivers, although Kafountine and Abené are on the coast with good beaches. Profits fund health clinics, schools or other community projects. The scheme has also inspired a number (43 at the last count) of private *campements*. Adama Goudiaby, the scheme's director, has a private guesthouse in Ziguinchor (**Aw Bay**, tel: 0936 8076) with information on other *campements*, or see *The Rough Guide to West Africa*.

■ Adama Goudiaby: Centre Artisanal, BP567 Ziguinchor, Casamance, Senegal

❶ 0991 1980; 0991 3514 ❶ 0991 2804

Crossing Cultures Programme   TOUR/VOL
Arranges village stays in Senegal with study courses in arts and traditional culture on request (dance, medicine, etc). Volunteering opportunities.

■ In the US: Janet L Ghattas: Intercultural Dimensions Inc, PO Box 391437, Cambridge, MA 02139-0015

❶ +1 617 864 8442 ❶ +1 617 868 1273

🅴 janetid@aol.com

Karamba Ltd   TOUR
Music and dance holidays based in the village of Abéné in southern Senegal. Djembe, sabar, talking drum and kora workshops with local musicians. For all levels from complete beginner to experienced. As well as music, there is a good beach, canoeing, birdlife, excursions to markets and the chance to see rural West African life. A 14-day tour costs £785, excluding flights.

■ In the UK: Gary Newland: Ollands Lodge, Heydon, Norwich, Norfolk NR11 6RB

❶ + ❶ +44 (0)1603 872402

🆆 www.karamba.co.uk 🅴 karamba@gn.apc.org

SOLOMON ISLANDS

International dialing code +677.

The Solomon Islands, in the South Pacific, offer superb and uncrowded diving and snorkelling, with stunning reefs and World War II wreckages in abundance. Above water, there is magnificent tropical forest, rich birdlife and white-sand beaches.

Facilities are usually basic but the friendly welcome, fascinating local customs and the beauty of the lagoons, hills and rainforests are worth a little discomfort. Travel is by boat, canoes and small planes – only the islands of Malaita and Guadalcanal have rough roads.

Most islanders live by fishing and farming. There has been some logging, although this has now slowed and there is still superb primary forest. The country used to be the epitome of peacefulness, but the island of Guadalcanal (which includes the capital, Honiara) was recently unsafe due to an inter-island dispute – check the current situation. The main tourist region of Western Province is unaffected.

The **Solomon Islands Visitors Bureau** (PO Box 321, Honiara; tel: 022 442; fax: 023 986; www.spto.org; visitors@welkam.solomon.com.sb) has details of village stays and community-run lodges, including those listed below. The **Solomon Islands Development Trust** (Silverio Wale/Francis Tarihao; tel: 21131) also helps to develop community tourism.

Makira Hilltribes Tour   TOUR
An adventurous seven-day trek into the Makira highlands through beautiful rainforest and traditional highland villages. Excellent birdlife.

■ In the US: Conservation International (see Outbound operators)

■ In Australia: Oxfam Community Aid Abroad Tours (see Outbound operators) or Ecotour Travel (see Australia, above)

Solomons Village Stay   ACCOM+
An agency that organizes stays with local families, mostly in coastal villages. Fishing, bushwalking, canoeing, snorkelling (bring your own gear), swimming, climbing and caving. Contact the **Visitors Bureau** (above) for details.

Vanua Rapita Lodge   ACCOM+
A community-owned lodge in beautiful Marovo Lagoon. Excellent snorkelling and diving (with a dive lodge nearby), plus guided rainforest walks, river trips, fishing and village tours. Supported by WWF. British Airways Tourism for Tomorrow Awards, highly commended 1998.

■ Vanua Rapita Lodge, Seghe Postal Agency, Marovo Lagoon

✆ 60191 ✆ 60294

SOUTH AFRICA

International dialing code +27.

The 'rainbow nation' is huge and diverse, with eleven official languages. A fine climate, a fascinating mix of cultures, superb wildlife parks, wild coastline, lovely scenery and beaches combine with the continent's best travel infrastructure to make it one of Africa's fastest-growing tourist destinations.

Cape Town is the most attractive city for tourists, with good nightlife and a spectacular setting. Near Cape Town, there is whale watching, plus popular touring around the Paarl and Stellenbosch vineyards and the scenic Garden Route. Further north, towards Namibia, there are austere rust-red deserts and the Kalahari-Gemsbok National Park. In the north-east, Kruger is one of the continent's premier safari parks, although others, such as Kwazulu-Natal's Hluhluwe-Umfolozi, offer excellent wildlife viewing. Kwazulu Natal also contains the beautiful Drakensberg mountains, with superb scenery and hiking.

Despite the end of apartheid, South African tourism remains predominantly white-run. Black-owned businesses lack capital, experience and contacts and find it hard to break into the mainstream. But black tourism businesses are emerging, from township tours to 'cultural villages' and rural village homestays. In the townships, most are run by individuals: only in rural areas is there community-owned tourism as defined elsewhere in this book.

There are township tours and guesthouses in Cape Town, Port Elizabeth, Johannesburg (Soweto) and elsewhere – ask local tourist offices for details. You can visit a shebeen (a cross between a nightclub and a houseparty) and hear South Africa's vibrant music, from township jazz to mbanqanga.

Is South Africa dangerous? Most rural areas are safe but it's best not to visit townships without guides, and to be careful in cities at night.

Cultural Tourism in South Africa, by Sue Derwent (Struik Publishers, PO Box 1144, Cape Town, 1999) is a useful guide to community/black tourism in South Africa.

Amadiba Adventures   TOUR/TREK
Four- or six-day horse trails and hikes, staying in Pondo villages along the Wild Coast south of Durban, one of South Africa's most beautiful and unspoilt stretches of coastline. Superb beaches, waterfalls, forest and archaeological sites. Six-day horse trail, R1350. The project is owned by the local Pondo community and supported by a local NGO, **PondoCROP**.

■ PO Box 588, Port Edward 4295, Transkei

☏ 039 305 6455/7 ☏ 039 305 6456

ⓔ cropeddy@iafrica.com *or* amadiba@euwildcoast.za.org

Calabash Lodge and Tours   ACCOM/DAY
A guesthouse in Port Elizabeth offering day trips and three- to five-day tours
including townships, community projects, homestays and cultural villages.

■ 8 Dollery Street, Central, Port Elizabeth, 6001

☎ 041 585 6162 ❶ 041 585 0985

Ⓦ www.axxess.web.za/calabash/ ❺ calabash@iafrica.com

Cape Town
For tours of Cape Town townships, try **Bonani 'Our Pride' Tours** (tel: 021 531
4291; ourpride@mweb.co.za), **One City Tours** (tel: 021 387 5351) or **Tsoga
Tours** (tel: 021 694 9106; nosipdil@iafrica.com). If you want to stay in a
township, try **Kopanong B&B** (C329 Velani Crescent; tel: 021 361 2084;
kopanong@xsinet.co.za), **Vicky's B&B** (tel: 021 387 7104;
vickysbandb@yahoo.com) or **Majoro's B&B** (69 Helena Crescent, Graceland; tel:
021 361 3412), all in Khayelitsha. **Lelapa Restaurant** (49 Harem Avenue; tel:
021 694 2681) in Langa is a good place to try township food. Former inmates
guide day tours to **Robben Island** (tel: 021 409 5169; www.robben-island.org.za),
where political prisoners such as Nelson Mandela were imprisoned.

■ All of the above can be booked through **Township Music Tours** (tel: 021 919 9168;
muse-art@iafrica.com) or **Cape Town Tourism** (tel: 021 426 4260;
info@cape-town.org).

■ In the UK: Rainbow Tours (see below)

CCAfrica (*formerly* **Conservation Corporation Africa**)   LUXURY/SAFARI
An upmarket safari operator that owns **Tau Lodge** in Madikwe (see below),
Phinda Private Game Reserve, Londolozi and **Ngala Private Game Reserves** in
Kruger, plus **Kichwa Tembo** and **Bateleur Camp** in southern Kenya and
Mnemba Island (in Zanzibar), **Ngorongoro Crater Lodge, Grumeti River
Camp, Maji Moto Tented Camp** and **Klein's Camp** in Tanzania. The company
has supported local communities and set up the Africa Foundation, which has
given more than $1 million to villages near its lodges.

■ CCAfrica: Private Bag X27, Benmore 2010

☎ 011 775 0000 ❶ 011 784 7667

Ⓦ www.ccafrica.com ❺ information@ccafrica *or* reservations@conscorp.ca.za

■ In the UK: Discovery Initiatives (see Outbound operators) are agents for Phinda
Reserve

Dreamcatcher   TOUR
A tour operator that designs customized itineraries incorporating community
tourism projects, township tours, ecotourism and black-run tourism businesses.

■ 6 Hartford Grange, Bokmakierie Av, Sonstraal, Durbanville, 7550, Cape Town

❶ + ❶ 021 976 9372

Ⓦ www.dreamcatcher.co.za Ⓔ info@dreamcatcher.co.za

■ In the UK: Rainbow Tours (see below)

Fair Trade in Tourism South Africa (FTTSA) ORG
A non-profit organization that works with the IUCN (World Conservation
Union) to help disadvantaged communities develop tourism projects in South
Africa. At present, they work with One City Tours in Cape Town, Amadiba
Adventures, Ribolla Tourism Association and Ukhahlamba Tourism Association
(all listed in this section).

■ Carine Munting: Kutlwanong Democracy Centre, 357 Visagie Street (PO Box 11536, Hatfield), Pretoria 0028

❶ 012 322 2106 ❶ 012 320 2414

Ⓦ www.fairtourismsa.org.za Ⓔ info@fairtourismsa.org.za

Fundani DAY
Township tours in Port Elizabeth, including observing weddings, ancestral
rituals and funeral ceremonies, retracing Nelson Mandela's early life, night
tours to shebeens and nightclubs.

■ Xanti Singapi: PO Box 21715, Port Elizabeth

❶ 041 454 8194/5 ❶ 041 454 3312

Ⓔ cultours@iafrica.com *or* fundani@ecol.co.za

Knysna Township Trail/Khulani Xhosa Village DAY
Guided half-day walks through a Xhosa township on the 'Garden Route' in
the Western Cape, visiting traditional healers, schools, dancing. Income goes to
community projects. In nearby George, Khulani Xhosa Village offers Xhosa
singing, dancing, beadwork and crafts.

■ Knysna Township Trail: PO Box 897, Knysna 6570

❶ 083 269 8501 ❶ 0445 2 2609

■ Khulani Xhosa Village: Steam Museum, George

❶ + ❶ 044 880 2250

Ⓔ colline@xsinet.co.za

Madikwe Game Reserve SAFARI
A wildlife reserve in North-West province on the Botswana border.
Accommodation is at **Madikwe River Lodge** (tel: 014 778 0891; www.three-
cities.co.za; lodge@madikwe.threecities.co.za) or **Tau Lodge** (tel: 014 067 2030;
www.ccafrica.com). Local communities participate in the park management
and receive a share of park fees.

📞 014 665 5960/3 📠 014 665 5964

🌐 www.parks-nw.co.za/madikwe

⬛ In the UK: Tribes Travel (see Outbound operators)

Nqutu Zulu Cultural Tours   DAY
Battlefield and cultural tours and home visits in Zulu and Basotho villages. From R100 per day.

⬛ Bethuel/Dudu Manyathi: PO Box 288, Nqutu 3135, Kwazulu Natal

📞 + 📠 034 271 9710; 088 130 0573

Rainbow Tours   TOUR
A UK-based tour operator that works with many of the community-based lodges, hotels and businesses in this section and can build township tours and community tourism projects into a customized South African itinerary. ATOL bonded. Brochure available.

⬛ In the UK: Roger Diski: Canon Collins House, 64 Essex Rd, London N1 8LR

📞 +44 (0)20 7226 1004 📠 +44 (0)20 7226 2621

🌐 www.rainbowtours.co.uk 📧 info@rainbowtours.co.uk

Ribolla Tourism Association/Shiluvari Lodge/Kuvona Tours   ACCOM/DAY
Shiluvari Lodge is a country lodge with thatched chalets in the Soutpansberg district of the Northern Province. From R180 per night. **Kuvona Tours** offers guided tours (bookable at the lodge) to local Shangaan and Venda villages to see craftpeople working and to learn about local communities. Plus local crafts projects.

■ Ribolla Tourism Association: PO Box 155, Elim Hospital 0960 *or* via Shiluvari Lodge.

■ Shiluvari Lodge: PO Box 560, Louis Trichardt 0920, Northern Province

❶ 015 556 3406   ❶ 015 556 3413

❷ shiluvar@lantic.net

Sibaya Lake Lodge   ACCOM/SAFARI
A community-owned lodge in Maputaland, Kwazulu Natal. Canoeing, snorkelling, dhow trips, fishing, bushwalks, birds, turtles, wildlife and Indian Ocean beaches at Kosi Bay. R845 per night.

■ PO Box 19233, Fishershill 1408, Johannesburg

❶ 011 616 9950   ❶ 011 616 8232

Ⓦ www.lake-sibaya.co.za   ❷ sibayi@iafrica.com

■ In the UK: Rainbow Tours (see below)

Ukhahlamba Tourism Association (UTA)   ACCOM+
A group developing community tourism in the foothills of the dramatic Drakensberg mountains, with Sotho, Xhosa, Griqua and white communities. Fishing, camping, village stays, hiking, birdwatching, rock art and local culture. The association is helped by a local NGO called **Environmental and Development Agency (EDA)**.

■ UTA: Fezeka Mfihlo: PO Box 1354, Matatiele 4730

❶ + ❶ 039 737 4176

❷ uta@icon.co.za

■ EDA: Nicky/Zandile: PO Box 1354, Matatiele 4730

❶ 039 737 3591   ❶ 039 737 3409

❷ zoleka@edamatat.org.za

Vulindlela Community Tours and Guesthouse   ACCOM/DAY/TOUR
A guesthouse plus day trips and overnight cultural tours to townships and Zulu villages near Ramsgate, on the coast south of Durban.

■ 75 Marine Drive, Ramsgate (PO Box 781, Margate 4275)

❶ 039 317 1328/4473   ❶ 039 317 1328/4498

❷ afritours@telkomsa.net *or* spiwe@sn.apc.org

Wilderness Safaris (Ndumo Wilderness Camp/Rocktail Bay Lodge) LUXURY/SAFARI
A commercial operator that encourages community partnerships. Their South African lodges are co-owned by local communities, including **Ndumo Wilderness Camp** in Maputaland, northern KwaZulu Natal (over 400 bird species plus good wildlife) and remote **Rocktail Bay Lodge** on a stretch of wild Maputaland coast (with deserted beaches, good birdwatching, forest wildlife, snorkelling and diving). Also **Damaraland Camp** in Namibia (see above).

■ PO Box 78573, Sandton, 2146

❶ 011 883 0747 ❶ 011 883 0911

Ⓦ www.wilderness-safaris.com Ⓔ info@sdn.wilderness.co.za

■ In the UK: Rainbow Tours (see above)

SRI LANKA

International dialing code +94.

The Garden of Eden, the Land of Serendipity, colonial Ceylon, war zone – you could be forgiven for being confused about Sri Lanka. The civil war mainly affects the north. The rest of the country is usually peaceful, although you should check the situation before travelling. The pace is less hectic than neighbouring India, with fine beaches – especially on the south and west coasts – and, inland, the cool hills of Uva province, with forest and tea plantations. Running through this province, the Colombo–Kandy–Badulla 'tea railway' is a scenic highland route. Although there are Hindus, Muslims and Christian communities, Sri Lanka is predominantly a Buddhist country. The Temple of the Sacred Tooth (one of the Buddha's) in Kandy is its foremost religious monument.

Federation of Entrepreneurs in Sustainable Tourism of Uva (FESTU)/Woodlands Network ACCOM+/AGRI/ORG/TOUR
ToDo! Award winner
FESTU promotes community-based guesthouses and tours in Uva province in central Sri Lanka. It can arrange guided tours, guesthouses and homestays in rural villages and tea plantations. Activities include walking, tea plantations, ancient monuments, birdwatching, organic farming, handicrafts and learning about Ayurvedic medicine or Buddhism. FESTU projects include: **Forests for People, Tanamalvila; Forest Park Country Home** (tel: 072 666 608), an old hunting lodge in Keppetipola, between Nuwara-Eliya and Bandarawela; **Green Field Bio Plantation, Haputale** (tel/fax: 057 68102), a tea plantation on the Colombo-Kandy-Badulla 'tea railway' line; **Uva Herbarium** (tel: 057 45033) and **Jungle Exploration Home** (tel: 072 658 823). FESTU was set up by

Woodlands Network, a local women's organization, which also has its own farm with visitor accommodation.

◼ Sarojinie Ellawela: 38/1c Esplanade Road, Bandarawela

☏ 057 32328; 057 32668 ☏ 057 32328

ⓦ www.uvanetwork.lk ⓔ haas@sltnet.lk

◼ In the UK: Travel Friends International (see Outbound operators)

Karuna Sevana (Haven of Kindness)   ACCOM

Accommodation near Colombo (3km from the airport) in a community project that also provides vocational training for homeless boys.

◼ Centre for Society and Religion Farm, Andiambalama, Colombo

☏ 01 074 831 195 ☏ 01 682 064

ⓔ csrlibra@slt.lk

SWAZILAND

International dialing code +268.

Like many other southern African nations, the main focus of tourism in tiny Swaziland is wildlife in national parks such as Mkhaya. Most of the country, however, is agricultural land: the project below also allows you to experience rural Swazi life.

Woza Nawe Tours/Liphupho Lami   ACCOM+/TOUR

Liphupho Lami homestead provides accommodation on a community-owned farm in Kaphunga, a village 65km south of Manzini. **Woza Nawe Tours** offers walking and cycling in the hills around Kaphunga plus tours around Swaziland that feature visits to markets, schools and community projects.

◼ Mxolisi Mdluli: PO Box 2455, Manzini M100

☏ 50 58363

ⓦ www.earthfoot.org ⓔ mzn136@postcafe.co.sz *or* wozanawe@realnet.co.sz

HELP US UPDATE

If you know of similar community tourism projects or changes to these listings, please email Tourism Concern at info@tourismconcern.org.uk – subject: community tourism.

TANZANIA

International dialing code +255.

Like Kenya, Tanzania has magnificent wildlife, Indian Ocean beaches, Rift Valley lakes, tribal cultures and Swahili towns. The Swahili island of Zanzibar has long been a favourite among backpackers for its enticing blend of beaches and Swahili culture and is now on the verge of mass tourist development.

On the mainland, Tanzania's wildlife is, if anything, superior to Kenya. Most tourists stick to the 'Northern Safari Circuit'. This includes Ngorogoro Crater – a 16km-wide volcanic crater packed with wildlife (and tourists) – the Serengeti National Park and Mt Kilimanjaro, Africa's highest peak.

However, there is good wildlife viewing, national parks and scenery throughout the country, as well as many interesting local cultures and the opportunity to see rural East African life away from the tourist regions.

Chole Mjini   ACCOM+/LUXURY
An upmarket ecolodge on a small island off the island of Mafia, south of Zanzibar. Great diving (PADI courses) and snorkelling, birdwatching, fishing, dhow trips, Swahili life, Swahili/Persian ruins. From $125 per night, including a payment to local community funds.

■ PO Box 20, Mafia Island

❶ + ❻ (in the UK) +44 (0)1737 241 892

❷ 2chole@bushmail.com

Dorobo Tours and Safaris   SAFARI+

A tour operator with a good record of working with local communities. Camping, wildlife viewing and walking trips with local Dorobo, Maasai, Hadza and Datoga people. Destinations include the wildlife-rich Soitorgoss area on the eastern Serengeti. Tailor-made itineraries available. $180–$300 per day.

■ David, Thad or Mike Peterson: PO Box 2534, Arusha

❶ 027 250 9685 ❻ 027 250 8336

❷ dorobo@yako.habari.co.tz

IntoAfrica   SAFARI/TOUR

Wildlife safaris, mountain climbing (Kilimanjaro, Meru and Crater Highlands) and adventure treks in northern Tanzania, with visits to Maasai and Chagga communities offering insights into local life and culture. A share of visitor fees are paid to community funds, plus donations to local health and education projects. Prices from £700 for a seven-day trip.

■ In Kenya: IntoAfrica Eco-Travel: PO Box 50484, Nairobi

■ In the UK: Chris Morris: 59 Langdon Street, Sheffield S11 8BH

❶ +44 (0)114 255 5610

Ⓦ www.intoafrica.co.uk ❷ enquiry@intoafrica.co.uk

Kilimanjaro Environmental Facility   TOUR

A local NGO running trips that combine wildlife and nature with visits to local villages and development and conservation projects around Mt Kilimanjaro. Farming, forest, walks, traditional medicine, crafts. Also trips to Zanzibar and the coast. From $150 per day; 12-day Mt Kilimanjaro climb, $2015. Income goes to village development projects.

■ Joseph Swai: PO Box 6928, Moshi

❶ 0744 298 429 ❻ 027 275 3638

Ⓦ www.kef.or.tz ❷ KEF_TZ@excite.com or ibc@eoltz.com

Multi Environmental Society (MESO)   TOUR

An NGO working with local communities to offer tours in northern Tanzania exploring local culture, wildlife and natural attractions (including Ngorongoro Crater, Serengeti, Lake Manyara and Tarangire). Tours, from a half-day to five days, start from Arusha or Karatu, 150km west of Arusha, and combine wildlife and Rift Valley scenery with homestays, visits to communities, markets, agriculture, rock art, caves. $40 per day.

■ Petro Ahham: next to Karatu Stores, Karatu or 1st floor, Ahmed Ghalib building, 14 Block H, Azimio Road, Bodeni Street (opposite Ijumaa mosque) (PO Box 8224), Arusha

❶ 027 254 8821; 07444 67472

📧 mesotz@hotmail.com

Safari Njema SAFARI+
A small UK operator running trips to Tanzania and Zanzibar combining wildlife (Ngorongoro, Serengeti) with an insight into local life, including visits to community-based projects.

■ Simon McGowan

❶ 0115 929 8785; 07733 021769

🌐 www.safarinjema.com 📧 simon@safarinjema.com

Simply Tanzania Tour Company SAFARI/TOUR
Tailor-made 4WD tours run by an ex-VSO field director for Tanzania. Tours combine wildlife with off-the-beaten-track destinations, communities and development projects. Specialists in the 'southern circuit' including Selous/Ruaha National Park and Mtwara, plus walking in the Iringa/Mbeya mountain and Sisi Kwa Sisi (see below). From £950 for a two-week tour, excluding international flights; shorter trips available.

■ In the UK: Tony Janes: 54 Cotesbach Road, Clapton, London E5 9QJ

❶ + ❶ +44 (0)20 8986 0615

🌐 www.simplytanzania.co.uk 📧 enquiries@simplytanzania.co.uk

Sisi Kwa Sisi BUDGET/ORG/TOUR
Community-based guesthouse, homestays and tours in Mbeya, near the border with Zambia and Malawi. Attractions include mountains, bush, forest hikes, Rift Valley scenery, hot springs, traditional healers and local life.

■ Nicholas Amandus Ntinda: near bus station next to Japan-Tanzania Monument (PO Box 2869), Mbeye

📧 sisikwasisi@hotmail.com

Tanzania Association of Cultural Tourism Organizers (TACTO) BUDGET/ORG/TOUR
Formerly known as **The Cultural Tourism Programme**, **TACTO** offers village-based tours, homestays and guesthouses, mainly in northern Tanzania. Member projects offer walking safaris, hiking (forest and hills), learning about local Maasai culture, traditional healers, storytelling, visiting village projects and farms, birdwatching, caves, waterfalls, fishing, ruins and (at Mkuru) camel safaris. Income goes to schools, irrigation canals, cattle dips, etc. Communities with projects include the **Usambara Mountains** (secap@tanga.net), the

Northern and Southern Pare Mountains (tel: 027 58176), **Kisangara** (tel: 027 275 7822), **Longido** (tel: 027 539 201), **Machame** (tel: 027 275 7033; fax: 027 275 1113), **Monduli Juu** (tel: 0741 510 170; ctpmonjuu@yahoo.co.uk), **Ng'iresi** (tel: 07411 337 889), **Mto wa Mbu, Engaruka, Mamba** and **Marangu, Mkuru, Ilkiding'a** (enmasarie@yahoo.com), **Mto wa Mbu, Babati/Hanang** (Joas Kahembe: tel: 027 253 1088; lsobabati@habari.co.tz) and **Mulala** (tel: 0744 372 566). On the coast, **Gezaolole** and **Pangani** have good beaches, snorkelling and Swahili/Ujamaa culture. **Sisi Kwa Sisi** (see above) is also part of the scheme. Helped by Dutch development agency SNV.

■ Thomas Ole Sikar: AICC, Ngorongoro Wing, Room 430 (PO Box 10455), Arusha

❶ + ❶ 027 253 9209

Ⓦ www.tourismtanzania.org Ⓔ info@tourismtanzania.org

■ Tanzania Tourist Information Centres: Boma Road, Arusha (tel: 027 250 3842/3) *or* Samora Avenue, Dar es Salaam (tel: 022 120 373).

■ In the UK: Simply Tanzania (see Outbound operators)

Trade Aid Mikindani   ACCOM

A project to encourage community-run tourism in the town of Mikindani on the southern coast. A colonial German fort has been restored and turned into a hotel.

■ Trade Aid Mikindani: PO Box 993 Mtwara

❶ 023 2333 875

Ⓔ tradeaid@raha.com

■ In the UK: Trade Aid UK: Burgate Court, Burgate, Fordingbridge, Hampshire SP6 1LX

❶ +44 (0)1425 657 774

Ⓔ tradeaid@netcomuk.co.uk

Zanzibar Travel   TOUR

A UK-based tour operator that uses locally-owned hotels and operators and can arrange village tours, meals with families, etc.

■ In the UK: Michael Sweeney: Reynards House, Selkirk Gardens, Cheltenham, Gloucestershire GL52 5LY

❶ + ❶ +44 (0)1242 222 027

Ⓦ www.zanzibartravel.co.uk Ⓔ info@zanzibartravel.co.uk

HELP US UPDATE

If you know of similar community tourism projects or changes to these listings, please email Tourism Concern at info@tourismconcern.org.uk – subject: community tourism.

Zanzibar Travel

Tailor-made holidays to this exotic tropical island

Our knowledge of Zanzibar means we can arrange a holiday on this intriguing unspoilt island to meet your interests and requirements... ...and we promote tourism which benefits and respects the people of Zanzibar

Contact Michael Sweeney at Zanzibar Travel
Tel/fax: 01242 222027
www.zanzibartravel.co.uk   sweeney@zanzibartravel.co.uk
Reynards House, Selkirk Gardens, Cheltenham, Gloucestershire GL52 5LY

Travel Trust
Association
No T6869

THAILAND

International dialing code +66.

Thailand is one of the most popular destinations in Asia for British tourists, attracted by a superb cuisine, a rich culture, Buddhist temples, royal palaces and a friendly and proud people. There are hilltribes and forested mountains in the north, and tropical beaches and islands in the south. Thailand also offers fascinating cultural opportunities, from silent meditation retreats in Buddhist monasteries to courses in Thai cookery, massage or even boxing.

The Thais, the only South-East Asian nation never to have been colonized, are an independent people with a resilient cultural identity. Tourism has brought money into the Thai economy without destroying Thai culture, and there are many locally-run guesthouses and tour agencies. On the other hand, it's estimated that 60 per cent of tourist spending in Thailand leaves the country. Poorly-regulated tourism development in places such as Phuket, Ko Phi Phi, Ko Samui and Pattaya has created environmental problems, and the country has a flourishing sex (and child-sex) tourism industry – in the UK, ECPAT (see Resources directory) campaigns to end sex tourism.

Tourists visiting hilltribes should ask if their guide is doing anything to ensure that the villagers benefit from tourism. Village hosts are often paid as little as 20 baht per visitor, less than the true cost of providing food and lodging, yet traditional hospitality makes it hard for them to refuse to take in visitors. Is the number of trekking agencies in an area low enough to minimize disruption to villages? And bear in mind that village boys assigned to smoke opium with tourists often end up as addicts.

Remember, too, that a number of foreigners are serving lengthy sentences in Thai prisons for drug possession.

In north-west Thailand, Padaung women, refugees from Burma, wear neck rings that stretch their necks. Although they earn an income from tourism, the rings also cause health problems and the practice might have died but for tourism. We suggest you don't visit Padaung 'attractions'.

Jorkoe EcoTrek   TOUR

A trekking agency set up by the **Project for Recovery of Life and Culture (PRLC)**, an NGO in Mae Hong Son. Tours visit the hilltribe villages of **Baan Huay Hee, Baan Huay Tong Kaw** and **Baan Huay Kung** in a rugged and scenic part of northern Thailand. Homestays, hiking in forested hills, local life and culture, rafting, elephant rides, birdwatching. Income stays in the villages or goes to PRLC's development and conservation work. From $27 per day.

■ 51 Khunlumprapas Rd, Tambon Jongkham, Amphur Muang, Mae Hong Son 5800

❶ + ❶ 53 620 511

❷ jorkoe_ecotrek@yahoo.com

■ Also marketed by REST (see below)

Khao Nor Chuchi Lowland Forest Project   ACCOM/DAY

A rural development and reforestaton project 60km south of Krabi in southern Thailand. Bungalows and day tours including walking trails, swimming in forest pools, rubber-tapping, hot springs. Bungalows from 150 baht per night; tours 690 baht.

■ Chan Phen Tour travel agency: 145 Uttarakit Road, Krabi 81000

❶ 75 612004 ❶ 75 612661

❷ chanphentour@yahoo.com or chan_phen@hotmail.com

Lisu Lodge   ACCOM+

A small lodge in a Lisu village near Chang Mai that works with the local community. Rafting, biking, elephant rides, guided walks through villages, plus one- to four-day treks.

■ East West Siam: Building One, 11th Floor, 99 Wireless Road, Pathumwan, Bangkok 10330

❶ 02 256 6153/5, 6666/8 ❶ 02 256 7166/6665

Ⓦ www.lisulodge.com

❷ eastwest@east-west.com

Natural Focus Ecotours   TOUR/VOL

A tour agency set up by the **Hill Area and Community Development Foundation (HADF)**, with profits supporting HADF's work. Tours from 1 to 15 days visiting hilltribe villages near Chiang Rai. Hiking in the forest, learning about forest plants, cookery courses and crafts workshops (weaving, embroidery, metal smithing, etc). Also volunteer workstays in villages. From £22 per day.

■ Jahae Leeja: 129/1 Moo 4 Pa-Ngiw Rd, Soi 4, Tambon Robwiang, Amphur Muang, Chiang Rai 57000

Responsible Ecological Social Tours Project (REST)

109/79 Mooban Yucharoen Pattana, Ladprao Soi 18,
Ladyao, Chatuchak, Bangkok 10900, Thailand
Tel: +66-2-938 7007, Fax: +66-2-938 5275,
E-mail: rest@asiaaccess.net.th   http://www.ecotour.in.th

For community based tours and homestays in rural villages

☏ + **☏** 053 715 696; 053 758 658

ⓦ www.hadf.org **ⓔ** naturalfocus@hadf.org

PDA Tours & Travel   CENTRE/TOUR
The trekking company of the non-profit **PDA (Population and Community Development Association)** in Chiang Rai. Profits from treks go to hilltribe development projects. The trekking agency is above the **Hilltribe Education Centre**, a hilltribe culture museum and crafts shop.

▮ Hilltribe Museum and Education Centre: 3rd Floor, PDA Building (next to Cabbages and Condoms restaurant), 620/1 Thanon Thanalai, Chiang Rai

☏ + **☏** 053 740 088; 053 719 167

ⓦ http://homepages.msn.com/NonProfitBlvd/crpda/index.html

ⓔ crpda@hotmail.com

REST (Responsible Ecological Social Tours Project)   ORG/TOUR
A Bangkok-based community development NGO offering tours and homestays in rural villages. Opportunities to learn about farming, cookery, puppetry, trekking etc. REST also provides training in managing tourism for local communities and NGOs.

▮ 109/79 Moo Baan Yucharoeng, Patana, Lad Phrao Road, Soi 18, Chatuchak, Bangkok 10900

☏ 02 938 5275/7007 **☏** 02 938 5275

ⓦ www.ecotour.in.th **ⓔ** rest@asiaaccess.net.th

(John Gray's) SeaCanoe   DAY/TOUR
Guided sea-canoe trips in Phuket and southern Thailand, including hidden lagoons in the dramatic karst islands of Phang-Nga Bay, with an emphasis on environmental interpretation. Founded and managed by John 'Caveman' Gray, an American environmentalist, the company draws its staff from local fishing

villages, with outstanding employment practices. Also trips in Vietnam (HaLong Bay), Fiji and Hawaii.

☎ 076 254 505/6 ● 076 226 077

ⓦ www.johngray-seacanoe.com ⓔ info@johngray-seacanoe.com

Symbiosis   TOUR
A UK tour operator that runs a Thailand trip with a local Thai NGO featuring visits to herbal doctors in Mae Chaem province, plus homestays and visits to hilltribe villages in Mae Salong.

◼ In the UK: 113 Bolingbroke Grove, London SW11 1DA

☎ +44 (0)20 7924 5906 ● +44 (0)20 7924 5907

ⓦ www.symbiosis-travel.com ⓔ info@symbiosis-travel.com

Thai Tribal Crafts/Hilltribe Products Promotion Centre   CENTRE
Two non-profit outlets for hilltribe crafts in Chiang Mai are **Thai Tribal Crafts** (208 Thanon Bamrungrat, near McCormick Hospital; tel: 053 241 043) and the **Hilltribe Products Promotion Centre** (21/17 Thanon Suthep, near Wat Suan Dawk; tel: 053 277 743). Both have a good selection and good quality and more of your money goes to the craftspeople and/or hilltribe welfare projects.

Yad Fon   TOUR
A local development agency in the southern province of Trang that can organize study tours to rural and fishing villages.

◼ Mr Phisit

☎ 075 219 737; 075 214 707/8 ● 075 219 327

ⓔ yadfon@loxinfo.co.th

UGANDA

International dialing code +256.

Lush, green and fertile Uganda is one of East Africa's bread-baskets. The country suffered under the dictatorships of Idi Amin and Milton Obote in the 1970s and 1980s, but things have improved since Yoweri Museveni ousted Obote in 1986, with democratic elections and economic growth. The two outstanding problems today are AIDS and instability in neighbouring Rwanda, southern Sudan and the Congo (formerly Zaire). Uganda itself is generally safe and friendly, but check the situation before visiting western Uganda.

The west includes some of the country's natural highlights: the Bwindi and Mgahinga National Parks are hilly, forested parks famous for their gorillas. The

Rwenzori Mountains – the fabled 'Mountains of the Moon' – are a 5000-metre snowcapped range that offers great trekking. (At the time of writing, however, the Rwenzori National Park was closed to visitors.) There is also good walking in Mt Elgon National Park in eastern Uganda and near the spectacular Murchison Falls in the north west.

Uganda has a strong cultural heritage and offers a chance to experience East African life away from the tourist traps of Kenya and northern Tanzania.

Heritage Trails/Kabaka's Trail DAY
A range of cultural attractions near Kampala, including historic sites, music, dance, crafts and storytelling.

■ John Tinka/Louise Dixey: PO Box 29846, Kampala

❶ 077 468 113 (Heritage Trails); 041 273 600 (Kabaka Foundation).

Kabarole Tourism Association ORG/TOUR/ACCOM+
An association promoting local and community-based tours, guesthouses, campsites and handicrafts projects around Fort Portal in western Uganda. The area's attractions include Kibale National Park (with 13 primate species and other wildlife), good birdwatching, swimming in crater lakes, hot springs in the jungle of the Semliki valley, fishing on Lake Albert, attractive walking and the Rwenzori mountains.

■ Maurice Barnes

Ⓦ www.visituganda.com/uta/kabarole.htm Ⓔ ruwview@africaonline.co.ug

UCOTA (Uganda Community Tourism Association) ORG/ACCOM+
An association supporting community tourism projects in Uganda. The UCOTA members listed here all have accommodation (usually in thatched huts called *bandas*) and camping facilities: **Amajambwere Iwacu** in Mgahinga National Park; **Banana Village Retreat Centre** (tel: 077 501 953) between Entebbe and Kampala; **Buhoma Rest Camp** in Bwindi National Park; **Bushara Island Camp** (tel: 077 464 585; bushara@maf.org) on Lake Bunyoni in the south west; **Kaniyo Pabidi** and **Busingiro** in the Budongo Forest. The **Abanya Rwenzori Mountaineering Association** also provides guides for trekking in the Rwenzori Mountains (although the mountains have been closed to visitors) and the surrounding region. **Crow's Nest** (thecrowsnest@yahoo.com) and **Moses** campsites near Mt Elgon National Park offer cultural and nature walks to Sipi Falls. The **Kibale Association for Rural and Environmental Development (KAFRED)** (PO Box 700, Bigodi) offers tours in the Bigodi Wetland Sanctuary in west Uganda. Near Kampala, **Mabira Forest Ecotourism Project** runs birdwatching tours. Most of these projects include women's handicrafts groups.

■ Paul Mugisa/Sheba Hanyurwa: Adam House, Portal Avenue 1A (PO Box 27159), Kampala

☎ 041 230 805
Ⓦ www.visituganda.com/community/ucota.htm **Ⓔ** ucota@africaonline.co.ug

US – NATIVE AMERICAN TOURISM

International dialing code +1.

Statistics on health, mental illness and suicides show that Native Americans share many of the problems of other Aboriginal people, and of poor people throughout the developing world, despite living in one of the world's wealthiest nations. The situation is worst on the 300 or so reservations, home to roughly a quarter of Native Americans (437,000 people) and plagued by high unemployment, alcoholism, poverty and substandard health and education facilities.

Some reservations, especially in the South-West, are popular with tourists – Taos and Acoma pueblos, for instance, or the Hopi villages – and tourism can intrude on people's privacy. But, if the tribe manages tourism, income is usually reinvested in communal programmes and services. Tours are often timed to coincide with fairs (or 'pow-wows'), featuring traditional dances and costumes. At other times it is unrealistic to expect – as many tourists seem to – that a brief visit will be coincide with ceremonies and ritual dancing.

Many Native Americans feel strongly that it is inappropriate for tourists to participate in spiritual practices such as sweat lodges, or to be present at ceremonies. Similarly, in South Dakota, traditional Indian people do not support the Crazy Horse Monument and would like tourists not to hike on Bear Butte, a sacred site. There are Native-run companies listed below that do offer these features on some trips, but they are controversial and may create problems within their tribes, and tours with these features should probably be avoided.

Alaska and the South-West (Navajo, Ute, Hopi, Zuni, Pueblo, Apache, Hualapai and Havasupai) are the standout regions for visitors interested in Native American culture. But there are also Native-run tourism ventures in Montana, South Dakota, Florida and elsewhere – more than we have room to list. Useful guidebooks include the *Rough Guide to Southwest USA* and *Native Peoples of the Northwest: A Traveler's Guide to Land, Art and Culture* by Jan Halliday (see www.janhalliday.com).

There are also tribally-run casinos, golf courses and even ski resorts. Many of these are successful community businesses, although we don't include them here.

Alaska
Alaska state code 907.

Alaska is a superb outdoors destination with wilderness, pristine forests and rivers, soaring mountains (including Mt McKinley, the highest peak in the US), frozen tundra and great wildlife (moose, caribou, bear, wolf, otter, beaver, eagles, etc) and whale watching. It has more coastline than all the other US states combined, with hundreds of inlets and islands that reach almost to Japan and Siberia.

Native Americans make up 16 per cent of Alaska's population, and the **Alaska Native Heritage Center** (8800 Heritage Center Drive, tel: 330 8000, 1-800 315 6608; www.alaskanative.net; info@alaskanative.net) in Anchorage is a good place to start exploring their culture. Other Native tourism in the state includes **Chugach Heritage Center** (tel: 224 5065) in Seward; **Eklutna Historical Park** (tel: 688 3824) near Anchorage and day tours in **Wrangell** on the Stikine river. The **Totem Heritage Center** (tel: 225 5900) in Ketchikan, and nearby **Saxman Native Village** (tel: 225 4421), feature collections of giant Totem poles.

Athabascan-run tours in the rugged interior include **Alexander's River Adventure**: day trips from Fairbanks to a salmon-fishing camp on the Tanana River (from $125; tel: 474 3924; alexriveradventure@gci.net); **Athabasca Cultural Journeys** (tel: 829 2261; 1-800 937 0899): three-day camping trips ($1650) from the village of Huslia into the Koyukuk National Wildlife Refuge; and **Yukon River Tours** (tel: 452 7162; www.mosquitonet.com/~dlacey/yrt.html): day and overnight boat trips on the Yukon River, four hours north of Fairbanks, plus hiking and canoeing and a cultural centre in Stevens Village.

Kodiak Native Tourism Association (tel: 486 5736; 1-888 288 5736) markets Native-run lodges, museums and tours on Kodiak Island, south-west of Anchorage. (Or call Kodiak Visitors Centre: 486 4782; 1-800 789 4782.) **St Paul Tours** (tel: 278 2312; www.alaskabirding.com) runs three- to eight-day tours to remote St Paul Island, 450km off the mainland with one of the world's largest seal and seabird rookeries. From $1200, including flight from Anchorage.

In Barrow, 500km above the Arctic Circle, there is **Tundra Tours** (two days $600, from Anchorage; tel: 852 3900; www.alaskaone.com/topworld) and the **Inupiat Heritage Center** (tel: 852 0422). Other Inuit tourism in northern Alaska includes **Tour Arctic** (three days, $544; www.tour-arctic.com) and the **Museum of the Arctic** in Kotzebue (tel: 442 3747) and **Gambell Village Tours** (tel: 276 7568) on St Lawrence Island – an island within sight of Siberia.

Most tours in Alaska only operate from May to September. For more information, see *Native Peoples of Alaska: A Traveler's Guide to Land, Art and Culture* by Jan Halliday (see www.janhalliday.com).

■ Alaska Airlines Vacations (for Barrow, Kotzebue, Kodiak)

✆ 1-800 468 2248

■ Southeast Alaska Visitor Center (for Saxman, Wrangell, Ketchikan)

✆ 228 6214

■ Alaska's Southwest (for St Paul Island)

✆ 562 7380

✉ info@swamc.org

Bear Print International   TOUR

Tours to Native American lands and communities run with tribal leaders and Native American educators and cultural representatives. Tours provide an insight into the history and life of contemporary Native Americans. Trips to different regions and tribes including the Navajo, Lakota (Sioux), Cheyenne and Blackfeet. Bear Print also publishes *The Trail of Many Spirits* by Serle Chapman, about Native American history and contemporary culture.

■ In the UK: PO Box 1, Wakefield, West Yorkshire WF4 4YB

✆ +44 (0)1924 840 111

✉ bearprint@bun.com

Havasupai Tourist Enterprise   ACCOM+

Havasu Canyon – an enchanting side canyon of the Grand Canyon – is part of the Havasupai reservation. It is a beautiful hidden oasis, famous for its turquoise waterfalls. In the canyon there's a lodge, campsite and tribally-run guiding services. The lodge is 12km from the road and access is by foot or mule only.

■ PO Box 160, Supai, AZ 86435

✆ 928 448 2141; 2120/1 (Lodge: 928 448 2111) 📠 928 448 2237

🌐 www.havasupaitribe.com ✉ touristoffice@havasupaitribe.com

Hopi   ACCOM+/DAY

The Hopi live in dramatic cliff-top villages in north-east Arizona. The **Hopi Cultural Center** has a motel and museum. There are tours of **Walpi** and **Oraibi** (Bertram Tsavadawa, tel: 928 734 9544). Other guides are **Ray Coin** (tel: 928 734 6699) and **Gary Tso** (tel: 928 734 2567). The **Hopi Learning Center** in the Hyatt hotel at Gainey Ranch, Scottsdale, Phoenix (tel: 480 991 3388) is also well worth visiting.

■ Hopi Cultural Center, Second Mesa

✆ 928 734 2401 📠 928 734 6651

🌐 www.hopionline.com ✉ hopiculturalcenter@hotmail.com

Hualapai Lodge/Grand Canyon West/River Runners   ACCOM+/DAY
The Hualapai run a lodge in Peach Springs (doubles $75), a two-hour guided tour on the rim of the Grand Canyon at Grand Canyon West and whitewater rafting trips through the Grand Canyon (March–September, $275).

■ Ed Rosenfeld: PO Box 369, Peach Springs, AZ 86434

❶ 1-888 255 9550 ❶ 928 769 2410

Ⓦ www.hualapaitours.com

Indian Country Tourism   TOUR
Customized Native-run tours focusing on Native American destinations, culture and history. They are also producing a guidebook to Native American tourism, due out in 2002.

■ Ben Sherman/Dana Echohawk

❶ 303 661 9819 ❶ 303 664 5139

Ⓦ www.indiancountrytourism.com ⓔ dechohawk@indiancountrytourism.com

■ In the UK: People and Places: Kate Stefanko

❶ +44 (0)1795 535 718

ⓔ kate@travelpeopleandplaces.com

Moccasin Tracks Tours   TOUR
Tours to the San Carlos Apache and Fort Apache Reservations in Arizona led by an Apache storyteller. Rodeos, camping, ceremonial dances and archaeological sites.

■ Irma Bell Kitcheyan: PO Box 80982, Phoenix, AZ 85060-0982

❶ 602 294 9320

Ⓦ www.ncaied.org/moccasintrackstour

Native Tours   DAY/TOUR
Native-run tour agency with tours to various regions of the US, including pow-wows, Alaskan cruises, golf tours and hiking trips. Plus day tours from Minneapolis.

■ Sonja Tanner: 6875 Highway 65 NE, Minneapolis, MN 55432

❶ 763 571 8184; 1-800 489 6583 ❶ 763 571 7889

Ⓦ www.nativetours.com ⓔ fly@tttravelinc.com

Navajo Nation
The Navajo are the largest Native American nation in the US, and one of the few who still occupy their traditional homelands – in north-east Arizona and north-west New Mexico. The reservation borders the Grand Canyon and Lake

Powell and contains spectacular South-West scenery including Monument Valley, Antelope Canyon, the Painted Desert and Rainbow Bridge. There are ancient Anasazi ruins at Canyon de Chelly, Navajo National Monument and Chaco Canyon. Navajo-owned **Largo NavajoLand Tours** organizes tours of the region, plus backcountry hiking and customized itineraries. The **Navajo Tourism Department** can supply information about local attractions, dates of the annual Navajo Fair and similar events, plus details of other Navajo guides offering jeep, horse-riding and overnight camping tours, mainly in Monument Valley and Canyon de Chelly.

■ Navajo Tourism Department: Economic Development Building, Highway 264 (PO Box 663), Window Rock, AZ 86515

☻ 928 871 6436 ☻ 928 871 7381

Ⓦ www.DiscoverNavajo.com Ⓔ ntourism@discovernavajo.com

■ Largo Navajoland Tours: John Largo: PO Box 3244, Gallup, NM 87305

☻ 505 863 0050; 1-888-726 9084

Ⓦ www.navajolandtours.com Ⓔ jlargo@cia-g.com

Pueblos, New Mexico   DAY/TOUR

There are 19 Pueblo communities in New Mexico, mostly along the Rio Grande near Santa Fe, including **Taos** and **Ácoma**. Most are open to visitors and have crafts shops. Many charge a small admission and a separate fee to take photographs. The Pueblo Cultural Center in Alburquerque has displays on Pueblo culture and visitor information for all the pueblos. The *Rough Guide to Southwest USA and Touring the Pueblos: A Travel Guide* (Ron Swartley, $10.95, Frontier Image Press) are useful guidebooks.

■ Pueblo Cultural Center: 2401 12st Street NW (one block north of I-40), Albuquerque, New Mexico 87104

☻ 505 843 7270; 1-800 766 4405

Ⓦ www.indianpueblo.org Ⓔ info@indian.pueblo.com

■ Eight Northern Indian Pueblos

☻ 505 852 4265; 1-800 793 4955

Rising Wolf Wilderness Adventures   TOUR/TREK

Rugged women-only camping and hiking trips run by Blackfeet women into beautiful alpine wilderness on the edge of East Glacier Park, Montana, on the Blackfeet Indian Reservation. Five-day trip, $895. June to August.

■ PO Box 203, East Glacier Park, Montana 59434

☻ 406 338 3016

Ⓔ risewolf@3rivers.net

Seminole Tours   DAY/TOUR
Day and overnight Everglades tours on the Big Cypress Seminole Indian Reservation in Florida, including airboat rides, night wildlife viewing and the tribal Ah-Tah-Thi-Ki Museum.

■ 12261 SouthWest 251 Street, Miami, Florida 33032

☎ 305 257 3737 ✆ 305 257 2137

🌐 www.seminoletours.com ✉ info@seminoletours.com

Ute Mountain Ute Tribal Park   DAY/TOUR
An Anasazi cliff-dwelling site in south-west Colorado near the Four Corners state junction, similar to nearby Mesa Verde but less visited. June-September. Half-day $18; day tours $60.

■ PO Box 109, Towaoc, CO 81344

☎ 303 565 3751; 1-800 847 5485 ✆ 303 565 7412

🌐 www.utemountainute.com ✉ utepark@fone.net

Vernell White Thunder   ACCOM+/SCHOOL
Horseriding trips with a Lakota guide.

■ PO Box 155, Kyle, South Dakota 57752

☎ 605 455 2343

✉ whitethunderranch@yahoo.com

Walk Softly Tours   TOUR
A non-Indian company that runs tours to the Navajo and Hopi reservations and other South-West destinations using Native American guides.

■ PO Box 5510, Scottsdale, AZ 85261-5510

☎ 602 473 1148 ✆ 602 473 1149

🌐 www.walksoftlytours.com ✉ round_up@msn.com

■ In the UK: Tribes Travel and Muir's Tours (see Outbound operators)

HELP US UPDATE

If you know of similar community tourism projects or changes to these listings, please email Tourism Concern at info@tourismconcern.org.uk – subject: community tourism.

VENEZUELA

International dialing code +58.

Venezuela has coral reefs and palm-fringed Caribbean beaches, wildlife-rich plains, snowcapped mountains and tropical rainforest. Most Venezuelans live near the Caribbean coast, with its fine beaches and national parks such as Morrocoy, Mochima or the Islas Los Roques. Isla Margarita, in the Caribbean, is the country's most developed beach destination.

The pleasant town of Mérida in the Andes has good hiking, with many tour agencies and backpacker hostels. To the south-east lies Los Llanos, an open savannah comparable to the East African plains and one of the best places in South America to see wildlife, and the wild, roadless rainforests of Amazonas. The vast, hauntingly beautiful, thinly populated Gran Sabana in the far south-east is a mix of rainforest and open plains interspersed by ancient *tepuis* – towering flat-topped mountains with sheer cliffs on all sides. Huge waterfalls tumble over these cliffs, including Angel Falls, the world's tallest. Roraima, on the border with Brazil, is the highest of the *tepuis* and said to be the inspiration for Arthur Conan Doyle's novel, *The Lost World*. The Gran Sabana is the homeland of the indigenous Pemon.

Canaima/Angel Falls region
Canaima, in the Gran Sabana, is the main tourist base for visiting the Angel Falls. Many tour agencies in Caracas, Porlamar, Ciudad Bolívar and Canaima offer trips to the falls but all the agencies and lodgings in this section are Pemon-run. In Canaima itself, Pemon agencies include **Kamarakoto Tours** (tel/fax in Puerto Ordaz: 086 27680) and Nasario Rosi's **Iwana Meru** (tel: 014 853 2296 or 014 884 0519), or his cousin Reynaldo's **Kaikarwa**. These agencies offer basic two-day river trips to Angel Falls (May–December, from $50 per day) or longer six-day trips which finish in the Pemon village of **Kamarata**. In Kamarata, a cooperative of Pemon guides called **Macunaima** (Tito Abati: tel: 086 620443) does the same route in reverse. There are also community-owned cabañas in nearby **Kavak**, another Pemon settlement close to the impressive Kavak Canyon. There are no roads in this region: flights to Canaima or Kavak from Ciudad Bolívar cost approximately $50 one-way.

Encuentro Paria (formerly CorpoMedina)   ACCOM/ORG/TOUR
ToDo! Award winner
A network of community-owned businesses on the Paria peninsula in north-east Venezuela, which has beautiful beaches, cloudforest-covered mountains and wet savannah. There are two small beach resorts – **Playa Medina** (double from $132 a night) and the cheaper **Playa Puipuy** – plus a small hotel, **Posada La Colina**, in Carúpano, the peninsula's main town (and home to the country's

most colourful Carnival). Other projects include the **Jardín Botánico El Pilar**, hot springs and a guesthouse at Agua Santa (tel: 016 615 6051) and accommodation at the **Hato Río de Agua** buffalo ranch. Corpomedina can also arrange trips to the Orinoco Delta and other regional attractions. **Fundación Proyecto Paria** (50 Calle Rivero, Río Caribe; tel 094 61883; fax: 094 61223; fpprio@telcel.net.ve) has helped fund many small community projects, including tourist ventures, in the region.

■ Wilfried Merle: Callejon Santa Rosa 9, Casa del Cable, Carúpano, Estado Sucre

❶ 094 315 241; 094 312 283 + ❶ 094 313 847 ❶ 313 021

❸ playamed@telcel.net.ve *or* wilfried@telcel.net.ve

Mawadianojodo   RAINFOREST
A basic rainforest camp in Amazonas, run by local Yekuana Indians, on the Río Cunucunuma, a tributary of the Orinoco. The camp is about three-quarters of the way to La Esmeralda from San Fernando de Atabapo, and close to 2396m Cerro Duida. Sleeping is in camp beds or hammocks under thatched *churuatas*.

❶ 02 251 0990

Piedras Blancas Ecological Refuge   TREK/ACCOM
A posada near Mérida, run by the **Programa Andes Tropicales**. Hiking on the Andean páramo, plus guided hikes or horse-treks into the Sierra de la Culata, with homestays in rural villages.

■ Yves Lesenfants

❶ + ❶ 074 638 633

❸ patven@telcel.net.ve

Roraima Tours/Paraitepui   BUDGET/TOUR
In the southern Gran Sabana, you can hire guides for the six-day hike to the top of Roraima from Pemon-run **Roraima Tours** (Ana Fernández, tel: 088 951 283, 014 864 323 or 014 886 3405) in San Francisco de Yuruani, or in the Pemon village of **Paraitepui** (ask for 'El Capitán'). Village men work as guides on a rota system, with communally-set rates (currently $25 per day).

Vuelta Larga   ACCOM/TOUR
A buffalo ranch and ecolodge near El Pilar on the Paria peninsula. The owner, Klaus Múller, organizes tours to nearby cloudforest and works with indigenous Warao communities.

■ Calle Bolivar 8, Guaraúnos

❶ 094 69052; 094 647 292 ❸ vueltalarga@cantv.net

VIETNAM

International dialing code +84.

The Vietnamese liken the shape of their country to the pole that peasants traditionally carried across their shoulders, a rice basket suspended from each end. The southern basket (Saigon and the Mekong Delta) and the northern one (around Hanoi) are connected by a narrow coastal strip that squeezes past the mountains of Laos. While the south feels tropical, the north is cooler and more mountainous, home to the hilltribes who have also spread from China into northern Laos and Thailand. Culturally, too, north and south are distinct, the south historically falling within the cultural orbit of India, the north of China.

Most of Vietnam's greatest historical sites, such as Hué, were bombed during the Vietnam War, and its beaches do not compare to Thailand's, but Vietnam is vibrant and fascinating, as its leaders seek to balance socialism with the open market. In the south, there is colourful rural life along the Mekong Delta waterways, while the northern highlands are strikingly beautiful. HaLong Bay, dotted with thousands of craggy limestone rocks and islands, is a natural wonder. The railway journey between Saigon and Hanoi is a popular trip, and cycling is also an excellent way to explore.

Sapa   ACCOM/BUDGET/TREK
Surrounded by Vietnam's highest peaks and hilltribe villages, the northerrn market town and hill-resort of Sapa has become a popular tourist destination. An **SNV/IUCN** project is developing sustainable trekking routes with local villages. There are also homestays in the Tay villages of Ban Ho and Thanh Phu (£1 per night).

■ Centre of Culture, Information, Sport and Tourism, Sapa

❶ 4 20871 975　❶ 4 20871 936

✉ spstpo@hn.vnn.vn

■ IUCN: Toot Oostveen/Nguyen Van Lam: tourism@iucn.org.vn

ZAMBIA

International dialing code +260.

Zambia is one of the less-established Southern African destinations, but its wildlife compares favourably with its neighbours. With plains and woodlands enclosed by steep escarpment walls, the Luangwa valley is one of Africa's richest wildlife areas. Two national parks (North and South Luangwa National

Parks) contain huge herds of elephant and buffalo, lion, leopard, hyena, impala, etc. These parks are known for walking safaris, which were pioneered here. Zambia's other big attraction is the Victoria Falls, which it shares with Zimbabwe.

Zambia is a poor country with high unemployment, a national economy crippled by debt repayments, a crumbling mining industry and an terrible AIDS problem. The government sees tourism as an important potential income earner

Kawaza Village   ACCOM+/DAY
A Kunda village in the Luangwa Valley offering day tours ($10) and overnight stays in local-style huts ($40 per night including food and activities. Camping $12.) Visitors can meet craftspeople, the chief and the traditional healer, and visit the school or tour other villages. Plus dancing, drumming and storytelling. The village works with Robin Pope Safaris, a safari operator in nearby South Luangwa National Park.

■ PO Box 15, Mfuwe

Ⓦ www.ftsl.demon.co.uk/KVTP.HTM

■ Robin Pope Safaris: PO Box 80, Mfuwe

❶ 62 45090 ❶ 62 45051

ⓔ rps@super-hub.com

■ In the UK: Sunvil Discovery and Discovery Initiatives (see Outbound operators)

Mukuni Village/Songwe Point   DAY
Songwe Point is a hotel overlooking Victoria Falls, which runs tours to 700-year-old Mukuni village. There are also archaeological sites nearby. The local community co-owns the business.

■ In South Africa: Kwando Safaris

❶ +27 11 886 9925 ❶ +27 11 886 6031

ⓔ reservations@kwando.co.za

■ In the UK: Sunvil Discovery and Tribes Travel (see Outbound operators)

Nsendamila Village   DAY
Day tours of another Kunda village near South Luangwa National Park, offering a glimpse of rural Zambian life. $5 entry. Ask for directions from Mfuwe.

ZIMBABWE

International dialing code +263.

Incoming foreign tourism supports an estimated 100,000 jobs in Zimbabwe and a third of all visitors are British. As in most African countries, safaris are the mainstay of tourism in Zimbabwe: over 95 per cent of Zimbabwe tourism is nature-based. Hwange National Park is the star, with over 100 animal species and huge elephant herds. The country has other attractions, of course. Most tourists find time to visit the mighty Victoria Falls, and the adventurous among them bungee-jump or whitewater raft on the Zambezi River near the Falls. In Great Zimbabwe, the country has one of Africa's most impressive and mysterious archaeological sites. The Chimanimani mountains in the eastern highlands have lovely hiking, while the Matobo Hills National Park contains a unique landscape of giant scattered boulders, as well as rock art.

The conflict between white farmers and the government has hit tourism hard, and you should check out the security situation before travelling.

CAMPFIRE (Communal Areas Management Programme for Indigenous Resources) ORG

A government scheme to promote rural development. The following community-owned CAMPFIRE ventures offer *rondavels* or camping, wildlife and birdwatching plus the chance to see rural life, traditional healers and local crafts: **Sanyati Bridge Camp** (Wildlife & Environment Zimbabwe: fax: 04 747 174) near Matusadona National Park, between Karoi and the Bumi Hills; **Sunungukai Camp** (tel: 078 2439/2591) in northern Zimbabwe, near the Umfurudzi Safari Area; and **Mavuradonha** campsite in the mountainous Mavuradonha Wilderness Area in northern Zimbabwe, with excellent hiking. **Chesvingo**, **Mahenye** and **Chilo** (all below) are belong to CAMPFIRE.

■ Campfire: Mukuvisi Woodlands, cnr Glenara Ave, South/Hillside Rd (PO Box 661), Harare

❶ 04 747 422/9 ❶ 04 747 470

Ⓦ www.campfire-zimbabwe.org Ⓔ campfire@internet.co.zw

■ Africa Resources Trust: PO Box A860, Avondale, Harare

❶ 04 732 625 ❶ 04 704 717

Ⓔ machena@art.org.zw

■ In the UK: Zimbabwe Trust: Rob Monro: The Old Lodge, Christchurch Road, Epsom, Surrey KT19 8NE

❶ +44 (0)1372 741 237

Ⓔ r.monro@virgin.net

Chesvingo Lakeside Village (Masvingo)   ACCOM+/BUDGET

Near Great Zimbabwe, with attractive lake and mountain scenery. Simple lodgings, guided walks, rock art. Run by the local Shona community.

■ PO Box 773, Masvingo

☏ 039 7157; 091 406 697

■ Travel World: Masvingo

☏ 039 62131 ☏ 039 64205

Chilangililo   ACCOM/DAY

A Tongan cooperative in Binga that offers low-cost stays in traditional stilt houses on the shore of Lake Kariba, plus guided visits to Tonga villages and local handicrafts.

■ Peta Jones: Private Bag 5713, Binga

☏ 015 2407

Emadwaleni Tours (Matobo Hills, Bulawayo)   ACCOM+

Homestays in a Ndebele village in the Matobo Hills outside Bulawayo, with guided tours visiting craftspeople, traditional doctors, etc. Also walking safaris, horseback trails.

■ 1 McNeillie Road, Riverside, Bulawayo

☏ + ☏ 09 48889

Inyathi Valley Motel (Victoria Falls)   ACCOM/BUDGET

Rondavel and dormitory accommodation, mainly for school and youth groups, developed by ex-combatants through the **Zimbabwe Project Trust**.

■ Ronnie Patel: 951 Parkway Drive (PO Box CT300), Victoria Falls

☏ 013 2345

@ inyathiv@telcovic.co.zw

Kunzwana Trust/Siachilaba Community Tourism Project   TOUR

Kunzwana Trust is an NGO promoting Zimbabwean music. It runs two- to three-day trips to the Tonga village of **Siachilaba**, near Binga in north-west Zimbabwe. Music plus crafts (basketwork, beadwork, drums), village life, community projects, etc.

■ Kunzwana Trust: Penny Yon: 4 Nettleton Road, Braeside (PO Box MP349, Mt Pleasant), Harare

☏ 04 725 166; 02 791 649

@ kunzwana@pci.co.zw

Mahenye Lodge/Chilo Lodge/Savé Conservancy — SAFARI/LUXURY

Mahenye and Chilo lodges, near Gonarezhou National Park in south-east Zimbabwe, are co-owned by local CAMPFIRE villages (see above) and **River Lodges of Africa (RLOA)**, which also owns **Senuko Lodge** in nearby **Savé Valley Conservancy**. Savé is Africa's largest private reserve, with cheetah, leopard, wild dog and black rhino, and works with local communities.

■ RLOA: Clive Stockil: Private Bag 7138, Chiredzi

☎ 031 7242; 031 7243 ✆ 031 7244

✉ rloa@mweb.co.zw

■ Bookings through Armadillo Travel

☎ + ✆ 04 305 878

✉ armadilo@mweb.co.zw

Monde Village (Victoria Falls) — ACCOM/DAY

Guided village tours plus simple accommodation in a village near Victoria Falls. Local customs, history, architecture, etc. Run jointly by the community and **Baobab Safaris**.

■ Baobab Safaris: Steve Bolnick: PO Box 196, Victoria Falls

☎ 013 4283

🌐 www.baobabsafari.com ✉ safaris@telconet.co.zw

Nduna Safari Lodge — LUXURY/SAFARI

A luxury lodge on the Mozambique border, owned by the **Malilangwe Conservation Trust**. Income helps fund the reserve and community projects. Good wildlife and birdwatching.

■ 1 Zermatt Court, cnr Baines Avenue and 7th Street (PO Box MP845), Mt Pleasant, Harare

☎ 04 725 797/9 + ✆ 04 722 983

🌐 www.malilangwe.co.zw ✉ mctsales@africaonline.co.zw

HELP US UPDATE

If you know of similar community tourism projects or changes to these listings, please email Tourism Concern at info@tourismconcern.org.uk – subject: community tourism.

HOLIDAY-FINDER INDEX

This index will help you find holidays that match your interests. Projects may be listed in more than one category. These indexes are selective: just because a project is not listed under 'birdwatching', for instance, it doesn't mean that you won't see any birds, but we've tried to highlight some of the best tours and projects in each category.

AGRITOURISM

Agritourism means participating in or learning about local farming methods and related traditions and lifestyles, although most village-based projects offer the chance to see rural lifestyles.

Costa Rica	CODECE, COOPRENA, Finca La Flor de Paraíso
Guatemala	Eco-Escuela (Bio Itza School)
India	Alternative Travels, ROSE
Indonesia	Mitra Bali
Jamaica	Countrystyle
Mexico	Las Canadas, Yucatan (Nacajuc)
Peru	Granja Porcon
Sri Lanka	FESTU
Tanzania	Cultural Tourism Programme
Thailand	REST
Outbound	IVEX

ARCHAEOLOGICAL AND HISTORICAL SITES

Belize	SPEAR
Ecuador	Huacamayos
Egypt	Wind, Sand & Stars
Guatemala	EcoMaya
Indonesia	Bina Swadaya
Mexico	Agua Selva, Chiapas
Peru	Llama Trek, Ollantaytambo Heritage Trails
Tanzania	Trade Aid Mikindani

Uganda	Heritage Trails
US	Hopi mesas, Navajo tourism, Ute Mountain Ute
Zambia	Mukuni
Outbound	Earthwatch, Make a Difference, Symbiosis, Wind, Sand & Stars, Multatuli

ARTS AND CRAFTS

Many community projects have small shops selling local artwork, clothes and crafts, but the following projects and trips put a particular emphasis on explaining or teaching traditional crafts.

Belize	Toledo Ecotourism Association
Canada	Anishinabe Experience, Shawenequanape Kipichewin, Tours Innu
Gambia	Tumani Tenda
Grenada	Grenada Homestays
Guatemala	Totonicapan
India	Ananda
Indonesia	Mitra Bali, Sua Bali
Kenya	Tawasal Institute
Mexico	Union de Museos Comunitarios de Oaxaca
New Zealand	Main Street (Tuku Wairua Centre), Rotorua
Senegal	Crossing Cultures
South Africa	Knysna, Ribolla
Sri Lanka	FESTU
Thailand	PDA Tours, Thai Tribal Crafts
Zimbabwe	Emadwaleni

BACKPACKERS/BUDGET GUESTHOUSES

Australia	Darlgunaya
Fiji	Abaca
Ghana	Bowiri, NCRC
Guatemala	Hotel Backpackers
Indonesia	Kandora
Mexico	Agua Selva, Maruata 2000, Oaxaca (Tourist Yu'u), Taselotzin
New Zealand	Main Street Backpackers
Senegal	Campement Villageois
Tanzania	Sisi Kwa Sisi
Vietnam	Sapa
Zimbabwe	Chesvingo, Chilangililo, Inyathi Valley

BEACHES

Australia	Kooljaman, Lombardina
Belize	SPEAR
Brazil	Prainha do Canto Verde
Costa Rica	ATEC, Matapalo
Egypt	Basata
Ghana	NCRC
Mexico	La Ventanilla, Maruata 2000, San José el Hueyate
Nicaragua	SELVA
Panama	San Blas Islands
Samoa	all listings
Solomon Islands	Vanua Rapita
South Africa	Eco-Escapes, Rainbow, Wilderness Safaris (Rocktail Bay)
Tanzania	Chole Mjini, TACTO (Gezaolole, Pangani), Zanzibar Travel
Venezuela	Corpomedina
Outbound	Symbiosis, Zanzibar Travel, Multatuli

BIRDWATCHING

Also, all tours in the Cloudforest and Rainforest sections (below) offer good birdwatching.

Belize	Belize Audubon Society
Ghana	Bowiri, NCRC
Ecuador	all listings
Peru	Casa Machiguenga, Manu Wildlife Centre, Tambopata
Philippines	Olongo Birds and Seascape Tour
Mexico	Grupo Ecologico Sierra Gorda, Chiapas
South Africa	Ukhahlamba, Wilderness Safaris (Ndumo)
Uganda	Kabarole
US	St Paul Island
Zimbabwe	Mavuradonha, Nduna

CANOEING/SEA-KAYAKING/ WHITEWATER RAFTING

Belize	TIDE
Canada	Nuuhchimi Wiinuu, Tours Innu

Samoa	Eco-Tour Samoa
Solomon Islands	Solomon Islands Village Stay
South Africa	Lake Sibaya Lodge
Thailand	SeaCanoe
US	Hualapai Lodge (River Runners)
Outbound	Wilderness Travel

CAVES

Australia	Mimbi Caves
Belize	Toledo Ecotourism Association
Ecuador	Huacamayos
Mexico	Sierra Tarahumara, Union de Museos Comunitarios de Oaxaca

CLOUDFOREST

Dominican Republic	Fundacion Loma Quita Espuela
Ecuador	Bellavista, Fundacion Golondrinas, Junin, Maquipucuna, Oyacachi
Honduras	Cusuco, El Carbon
Mexico	Grupo Ecologico Sierra Gorda, Las Canadas, Los Tuxtlas

CULTURE (LOCAL)

Most of the tours in this guide offer contact with local people and insights into local culture – this is one of the big attractions of community-based tourism. The following place a special emphasis on exploring of local culture. Also see Tribal culture.

Australia	all listings
Belize	Toledo Ecotourism Association
Botswana	Kalahari Sunset Tours, SNV, /Xai /Xai
Canada	Anishinabe Experience, Cowichan, Shawenequanape Kipichewin
Ghana	Exodus
Guatemala	Totonicapan
India	Alternative Travels, Insight India, Kolam
Indonesia	Bina Swadaya, Mitra Bali, Sua Bali
Kenya	Tawasal Institute

Mexico	Union de Museos Comunitarios de Oaxaca
Namibia	Lianshulu (Lizauli), Khowarib (Anmire), Tsumkwe
Palestine	Guiding Star, PACE
Peru	Ollantaytambo Heritage Trails, Taquile, Willoc, Winaymarka
Philippines	PRRM
Senegal	Campement Villageois
South Africa	Isinamva, Vulindlela
Sri Lanka	FESTU
Tanzania	TACTO, KEF, MESO
Thailand	JorKoe, REST, Symbiosis
Uganda	UCOTA
Zambia	Kawaza, Nsendamila
Zimbabwe	Kunzwana, Monde Village
Outbound	Dragoman, Exodus, IntoAfrica, Make a Difference, Muir's Tours, Rainbow, Safari Njema, Simply Tanzania, Symbiosis, Tribes, Cross-Cultural Solutions, Dreamweaver, Associazione RAM, Multatuli, Oxfam Community Aid Abroad Tours

DESERT

Australia	Aboriginal Arts and Cultural Centre, Anangu Tours, Desert Tracks
Botswana	Kalahari Sunset Tours
Egypt	Wind, Sand & Stars
India	Billion Star Hotel
Morocco	Tizi-Randonnées
Namibia	Damaraland, Etendeka, Kaokohimba, NACOBTA, Nyae Nyae
US	Havasupai, Navajo tourism
Outbound	Wind, Sand & Stars

DEVELOPMENT PROJECTS/ISSUES

Belize	SPEAR
India	Development Tourism, Equations, Kolam, Cross Cultural Solutions
Indonesia	Bina Swadaya, Mitra Bali
Kenya	Tawasal
Philippines	Biyaheng Pinoy, PRRM
South Africa	Calabash, Rainbow

Sri Lanka	FESTU
Tanzania	KEF, Simply Tanzania
Thailand	REST
Outbound	Simply Tanzania, Global Exchange, Community Aid Abroad Tours

FISHING

Australia	Kooljaman, Lombardina
Belize	TIDE
Canada	British Columbia (Wilp Sy'oon Lodge), Quebec (Nuuhchimi Wiinuu)
Costa Rica	ATEC
Solomon Islands	Solomon Islands Village Stay, Vanua Rapita
South Africa	Lake Sibaya Lodge
US	Alaska (Alexander's River Adventure), Athabasca Cultural Journeys, Yukon River Tours

HEALING (TRADITIONAL, PLANT)

Many of the tours listed under Culture and Rainforest include walks identifying traditional medicinal plants.

Canada	Anishinabe Experience, Shawenequanape Kipichewin
Botswana	Kalahari Sunset Tours
Ecuador	RICANCIE
Guatemala	Eco-Escuela (Bio-Itza School)
Honduras	El Carbon
Indonesia	Sua Bali
Mexico	CICE, Las Canadas
Namibia	NACOBTA (Purros)
Nepal	CCODER, The Nepal Trust
Peru	Eseturpal
South Africa	Eco-Escapes
Sri Lanka	FESTU
Tanzania	KEF, Sisi Kwa Sisi
Thailand	Symbiosis
Outbound	Symbiosis

HOMESTAYS

Belize	Toledo Ecotourism Association, TVIC
Cuba	Casa del Caribe
Fiji	Abaca
Ghana	Exodus
Haiti	Beyond Borders
Honduras	Rio Platano
India	Alternative Travels, Kolam, ROSE
Indonesia	Bina Swadaya, Mitra Bali
Jamaica	Countrystyle
Kenya	Tawasal
Peru	Amananti, Taquile, Winaymarka
Philippines	Biyaheng Pinoy
Russia	Eco-Travels
Samoa	all listings
Senegal	Campement Villageois, Crossing Cultures
Solomon Islands	Solomons Village Stay
Sri Lanka	FESTU
South Africa	Isinamva
Tanzania	TACTO, Sisi Kwa Sisi
Thailand	REST
Zambia	Kawaza
Zimbabwe	Chilangililo, Emadwaleni
Outbound	Dreamweaver

HORSERIDING

Belize	Toledo Ecotourism Association
Canada	Quaaout Lodge
Costa Rica	Matapalo
Dominican Republic	CEBSE
Ecuador	Casa Mojanda, Fundacion Golondrinas, Oyacachi
India	Alternative Travels
Lesotho	Malealea Lodge
Mexico	Grupo Ecologico Serra Gorda
South Africa	Amadiba
US	Navajo tourism, Vernell White Thunder
Outbound	Discovery Initiatives, Tribes, Wind, Sand & Stars

SPANISH LANGUAGE SCHOOLS

Costa Rica	Finca La Flor de Paraíso
Guatemala	Eco-Escuela, Quetzaltenango
Mexico	CICE
Nicaragua	Nicaragua Spanish Schools
Outbound	Caledonia

LUXURY

Botswana	Vumbura
Ecuador	Kapawi
Kenya	Il Ngwesi, Sarara
Namibia	Damaraland, Sunvil
South Africa	CCAfrica, Wilderness Safaris (Ndumo/Rocktail Bay), Rainbow
Tanzania	Chole Mjini
Zimbabwe	Mahenye, Nduna
Outbound	Rainbow, Sunvil, Tribes, Zanzibar Travel

MUSIC AND DANCE

Cuba	Caledonia, Karamba
Gambia	Tumani Tenda
Ghana	Academy of African Music and Arts, Kasapa
India	Ananda
Senegal	Karamba
South Africa	Knysna
Zimbabwe	Kunzwana
Outbound	Caledonia, Karamba

RAINFOREST

Community-based rainforest tours typically involve guided walks or canoe trips in the forest to look for birds and wildlife, plus explanations of indigenous customs and crafts and traditional uses of plants for medicine, materials and food.

Belize	Cockscomb, SPEAR, Toledo Ecotourism Association
Bolivia	Chalalan, Ville Amboro

Brazil   Aldeia dos Lagos, Uakari, Tataquera
Costa Rica   ATEC
Ecuador   most listings
Ghana   Kakum
Guatemala   EcoMaya, Eco-Escuela, Proyecto Eco-Quetzal
Honduras   Rio Platano
Indonesia   Bina Swadaya
Malaysia   Ulu Ai
Mexico   Chiapas, Los Tuxtlas
Papua New Guinea   Tubo Lodge
Peru   Casa Machiguenga, Eseturpal, InkaNatura, Posada
                       Amazonas
Philippines   Aeta Jungle Environment Survival Tour
Solomon Islands   Makira Hill Tribes Trek
Venezuela   Canaima
Outbound   Discovery Initiatives, Tribes, Conservation International,
                       Mesoamerican Ecotourism Alliance, The Nature
                       Conservancy, Tread Lightly, Wildland, Multatuli

SNORKELLING AND DIVING

Costa Rica   ATEC
Dominican Republic   CEBSE
Indonesia   Togean Ecotourism Network
Panama   San Blas
Philippines   PRRM
Samoa   all listings
Solomon Islands   Solomons Village Stay, Vanua Rapita
South Africa   Wilderness Safaris (Rocktail Bay)
Tanzania   Chole Mjini
Outbound   Symbiosis, Zanzibar Travel

TREKKING/HIKING

Most of the tours in this book are in rural areas, with attractive scenery and plentiful walking opportunities. This selection highlights those offering multi-day treks.

Canada   British Columbia, Quebec, Nunavut
Ecuador   Fundacion Golondrinas, Oyacachi, Piraña Tour
Egypt   Wind, Sand & Stars

India	Dhami Dham, Tashila Tours
Indonesia	Kandora Lodge
Kenya	IntoAfrica
Laos	Nam Ha
Lesotho	Malealea Lodge
Mexico	Sierra Tarahumara
Morocco	Tizi-Randonnées
Namibia	Kaokohimba Safaris, NACOBTA
Nepal	ACAP, CCODER, Explore Nepal, Muir's Tours, Nepal Trust, Specialist Trekking
Pakistan	Full Moon Night Trekking
Peru	Llama Trek
Philippines	Biyaheng Pinoy
Solomon Islands	Makira Hill Tribes Trek
South Africa	Amadiba
Tanzania	IntoAfrica
Thailand	JorKoe, Lisu Lodge, Natural Focus, PDA Tours, REST
Uganda	Kabarole, UCOTA
US	Rising Wolf
Venezuela	Roraima
Zimbabwe	Mavuradonha
Outbound	Full Moon Night Trekking, IntoAfrica, Muir's Tours, Specialist Trekking, Tribes, Wind, Sand & Stars, Wilderness Travel

TRIBAL CULTURE/LIFESTYLES

There are other projects run by or with tribal people, but which concentrate on wildlife viewing. The following contain a more cultural element.

Australia	all listings
Botswana	Dqãe Qare, Kalahari Sunset Safaris, Nqwaa Khobee Xeya, /Xai /Xai
Canada	most listings
Ecuador	Amarongachi, Apturc, ATACAPI, Cofan Dureno, Kapawi, Oyacachi, Piraña Tour, RICANCIE, SionaTour, Tropic, Tsanta
Kenya	Tawasal
Laos	Nam Ha
Malaysia	Ulu Ai
Namibia	NACOBTA, Nyae Nyae

Papua New Guinea	Enga Experience
Philippines	Aeta, PRRM
Solomon Islands	Makira Hill Tribes Trek
Tanzania	MESO, TACTO
Thailand	JorKoe EcoTrek, Lisu Lodge, PDA Tours, REST, Symbiosis
Outbound	Bear Print, Tribes

URBAN TOURS

Australia	Dharawal Tours, Sydney Aboriginal Discoveries
Brazil	Favelatour
Philippines	Biyaheng Pinoy
South Africa	Calabash, Cape Town, Dreamcatcher, Fundani, Rainbow

VOLUNTEERING

We include a few short-term volunteer placements but not long-term placements such as VSO. *The International Directory of Voluntary Work* (Victoria Pybus and Louise Whetter, £10.99, Vacation Work Publications) lists many volunteering opportunities.

Costa Rica	COOPRENA, Finca La Flor de Paraíso
Ecuador	Fundacion Golondrinas
Guatemala	Quetzeltenango
India	Cross-Cultural Solutions, ROSE
Kenya	Taita Discovery Centre
Nepal	Gift for Aid
Senegal	Crossing Cultures
Thailand	Natural Focus Ecotours
Outbound	Earthwatch, Nepal Trust, Cross-Cultural Solutions, IVEX

WHALE WATCHING

Canada	Nunavut (Toonoonik Sahoonik), Quebec (Tours Innu)
Dominican Republic	CEBSE
New Zealand	Whale Watch Kaikoura
Outbound	Discovery Initiatives, Dreamweaver

WILDLIFE

Most tours in the Rainforest section (above) also feature good wildlife.

Botswana	most listings
Canada	G Cook Tours, Nunavut, Qimutsik Eco-Tours, Tours Innu
Ghana	NCRC
Kenya	most listings
Namibia	most listings
South Africa	CCAfrica, Madikwe, Wilderness Safaris
Tanzania	most listings
Uganda	Kabarole
US	Alaska (St Paul Island, Athabasca Cultural Journeys)
Zimbabwe	Mahenye, Nduna
Outbound	Discovery Initiatives, Earthwatch, IntoAfrica, Rainbow, Safari Njema, Simply Tanzania, Sunvil, Tribes, The Nature Conservancy, Tread Lightly, Wilderness Travel, Wildland, Multatuli

WOMEN

Women-only trips or trips focusing on women's issues. (Many other tours offer insights into the situation of women in different societies and some, such as FESTU in Sri Lanka, are run by women's groups.)

India	Cross-Cultural Solutions
Nepal	The Nepal Trust
US	Native Tours, Rising Wolf
Outbound	Cross-Cultural Solutions

SECTION THREE

RESPONSIBLE TOURISM RESOURCES

RESOURCES DIRECTORY

CATEGORIES

Organizations and websites

- Members of TEN (Third World Tourism European Network)
- Responsible tourism: the West
- Responsible tourism: developing countries
- Ecotourism
- General travel
- Environment and conservation
- Indigenous people
- Development organizations

Books

- Books, magazines and reports
- Tourism Concern publications

KEY
■ contact name/address ❶ telephone ❶ fax Ⓦ website ❸ email

TOURISM CONCERN

■ Stapleton House, 277–281 Holloway Road, London N7 8HN, UK
❶ +44 (0)20 7753 3330 ❶ +44 (0)20 7753 3331
Ⓦ www.tourismconcern.org.uk ❸ info@tourismconcern.org.uk

MEMBERS OF TEN (THIRD WORLD TOURISM EUROPEAN NETWORK)

TEN is a loose association of NGOs with interests similar to those of Tourism Concern.

Arbeitskreis Tourismus und Entwicklung
Swiss NGO campaigning for fair trade and responsible tourism.

■ Missionsstrasse 21, CH-4003, Basel, Switzerland

❶ +41 (0)61 261 4742 ❶ +41 (0)61 261 4721

Ⓦ www.akte.ch ❸ info@akte.ch

Associazione RAM
An Italian NGO working for fair trade and responsible tourism. They also run trips to Thailand, Vietnam, Sri Lanka, Sikkim, Nepal and India.

■ Renzo Garrone: Via Mortola 15 I-16030, San Rocco di Camogli (GE), Italy *or* via Figari 76-16030, Ruta di Camogli (GE), Italy

❶ + ❶ +39 (0)185 773 061; 776 028; 0338 160 6910

Ⓦ www.associazioneram.it ❸ orzonero@hotmail.com

Informatie Verre Reizen
A Dutch publisher of alternative tourist guides.

■ PO Box 1504, NL-6501 Nijmegen, The Netherlands

❶ +31 (0)24 355 2534 ❶ +31 (0)24 355 2473

Ⓦ www.tegastin.nl ❸ IVR@xs4all.nl

respect/Austrian Centre for Tourism and Development
Austrian campaign for more sustainable tourism.

■ Christian Baumgartner: Diefenbachgasse 36/3, A-1150, Wien, Austria

❶ +43 (0)1 895 6245 ❶ +43 (0)1 812 9789

Ⓦ www.respect.at ❸ office@respect.at

Stichting Retour (Retour Foundation)
Dutch responsible tourism NGO and non-profit consultancy. Consultancy income is reinvested into campaigns/projects supporting communities affected by tourism.

■ PO Box 1570, 6501 BN Nijmegen, The Netherlands

❶ + ❶ +31 (0)24 360 6224

Ⓦ www.retour.net ❸ mail@retour.net

Studienkreis fur Tourismus und Entwicklung
German responsible tourism NGO. Organizes the ToDo! and Toura d'or Awards.

■ Kapellenweg 3, D-82541 Ammerland, Germany

☎ +49 (0)8177 1783 ☏ +49 (0)8177 1349

ⓦ www.studienkreis.org ⓔ studienkreistourismus@compuserve.com

Tourism Watch
German responsible tourism development and education NGO.

■ Church Development Service, Ulrich-von-Hassell-Strasse 76, 53123 Bonn, Germany

☎ +49 (0)228 81010

ⓦ www.tourism-watch.org ⓔ tourism-watch@eed.de

Transverses
French responsible tourism NGO.

■ 7 rue Heyrault, F-92100, Boulogne, France

☎ + ☏ +33 (0)1 4910 9084

ⓔ transverses@wanadoo.fr

RESPONSIBLE TOURISM: THE WEST

ACT (Action for Conservation through Tourism)
A charity that helps local communities, NGOs, governments and tour operators to develop and market sustainable tourism projects that benefit local communities.

■ Sue Hurdle: ACT, CREATE Centre, Smeaton Road, Bristol, BS1 6XN, UK

☎ +44 (0)117 927 3049 ☏ +44 (0)117 930 0076

ⓔ act@gn.apc.org

Centre for Responsible Tourism
Training, consultancy and research about sustainable tourism.

■ University of Greenwich, Medway Campus, Pembroke, Chatham Maritime, Kent ME4 4TB, UK

☎ +44 (0)20 8331 9800 ☏ +44 (0)20 8331 9805

ⓦ www.cfrt.org.uk ⓔ cm59@greenwich.ac.uk

C.E.R.T. (Centre for Environmentally Responsible Tourism)

Runs an award scheme for tour operators working towards high environmental standards.

■ Peter Chipperfield, Indaba House, 1 Hydeway, Thundersley, Essex SS7 3BE, UK

☎ +44 (0)1268 752827 ✆ +44 (0)870 139 2802

🕸 www.c-e-r-t.org ✉ cert.desk@virgin.net

Choose Climate

Information about climate change, including air travel and global warming. An interactive map lets you calculate the environmental impact of your air journey.

🕸 www.chooseclimate.org

Climate Care

A voluntary 'pay-as-you-pollute' scheme that funds renewable energy, energy efficiency and forest restoration projects. Travellers can donate to offset the global warming impact of air travel.

🕸 www.co2.org

ECPAT UK

A campaign to end child prostitution, pornography and trafficking, including child-sex tourism.

■ The Stable Yard, Broomgrove Road, London SW9 9TL, UK

☎ +44 (0)20 7501 8927 ✆ +44 (0)20 7738 4110

🕸 www.ecpat.org.uk ✉ ecpatuk@antislavery.org

Future Forests

Another scheme where travellers pay for trees to be planted to offset the environmental impact of (air) travel.

🕸 www.futureforests.com

Responsible Tourism Network (RTN)

Australian networking organization linked to Oxfam Community Aid Abroad Tours (see Outbound operators).

■ Brian Witty: PO Box 34 Rundle Mall, South Australia 5000, Australia

☎ +61 (0)8 8232 2727 (1-800 814 848) ✆ +61 (0)8 8232 2808

🕸 www.caa.org.au/travel/ ✉ info@tours.caa.org.au

Responsible Travel.com

A website featuring a selection of holidays from 'responsible' tour operators.

🕸 www.responsibletravel.com

Sustainable Travel and Tourism
An online and printed journal about sustainable tourism linked to the WTTC's Green Globe initiative. Features, news and links, but don't expect hard-hitting criticism of the tourism industry.

Ⓦ www.sustravel.com

RESPONSIBLE TOURISM: DEVELOPING COUNTRIES

Annapurna Conservation Area Project (ACAP)
A project of the **King Mahendra Trust for Nature Conservation (KMTNC)**, ACAP uses trekking fees to protect the environment and culture in the Annapurna region of Nepal. With Tourism Concern, ACAP has published the Himalayan Code for trekkers (see Responsible tourism codes).

▮ PO Box 183, Pokhara, Nepal

❶ +977 (0)61 21102; 28202 ❶ +977 (0)61 28203

Ⓦ www.kmtnc.org.np ❷ acap@mos.com.np

Asociacion Ecuatoriana de Ecotourismo (ASEC)
ASEC have published guidelines for ecotourism operators.

▮ Diego Andrade-Ubidia, Director Ejecutivo, ASEC, PO Box 17211798, Quito, Ecuador

❶ +593 (0)22 251 053; 253 539 ❶ +593 (0)22 253 540

Ⓦ www.ecoturismo-ecuador.com ❷ asec@accessinter.net

Bina Swadaya
One of Indonesia's largest community-development NGOs. They also run tours (see Local tours: Indonesia).

▮ Wisma Jana Karya: Jl Gunung Sahari III/7, Jakarta Pusat 10610 (PO Box 1456, Jakarta 10014), Indonesia

❶ +62 (0)21 420 4402; 425 5354 ❶ +62 (0)21 420 8412

❷ bst@cbn.net.id

Ecumenical Coalition on Third World Tourism
This Christian NGO was a founding light of the responsible tourism movement. It was set up at a conference in Manila in 1980, which published the *Manila Declaration on World Tourism* criticizing the impact of tourism in the developing world. The NGO publishes a magazine, *Contours*.

▮ Mr Tan Chi Kiong: CCA Centre, 96, 2nd District, Pak Tin Village, Mei Tin Road, Shatin, NT, Hong Kong SAR

☎ +852 (0)2602 3669 📠 +852 (0)2602 3649

🌐 www.pacific.net.hk/~contours ✉ contours@pacific.net.hk *or* contours@cca.org.hk

Equations
Indian responsible-tourism organization.

■ 198, 2nd Cross, Church Road, New Thippasandra, Bangalore, 560 075, India

☎ +91 (0)80 528 2313; 529 2905 📠 +91 (0)80 528 2313

🌐 www.equitabletourism.org ✉ admin@equations.ilban.ernet.in

Gambia Tourism Concern
Campaigns to bring more of the benefits of tourism in The Gambia to local people.

■ Adama Bah: Bakadaji Hotel (PO Box 4587), Bakau, The Gambia

☎ +220 (0)462 057 📠 +220 (0)466 180

🌐 www.gambiatourismconcern.com ✉ bahs@qanet.gm

Initiatives for International Dialogue (IID)
Philippine NGO that campaigns for more responsible tourism and promotes alternative tourism projects.

■ 27d Rosario Townhouse, Galaxy Street, GSIS Heights, Matina, Davao City, Philippines

☎ +63 (0)82 299 2574 📠 +63 (0)82 299 2052

🌐 www.skyinet.net/~iiddvo ✉ iid@skyinet.net *or* biyaheng-pinoy@skyinet.net

INDECON (Center for Indonesian Ecotourism Research, Training and Promotion)
A network set up by the **Institute for Indonesia Tourism Studies (IITS)**, **Conservation International** and **Bina Swadaya** (see above) to promote responsible ecotourism in Indonesia.

■ Jl Jati Padang 8, Pasar Minggu, Jakarta 12540, Indonesia

☎ + 📠 +62 (0)21 781 3712

🌐 www.ecotourism-indonesia.com ✉ indecon@cbn.net.id

International Porter Protection Group (IPPG)
A campaign to improve conditions and safety for trekking porters in the Himalaya. See the website for contacts in other countries.

■ Jim Duff

🌐 www.ippg.net (e) info@ippg.net

■ In Nepal: Prakash Adhikari: HRA, PO Box 4844, Thamel, Kathmandu

🄔 hra@aidpost.mos.com.np

◼ In the UK: Nayan Brown

🄣 +44 (0)7905 113067

🄔 nayanbrown@yahoo.co.uk

Himalayan Explorers Club

Information source and meeting place for travellers, volunteers and locals in the Himalayan region, with clubhouses in Islamabad, Pakistan and Kathmandu, Nepal. (See their website or Local tours: Pakistan and Nepal for clubhouse addresses.)

◼ Scott Dimetrosky: PO Box 3665, Boulder, CO 80307, USA

🄣 +1 303 998 0101 🄕 +1 303 998 1007

🅦 www.hec.org 🄔 info@hec.org

Kenya Tourism Concern

A Kenyan campaign for more sustainable tourism.

◼ Samuel Munyi: PO Box 22449, Nairobi, Kenya

🄣 + 🄕 +254 (0)2 535 850; +254 (0)2 793 495

Namibia Community-Based Tourism Association (NACOBTA)

An association representing community tourism projects in Namibia.

◼ Theo Ngaujake/Maxi Louis: PO Box 86099, 18 Lilliencron St, Windhoek, Namibia

🄣 +264 (0)61 250 558; +264 (0)61 221 918 🄕 +264 (0)61 222 647

🅦 www.nacobta.com.na 🄔 nacobta@iafrica.com.na

Uganda Community Tourism Association (UCOTA)

An association representing community tourism projects in Uganda.

◼ Paul Mugisa/Sheba Hanyurwa: Adam House, Plot 11, Portal Avenue, (PO Box 27159) Kampala, Uganda

🄣 +256 (0)41 230 805

🄔 ucota@africaonline.co.ug

ECOTOURISM

Conservation International

An environmental organization promoting conservation through community development, including a number of tourism projects.

■ Greta Ryan: 1919 M Street NW, Suite 600, Washington DC 20036, USA
☎ +1 202 912 1000x421 📠 +1 202 912 1044
🌐 www.ecotour.org ✉ g.ryan@conservation.org

Earthwise Journeys
A US website that lists 'responsible' tour operators and 'alternatives to mass tourism'.
🌐 www.teleport.com/~earthwyz

Ecotourism Resource Centre
An Australian ecotourism website with some useful links.
🌐 www.bigvolcano.com.au/ercentre/

Green Globe
A WTTC-backed environmental award scheme for tour operators.
■ 7 St Stephens Court, St Stephens Road, Bournemouth BH2 6LA, UK
☎ +44 (0)1202 312 001 📠 +44 (0)1202 312 002
🌐 www.greenglobe21.com ✉ info@greenglobe21.com

Green-Travel
A good starting-point for internet ecotourism links with an online mail-list for discussion of ecotourism.
🌐 www.green-travel.com

The International Ecotourism Society (TIES)
A US-based organization promoting ecotourism, which it defines as 'responsible travel to natural areas that conserves the environment and improves the well-being of local people'. The website contains valuable information and links.
■ PO Box 668, Burlington, VT 05401, USA
☎ +1 802 651 9818 📠 +1 802 651 9819
🌐 www.ecotourism.org ✉ ecomail@ecotourism.org

Planeta Platica
An excellent website on ecotourism in Latin America (particularly Mexico and Central America) maintained by US travel writer Ron Mader.
🌐 www.planeta.com ✉ ron@planeta.com

Sustainable Tourism Research Interest Group (STRING)
A Canadian website and listserv on sustainable tourism, with ecotourism links.

Ⓦ www.dkglobal.org/string

GENERAL TRAVEL

Access-able
Good US website about disabled travel.

Ⓦ www.access-able.com

ANTOR (Association of National Tourist Offices in the UK)
Links to a wide range of national tourist offices.

Ⓦ www.antor.com *or* www.tourist-offices.org.uk

Footprint guidebooks
UK-based guidebook publisher, with an excellent mix of cultural and historical background and practical detail and advice.

▇ 6 Riverside Court, Lower Bristol Road, Bath BA2 3DZ, UK

❶ +44 (0)1225 469141 ❶ +44 (0)1225 469461

Ⓦ www.footprintbooks.com

Foreign and Commonwealth Office
The travel section of the website provides useful travel advice plus warnings of any trouble hotspots.

Ⓦ www.fco.gov.uk

Mountain Institute
Promotes the conservation of mountain regions worldwide, with offices in the US, Peru and Nepal.

▇ PO Box 2414, Purcellville, VA 20134, USA

❶ 540 338 8088 ❶ 703 443 8891

Ⓦ www.mountain.org ⊖ summit@mountain.org

Rough Guides
UK guidebook publishers. Their website contains text from their guidebooks and other internet links.

▇ 62–70 Shorts Gardens, London WC2H 9AH, UK

❶ +44 (0)20 7556 5000 ❶ +44 (0)20 7556 5050

Ⓦ http://travel.roughguides.com ⊖ mail@roughguides.co.uk

South American Explorers' Club (SAEC)

The SAEC website and clubhouses in Lima and Cuzco in Peru and Quito in Ecuador are excellent sources of advice about travel in South America. (See Local tours: Peru and Ecuador sections for addresses of clubhouses.)

■ 126 Indian Creek Road, Ithaca, New York 14850, USA

☎ +1 607 277 0488 ✆ +1 607 277 6122

🖥 www.saexplorers.org ✉ explorer@saexplorers.org

Tourism Information Network

A Canadian website with extensive tourism links for academics and researchers.

🖥 http://webhome.idirect.com/~tourism

Tourism Research Links

A huge list of useful tourism research websites.

🖥 www.waksberg.com

Travel Mole

A networking and news website for people in the travel industry.

🖥 www.travelmole.com

UNESCO World Heritage Sites

A complete list of world heritage-listed sites with links to national parks, etc.

🖥 www.unesco.org/whc/

Whatsonwhen.com

A website that lists a huge number of events, festivals and natural phenomena around the world.

🖥 www.whatsonwhen.com

ENVIRONMENT

This is a selective list of environmental organizations that sometimes deal with tourism issues.

Caribbean Environmental Reporters' Network (CERN)

Web news service on environmental issues in the Caribbean.

■ Zadie Neufville: PO Box 461, Bridgetown, Barbados

☎ + ✆ +1 435 304 5290

🌐 http://website.lineone.net/~cernnet/

📧 cernnet@appleonline.net *or* cernnet@madhousenet.co.uk

Conservation Foundation
UK-based environmental organization. Their website includes a weekly roundup of environmental news, plus links.

⬛ 1 Kensington Gore, London SW7 2AR, UK

📞 +44 (0)20 7591 3111 📠 +44 (0)20 7591 3110

🌐 www.conservationfoundation.co.uk 📧 conservef@gn.apc.org

Earth Pledge Foundation
US organization that promotes sustainable development.

⬛ Leslie Hoffman, executive director: 149 East 38th Street, New York, NY 10016, USA

📞 +1 212 573 6968 📠 +1 212 808 9051

🌐 www.earthpledge.org 📧 lhoffman@earthpledge.org

Earthscan
Publishers of a wide range of books (including this one, *The Green Travel Guide* and *A Trip Too Far*) on the environment, development, globalization, economic alternatives, etc.

⬛ 120 Pentonville Road, London N1 9JN, UK

📞 +44 (0)20 7278 0433 📠 +44 (0)20 7278 1142

🌐 www.earthscan.co.uk 📧 earthinfo@earthscan.co.uk

Earth Times
US environmental newspaper, with a daily online version. The print version is available on subscription from Earth Times (Subscription Department).

⬛ 205 East 42nd Street, Suite 1316, New York, NY 10017, USA

🌐 www.earthtimes.org

The Ecologist
UK environmental magazine.

⬛ Unit 18, Chelsea Wharf, 15 Lots Road, London SW10 0QJ, UK

📞 +44 (0)20 7351 3578 📠 +44 (0)20 7351 3617

🌐 www.theecologist.org

Environmental News Network
Online news reports on environmental issues.

🌐 www.enn.com

Environmental News Service
Internet environmental news roundup and search engine, now part of Lycos. Updated daily.

ⓦ http://ens.lycos.com

Friends of the Earth (UK)
Environmental pressure group.

■ 26–28 Underwood Street, London N1 7JQ, UK

ⓣ +44 (0)20 7490 1555 ⓕ +44 (0)20 7490 0881

ⓦ www.foe.co.uk (e) info@foe.co.uk

Greenpeace (UK)
UK branch of the environmental pressure group.

■ Canonbury Villas, London N1 2PN, UK

ⓣ +44 (0)20 7865 8100 ⓕ +44 (0)20 7865 8200

ⓦ www.greenpeace.org.uk ⓔ info@uk.greenpeace.org

International Bicycle Fund
Promotes sustainable transport, with cycling holiday ideas and links.

■ 4887 Columbia Drive South, Seattle, Washington 98108-1919, USA

ⓣ + ⓕ 206 767 0848

ⓦ www.ibike.org ⓔ ibike@ibike.org

International Institute for Environment and Development (IIED)
Publishes an online database of literature on the environment and development.

■ 3 Endsleigh Street, London WC1H 0DD, UK

ⓣ +44 (0)20 7388 2117 ⓕ +44 (0)20 7388 2826

ⓦ www.iied.org ⓔ info@iied.org

The Nature Conservancy (TNC)
This large US conservation organization has a project to develop community-based ecotourism as a conservation tool.

■ Andy Drumm, Ecotourism Director: Suite 100, 4245 North Fairfax Drive, Arlington, VA 22203-1606, USA

ⓦ www.nature.org/ecotourism ⓔ ecotourism@tnc.org

peopleandplanet.net
An online magazine with sections exploring environmental issues, including a section on ecotourism
Ⓦ www.peopleandplanet.net

Planet Ark
The website of this Australian environmental organization contains a useful global environmental news service, updated daily with stories from the Reuters press agency.
Ⓦ www.planetark.org/index.cfm

Reef Check
An international volunteer network for recreational divers to help monitor the health of coral reefs worldwide.
◼ Jennifer Liebeler: Institute of the Environment, 1652 Hershey Hall, UCLA, Los Angeles, CA 90095-1496, USA
❶ +1 310 794 4985 ❶ +1 310 825 0758
Ⓦ www.reefcheck.org ❸ Rcheck@ucla.edu

INDIGENOUS PEOPLES

Amazon Alliance
A coalition of 80 organizations and NGOs representing indigenous Amazonian peoples, including links to member organizations' own websites.
◼ 1367 Connecticut Avenue, NW Suite 400, Washington DC 20036, USA
❶ +1 202 785 3334 ❶ +1 202 785 3335
Ⓦ www.amazonalliance.org ❸ amazon@alliance.org

Cultural Survival
US-based campaign for the rights of indigenous peoples.
◼ 215 Prospect St, Cambridge, MA 02139, USA
❶ +1 617 441 5400 ❶ +1 617 441 5417
Ⓦ www.cs.org ❸ csinc@cs.org

Indigenous Environmental Network
Environmental campaigns and news from Native American groups in the US.
◼ PO Box 485, Bemidji, MN56619, USA
Ⓦ www.ienearth.org ❸ ien@igc.org

NativeWeb
Native American networking website.

ⓦ www.nativeweb.org

Rethinking Tourism Project
An indigenous peoples' organization focusing on education and networking on tourism issues to protect and preserve indigenous lands and cultures.

◼ Deborah McLaren (Director): 366 North Prior Ave, Suite 203, St Paul, MN 55104, USA

ⓣ +1 651 644 9984 ⓕ +1 651 644 2720

ⓦ www.rethinkingtourism.org ⓔ info@rethinkingtourism.org

Survival
A worldwide organization campaigning for the rights of tribal peoples.

◼ 5 Charterhouse Buildings, London EC1M 7ET, UK

ⓣ +44 (0)20 7687 8700 ⓕ +44 (0)20 7687 8701

ⓦ www.survival-international.org ⓔ info@survival-international.org

DEVELOPMENT

A selective list of (mainly UK-based) NGOs involved with tourism, fair trade, development, etc.

ActionAid
A poverty relief agency that works on community tourism with RICANCIE in Ecuador.

◼ Hamlyn House, Macdonald Road, London N19 5PG, UK

ⓣ +44 (0)20 7561 7614 ⓕ +44 (0)20 7561 7640

ⓦ www.actionaid.org ⓔ mail@actionaid.org.uk

Action for Southern Africa (ACTSA)
UK-based organization working on development issues in southern Africa. Has a campaign for 'people-first tourism' in the region.

◼ Aditi Sharma, 28 Penton St, London N1 9SA, UK

ⓣ +44 (0)20 7833 3133 ⓕ +44 (0)20 7837 3001

ⓦ www.actsa.org (e) actsa@actsa.org

International Federation for Alternative Trade (IFAT)

The world's largest network of fair trade organizations, including both producers and retailers.

■ 30 Murdock Road, Bicester, Oxon, OX26 4RF, UK

❶ +44 (0)1869 249 819 ❶ +44 (0)1869 216 819

Ⓦ www.ifat.org Ⓔ info@ifat.org.uk

GreenNet

UK-based webserver that hosts the websites of many environment, human rights and development organizations.

Ⓦ www.gn.apc.org

Latin American Bureau

Non-profit organization that publishes books and runs workshops about Latin America and the Caribbean, aimed at raising awareness of social justice and human rights issues.

■ 1 Amwell Street, London EC1R 1UL, UK

❶ +44 (0)20 7278 2829 ❶ +44 (0)20 7278 0165

Ⓦ www.lab.org.uk Ⓔ info@lab.org.uk

OneWorld

Another UK-based webserver for many organizations concerned with development, social justice, etc. The OneWorld homepage features environmental and development news, updated daily.

Ⓦ www.oneworld.org

Oxfam

Works to relieve developing world poverty and is one of the driving forces in the UK fair trade movement.

■ 274 Banbury St, Oxford, UK

❶ +44 (0)1865 311 311 ❶ +44 (0)1865 313 770

Ⓦ www.oxfam.org.uk Ⓔ oxfam@oxfam.org.uk

SNV

Dutch development agency that supports community tourism in Botswana, Tanzania, Ghana, Uganda, Nepal, Laos, Vietnam and elsewhere.

■ Marcel Leijzer, Tourism officer: Bezuidenhoutseweg 161, 2594 AG, The Hague, The Netherlands

❶ +31 (0)70 344 0139

Ⓦ www.snv.nl Ⓔ tourism@snv.nl or informatie@snv.nl

TWIN/Twin Trading Ltd

TWIN (Third World Information Network) is a development charity that develops fairly traded products such as Café Direct and The Day Chocolate Company. Twin Trading is the organization's trading arm.

■ 1 Curtain Road, London, EC2A 3LT, UK

❶ +44 (0)20 7375 1221 ❶ +44 (0)20 7375 1337

ⓔ info@twin.org.uk

Voluntary Services Overseas (VSO)

Places volunteers with development projects in the South, including some with community tourism projects.

■ 317 Putney Bridge Road, London SW15 2PN, UK

❶ +44 (0)20 8780 7500 ❶ +44 (0)20 8780 7300

Ⓦ www.vso.org.uk ⓔ enquiry@vso.org.uk

World Development Movement (WDM)

A campaigning organization tackling the root causes of poverty in the global economy.

■ 25 Beehive Place, Brixton, London SW9 7QR, UK

❶ +44 (0)20 7737 6215 ❶ +44 (0)20 7274 8232

Ⓦ www.wdm.org.uk ⓔ wdm@wdm.org.uk

BOOKS, MAGAZINES AND REPORTS

The publications listed below provide more in-depth discussion of the issues raised in this book.

Alternative Travel Directory

A US directory of organizations around the world facilitating alternative travel, such as teaching English, language schools, volunteer and study programmes, living abroad, etc.

■ Available from Transitions Abroad (see below).

Community Based Sustainable Tourism Reader/Handbook

A set of two books from Philippines organization ASSET. The Handbook provides useful, easy-to-understand advice for launching and running a community tourism project.

■ Corazon T Urquico, ed (ASSET, 1998, asset@pacific.net.ph). Available from Tourism Concern, £14.

Community-Based Tourism for Conservation and Development: A Resource Kit

Practical advice for field-based professionals helping communities to develop tourism. $25 including p&p.

The Mountain Institute (Asia): PO Box 2875, Kathmandu, Nepal

☎ +977 (0)1 419 356 **✆** +977 (0)1 410 073

Ⓦ www.mountain.org **ⓔ** tmi@regional.wlink.com.np

The Earthscan Reader in Sustainable Tourism

A compilation of book extracts, case studies and papers covering destinations from the Isle of Man to Zimbabwe, Nepal and Kenya.

L France, ed (Earthscan, London, 1997)

Ecotourism: A Guide for Planners and Managers, volume 2

A mix of practical advice and assessment of industry trends. Although primarily about nature tours, much of this applies to community-based tourism as well. Volume 1 was published in 1993.

Lindberg, Epler Wood & Engeldrum, eds (The Ecotourism Society, Vermont, 1998)

Ecotourism and Sustainable Development

Analysis and case studies of ecotourism in the Galapagos, Costa Rica, Cuba, Tanzania, Kenya and South Africa. The book discusses how ecotourism relates to local communities.

Martha Honey (Island Press, Washington, 1999)

Ecotourism in the Less Developed World

Research paper with case studies of Costa Rica, Kenya, Nepal, Thailand, the Caribbean and the South Pacific.

D Weaver (CAB International, Wallingford, 1998)

The Green Travel Guide

A comprehensive guide to nature-based holidays both in the UK and abroad, from voluntary conservation work in the UK to jungle tours in the South American rainforest.

Greg Neale (Earthscan, London, 2nd edition 1999)

Last Resorts: The Cost of Tourism in the Caribbean

Examines the impacts of tourism on the Caribbean.

Polly Pattullo (Latin American Bureau, London, 1996). Available from Tourism Concern.

Pro-Poor Tourism Strategies: Making Tourism Work for the Poor
A study looking at how tourism affects, and could be used to benefit, the world's poor, with case studies from South Africa, Namibia, Uganda, Ecuador, Nepal and St Lucia.

■ Caroline Ashley, Dilys Roe, Harold Goodwin (Overseas Development Institute, 2000, www.odi.org.uk)

Rethinking Tourism and Ecotravel
A book critically reassessing tourism, including 'alternative' forms of tourism. Written by the director of the Rethinking Tourism Project.

■ Deborah McLaren (Kumarian Press, 1997)

Sustainable Tourism: A Geographical Perspective
Readable academic introduction including both environmental and social issues.

■ C Michael Hall and Alan Lew, eds (Longman, London, 1999)

Tourism and Sustainability: New Tourism in the Third World
Explores globalization, sustainability and global power in relation to tourism, and asks whether emerging forms of tourism (including community tourism) will help people in developing countries. Includes research from Central America and the Caribbean.

■ M Mowforth and I Munt (Routledge, London, 1998)

Transitions Abroad
US magazine devoted to alternative forms of travel, such as volunteer work, teaching and homestays.

■ PO Box 1300, Amherst, Massachusetts 01004-1300, USA

❶ +1 413 256 3414; 800 293 0373 ❶ +1 413 256 0373

Ⓦ www.transitionsabroad.com ℮ info@transitionsabroad.com

Travel Weekly
The trade newspaper of the UK tourism industry. The website contains an archive of articles.

■ Quadrant House, The Quadrant, Sutton, Surrey SM2 5AS, UK

❶ +44 (0)20 8652 3799 ❶ +44 (0)20 8652 3956

Ⓦ www.travelweekly.co.uk

Wanderlust
A magazine for the 'independent-minded' traveller, with the accent on cultural, wildlife and soft adventure travel, plus consumer issues and practical information.

■ PO Box 1832, Windsor, Berks SL4 6YP, UK

❶ +44 (0)1753 620 426

Ⓦ www.wanderlust.co.uk Ⓔ info@wanderlust.co.uk

TOURISM CONCERN PUBLICATIONS

The following reports and magazines can be purchased directly from Tourism Concern. Call +44 (0)20 7753 3330 or see the website – www.tourismconcern.org.uk – for details of these and other publications.

Beyond the Green Horizon: Principles for Sustainable Tourism
Introduces the principles and issues of sustainable tourism, with case studies. Published with WWF.

■ S Eber, ed 1992

Trading Places: Tourism as Trade
An introduction to tourism as trade, with case studies on The Gambia, Kenya, Turkey, Sri Lanka, Barbados, Egypt and the Philippines.

■ Badger et al, 1996

Tourism and Human Rights
Highlights human rights abuses connected with tourism and explores how tourism can affect local communities.

■ Jean Keefe and Sue Wheat, 1998

Tourism as Fair Trade: NGO Perspectives
Considers whether fair trade can be extended to tourism. The report focuses on the role of NGOs, with case studies from Tanzania, Nepal, the Philippines, The Gambia, South Africa, Namibia and Ecuador. The report is part of Tourism Concern's Fair Trade in Tourism Project.

■ Angela Kalisch, 2001

In Focus
Quarterly magazine for Tourism Concern members. Each issue focuses on a particular theme, such as guidebooks or backpacking. Back issues available from www.tourismconcern.org.uk.

THE TODO! AWARDS

The ToDo! Awards are the only awards that we know of dedicated specifically to socially responsible tourism. They are presented each year at the International Tourism Exchange in Berlin by the German NGO **Studienkreis fur Tourismus und Entwicklung**. The winners are described in more detail in the Holiday Directory and on the Studienkreis website (www.studienkreis.org). The award criteria are:

- raising awareness among local people of the impacts of tourism;
- participation of a broad range of local people in tourism;
- good working conditions for local employees, including pay, security, hours, training;
- reinforcement of local culture;
- minimization of the social and cultural damage caused by tourism;
- developing new partnerships between the tourist industry and local people;
- helping to develop socially responsible tourism in destination areas;
- environmental sustainability.

TODO! AWARDS ORGANIZER

Studienkreis fur Tourismus und Entwicklung

■ Kapellenweg 3, D-82541 Ammerland, Germany

❶ +49 (0)8177 1783 ❶ +49 (0)8177 1349

Ⓦ www.studienkreis.org ⓔ studienkreistourismus@compuserve.com

TODO! AWARDS WINNERS

2000

Tumani Tenda, The Gambia
Community-owned accommodation in an inland village on the Gambia river, with guided forest walks, river trips, crafts workshops, music, dance and story-telling.

Kasapa Centre, Ghana
A village-based centre on the coast near Accra, offering drumming, dance and cultural tours.

1999

Amigos de Prainha do Canto Verde, Brazil
A coastal village in north-east Brazil developing small-scale, community-based sustainable tourism in a region targeted for huge commercial tourism investment.

Cultural Tourism Programme, Tanzania
A programme of village-based tourism involving Maasai communities in northern Tanzania.

1998

Aboriginal Art and Culture Centre, Australia
Aboriginal-owned art gallery in Alice Springs which run tours to Aboriginal communities.

Corpomedina CA, Venezuela
A company facilitating a range of community-based tourism projects including guesthouses, tour agencies and micro-credit business support on the Paria peninsula in north-east Venezuela.

1997

Tropic Ecological Adventures (Huaorani tour), Ecuador
Five-day rainforest tours to Ecuador's Amazon, staying with an indigenous Huaorani community.

Shawenequanape Kipichewin (Anishinabe Village), Canada
A First Nations-owned camp, tipi village and cultural tours in Riding Mountain National Park, Manitoba.

1996

International Centre of Bethlehem, West Bank
A project to increase local benefit from tourism to Bethlehem.

Toledo Ecotourism Association, Belize
Tours and village stays with Mayan, Garifuna and Kekchi communities in southern Belize.

1995

Sua Bali, Indonesia
A small resort just south of Ubud in Bali that works closely with the local village.

Woodlands Network, Sri Lanka
A women's organization that arranges village stays in (mainly) rural Sri Lanka.

Note: Since this guide does not cover Europe, three European projects have been excluded from this list.

RESPONSIBLE TOURISM CODES

THE RESPONSIBLE TOURIST

People often phone Tourism Concern to ask 'how to behave responsibly' when on holiday. Here we list Tourism Concern's 'responsible travel' guidelines, plus three other codes. Two are for trekkers in the Nepalese Himalayas (or similar mountain regions). The final one is from Survival, an organization campaigning for the rights of tribal people.

These codes lay down broad principles: specific customs and values vary from country to country. On the whole, of course, if you are considerate and respectful to the people you meet, you probably won't go far wrong. That includes learning and observing basic local customs (such as covering bare flesh in religious buildings or not pointing your feet at someone). It means learning a few simple phrases of the local language, even if it's only 'hello' and 'thank you'. It means understanding and respecting the boundary between public and private space.

Leave behind the 'consumer mentality': think of yourself not simply as 'the paying customer', always demanding service. You are also a visitor in someone else's country, village or home. Remember, too, that the people you meet on holiday probably haven't had a say in whether tourists come to their town or village, and that most people you meet probably don't benefit from tourism.

Responsible tourism doesn't mean you can't enjoy yourself. It doesn't mean you can't have a laugh, or share a joke with the people you meet. It doesn't mean you can't simply lie on a beach. It doesn't even mean you can't get drunk or stoned, if that's what you want to do. (In some Mexican cantinas, it would be rude *not* to get drunk!) It simply means treating local people as *people* – not as beggars, nuisances, servants, con men, thieves or exotic photo opportunities.

TOURISM CONCERN

This code was drawn up in 2001 at a Tourism Concern conference for young travellers. It applies to all holiday-makers.

The cost of your holiday

- Think about where your money goes – be fair and realistic about how cheaply you travel. Try and put money into local people's hands; drink local beer or fruit juice rather than imported brands and stay in locally-owned accommodation.
- Haggle with humour and not aggressively. Pay what something is worth to you and remember how wealthy you are compared to local people.

How big is your footprint? Minimize your environmental impact

- Think about what happens to your rubbish – take biodegradable products and a water filter bottle. Be sensitive to limited resources like water, fuel and electricity.
- Help preserve local wildlife and habitats by respecting rules and regulations, such as sticking to footpaths, not standing on coral and not buying products made from endangered plants or animals.

Learn about the country you're visiting

- Start enjoying your travels before you leave by tapping into as many sources of information as you can.
- Use your guidebook as a starting point, not the only source of information. Talk to local people, then discover your own adventure!

Culture

- Open your mind to new cultures and traditions – it will transform your experience.
- Think carefully about what is appropriate in terms of your clothes and the way you behave. You'll earn respect and be more readily welcomed by local people.
- Respect local laws and attitudes towards drugs and alcohol that vary in different countries and communities. Think about the impact you could have.

Photography

- Don't treat people as part of the landscape; they may not want their picture taken. Put yourself in their shoes, ask first and respect their wishes.

THE HIMALAYAN CODE

The Himalayan Code was drawn up by Tourism Concern with British and Nepalese tour operators and the **Annapurna Conservation Area Project (ACAP)**, a Nepalese NGO. It is designed for trekkers in the Himalayas, but the principles apply to other high mountain environments, such as the Andes.

Protect the natural environment
- **Limit deforestation.** Make no open fires and discourage others from doing so on your behalf. Where water is heated by scarce firewood, use as little as possible. When possible, choose accommodation that uses kerosene or fuel-efficient wood stoves.
- **Remove litter.** Burn or bury paper and carry out all non-degradable litter. Graffiti is a permanent form of environmental pollution.
- **Keep local water clean.** Avoid using pollutants such as detergents in streams or springs. If no toilets are available, make sure you are at least 30 metres away from water sources and bury or cover wastes.
- **Plants** should be left to flourish in their natural environment. Taking cuttings, seeds and roots is illegal in many parts of the Himalayas.
- Help your **guides and porters** to follow conservation measures.

As a guest, respect local traditions and cultures and maintain local pride
- When taking photos, **respect privacy.** Ask permission and use restraint.
- **Respect holy places.** Preserve what you have come to see. Never touch or remove religious objects. Shoes should be removed in temples.
- Giving to children encourages begging. A **donation** to a project, health centre or school is a more constructive way to help.
- You will be accepted and welcomed if you **follow local customs.** Use only your right hand for eating and greeting. Do not share cutlery and cups, etc. It is polite to use both hands when giving or receiving gifts.
- **Respect local etiquette.** Loose, lightweight clothes are preferable to revealing shorts, skimpy tops and tight fitting 'action-wear'. Handholding or kissing in public are disliked by local people.
- **Observe standard food and bed charges** but do not condone over-charging. Remember, when you're shopping, the bargains you buy may only be possible because of low income to others.
- Visitors who **value local traditions** encourage local pride and maintain local cultures. And please help local people gain a realistic view of life in Western countries.

INTERNATIONAL PORTER PROTECTION GROUP

This code covers safety and working conditions for trekking porters in Nepal although, as with the Himalayan Code, it applies to any similar trekking region.

- That **adequate clothing** be available for protection in bad weather and at altitude. This should include adequate footwear, hat, gloves, windproof jacket and trousers, sunglasses, and access to a blanket and pad above the snowline.
- That leaders and trekkers provide the same standard of **medical care** for porters as they would expect for themselves.
- That porters **not be paid off because of illness** without the leader or trekkers being informed.
- That sick porters **never be sent down alone**, but with someone who speaks their language and understands the problem.
- That sufficient **funds** be provided to sick porters to cover the cost of their rescue and treatment.

SURVIVAL

This code is for tourists visiting tribal communities or their territories. It was drawn up by Survival, an organization campaigning for the rights of tribal peoples.

'Tourism need not be a destructive force for tribal peoples, but unfortunately it usually is: any tourism which violates tribal peoples' rights should be opposed. Tourism must be subject to the decisions made by tribal peoples themselves.'

Do...

- **Recognize land rights:** tribal peoples' ownership of the lands they use and occupy is recognized in international law. This should be acknowledged irrespective of whether the national government applies the law or not (governments are amongst the principal violators of tribes' rights). When in tribal lands, tourists should behave as they would on private property.

- **Ask permission:** the lands lived in or used by tribes should not be entered without the free and informed consent of the tribal peoples themselves. Obtaining this consent can be lengthy; it requires respect, tact and honesty. Bribery should never be used.

- **Pay properly:** tribespeople should be properly recompensed for their services and use of their territory. Payment should be agreed in advance with their legitimate representatives. (Bribery should never be used.) Where profits arise from using tribal areas, this should be properly explained to the tribes, who may want a share. Anyone who is not able to accept tribal peoples' own terms for payment should not be there.

- **Be respectful:** tourist companies should insist that their staff and clients behave respectfully towards tribal peoples. (In practice, many tourists who visit tribal areas simply have their false stereotypes reinforced.)

Don't...

- **Bring in disease:** care must be taken in areas where tribal peoples' immunity to outside diseases may be poor. Some contagious diseases (colds, influenza, etc) which affect tourists only mildly can kill tribespeople. Please also remember that AIDS kills.

- **Demean, degrade, insult or patronize:** all tourism and advertising which treat tribal people in an insulting, degrading or patronizing manner (for example, references to 'stone-age cultures', 'untouched by time', etc) should be opposed. They are demeaning and wrong.

GLOSSARY

This glossary defines terms as they are used in this book, which may not be exact dictionary definitions.

ABTA Association of British Travel Agents. The trade association of large tour operators.

ATOL Air Travel Organizers Licence. A bonding scheme run by the Civil Aviation Authority. If your tour operator is a member of ATOL, you are guaranteed a refund if the company goes into liquidation.

Aboriginal refers to the original inhabitants of a country and their descendants. The term is used mainly in Australia and Canada. See also **First Nations**, **indigenous people**.

all-inclusive a resort providing accommodation, food and all facilities (eg beach and watersports) internally, so that visitors have no need to leave the resort.

backpacker a (usually young) **independent traveller**; typically carries a rucksack and stays in cheap, locally owned accommodation.

community a mutually supportive, geographically specific social unit such as a village or tribe.

community tourism a shorter term for **community-based tourism**.

community-based tourism tourism that consults, involves and benefits a local **community**, especially in the context of rural villages in **developing countries** and **indigenous peoples**.

customized itineraries a holiday schedule drawn up by a tour operator specifically for one client or group, usually including flight, accommodation and transport. Sometimes called tailor-made holidays.

developed countries/world see **the West**.

developing countries/world the world's less wealthy nations, mostly former colonies: ie most of Asia, Africa, Latin America and the South Pacific. Also sometimes referred to as **the South**.

ecotourism	according to the US-based Ecotourism Society, 'Ecotourism is responsible travel to a natural area that conserves the environment and sustains the well-being of local people'. In the UK, the phrase **green travel** is sometimes preferred.
ethical tourism	see **responsible tourism**.
fair trade	equitable, non-exploitative trade between **developing world** suppliers and **Western** consumers. Tourism Concern is undertaking a three-year Fair Trade in Tourism project to consider whether the concept of fair trade can be applied to tourism.
First Nations	a collective term for the original, pre-European inhabitants of the US, Canada, Hawaii, Australia and New Zealand. In individual countries, different terms are sometimes used: eg **Aboriginal**, **indigenous**, **tribal**, Indian, First Peoples, Native American, AmerIndian.
green travel	a UK alternative to the American term **ecotourism**.
independent traveller	someone who travels without booking a **package tour**.
indigenous people	the original inhabitants of a country and their descendants. Indigenous communities are often, but not always, **tribal peoples** and the two terms are often and easily confused. (Note: there are points in this book that apply particularly to tribal people, others that apply to indigenous people in general, and still others that apply to all rural developing world communities. I've tried to use each term in its correct and precise sense. In the real world, of course, people stubbornly refuse to fit into such simplistic categories, and the distinctions between tribal, indigenous and non-indigenous communities may not always be crystal clear.) See also **First Nations, Aboriginal**.
local communities/people	people living in tourist destinations, especially in the rural **developing world**.
multinational corporation	see **transnational corporation**.
NGO	non-governmental organization: an independent pressure group or campaigning organization, usually non-profit.
Native Americans	a collective term for the **indigenous** peoples of the Americas. Also **First Nations**, AmerIndians, American Indians, Indians.

North, the	see **the West**.
package tour	a holiday combining transport and accommodation in an inclusive price.
responsible tourism	tourism that aims to avoid harmful impacts on people and environments. Sometimes referred to as ethical tourism. Other similar concepts include People First Tourism, reality tourism, etc.
South, the	see **developing countries**.
sustainable tourism	tourism that does not degrade the environment or local cultures/societies.
Third World, the	now generally referred to as either **developing countries** or **the South**.
tourists	holiday-makers, generally from the **West**. The term is sometimes used to distinguish **package tourists** from **independent travellers**, but I use it to mean anyone going on holiday.
transnational corporation	correctly, a large company with shareholders in more than one country. I use the term fairly loosely to mean any large, powerful, Western-owned company.
tribal peoples	people living in close-knit social units based on kinship ties and shared belief systems. While most remaining tribal communities are **indigenous**, not all indigenous people are tribal.
West, the	the world's rich nations: ie Western Europe, the US, Canada, Australia, New Zealand and (economically, although perhaps not culturally) Japan. Also referred to as the **North**, the **developed countries/world**.

2302